ANCIENT AS THE HILLS

Ancient as the Hills

DIARIES, 1973–1974

James Lees-Milne

JOHN MURRAY

Albemarle Street, London

First published in 1997
by John Murray (Publishers) Ltd,
50 Albemarle Street, London W1X 4BD

Reprinted 1997, 1998, 1999

Paperback edition 2000

A catalogue record for this book is available from the British Library

ISBN 0-7195-6200 7

Typeset by
Pure Tech India Ltd, Pondicherry
Printed and bound in the United Kingdom
at the University Press, Cambridge

For
ANNE HILL
with love

Contents

Preface

This volume is a chronological sequel to the final entries of *A Mingled Measure*, embracing as it does the two years 1973 and 1974. Alvilde and I were still living at Alderley Grange in Gloucestershire, she busy with her garden and embarking upon schemes and layouts for other people's gardens. I was fretting and fuming over my writing. At the back of both our minds was the knowledge that soon we would have to leave Alderley which we loved, I probably more than she for it was the first real home I had had since childhood. When we moved to Alderley in 1961 I was convinced that we would end our days there. It was not to be. By the end of 1974 we had packed up and gone.

I do not think Alvilde felt her tireless efforts in creating the Alderley garden had been wasted. They were a grade in the knowledge of horticulture which she was accumulating and which was to stand her in good stead in the coming years. Moreover she was fortunate in that our successors happened to be pre-eminent gardeners in their own right. Therefore her contribution to this lovely place had not been in vain. Far from it. It had been the proto-renaissance of its full flowering at this very time.

In a daze we moved to a flat in Bath, she momentarily relieved to be out of the endless and relentless battle with plants, I silently weeping. Within six months she was fed up with Bath and having no garden to wrestle with beyond a pocket handkerchief the other side of a black chasm which the estate agents denominated 'the patio'. And I had fallen in love with the early nineteenth-century library which had been created by William Beckford for his declining years. Within less than twelve months we moved back into the country, where she instantly began another albeit smaller garden in Badminton village. And I kept on Mr Beckford's library, commuting there to write. And so our mutually busy lives worked out very well.

In looking through these diary entries as they were prepared for publication I began to doubt whether they could possibly be of interest to anyone but me; then I came upon this fragment from the Memoirs of Alexander Herzen:

In order to write one's reminiscences it is not at all necessary to be a great man, nor a notorious criminal, nor a celebrated artist, nor a statesman – it is quite enough to be simply a human being, to have something to tell, and not merely to desire to tell it but at least have some little ability to do so.

Every life is interesting; if not the personality, then the environment, the country are interesting, the life itself is interesting. Man likes to enter another existence, he likes to touch the subtlest fibres of another's heart, and to listen to its beating . . . he compares, he checks it by his own, he seeks for himself confirmation, sympathy, justification . . .

But may not memoirs be tedious, may not the life described be colourless and commonplace?

Then we shall not read it – there is no worse punishment for a book than that.

                                                        J.L.-M., 1996

And there were gardens bright with sinuous rills,
Where blossomed many an incense-bearing tree;
And here were forests ancient as the hills,
Enfolding sunny spots of greenery.

Samuel Taylor Coleridge, *Kubla Khan*

1973

Friday, 5th January

This morning the new farmers' syndicate here gave a New Year's
party to the village and neighbourhood. To curry favour. Rather
cheek I thought. I went reluctantly because I hate cocktail parties
and also strongly disapprove of the new complex of buildings with
which the syndicate are going to ruin this valley. They – called
Bernays* – are however nice people, which is a change. Ironical that
the nicest farmers since we have been here are about to commit the
greatest mischief, which we cannot prevent. Mrs Bernays told me
that after her husband Rob's death, Harold Nicolson† looked at
preparatory schools for her boys. Together they went to Rosehill
in this village. Strange to think of dear Harold in Alderley long
before we came to live in it. They went round the school and in the
garden the then headmaster showed them the great fir tree. The
headmaster explained that it had recently been struck by a thunderbolt, which was to be seen beside the tree. Harold asked where the
thunderbolt now was. The headmaster said it had gone, he didn't
know where. When they left Mrs Bernays said she quite liked the
school and asked Harold whether she should send her boys to it.
'No,' said Harold. 'Either the headmaster is a liar, or he lacks
curiosity.' Gilbert Wheat, the present headmaster, to whom she told
this story, agreed that Harold was right. Harold also remarked to Mrs
Bernays that he could not decide, were he able to summon one
person back to life for an hour, whether to choose Shakespeare or
Rob.

Robin Fedden‡ has been appointed CBE. I immediately sent him
the most congratulatory letter of affection that I knew how to write.
I would simply hate him or anyone to suppose that I am not
delighted. What are my feelings? No resentment at all, and only the

---

* R. Bernays, son of late Robert H. Bernays, MP, and his widow Nan; godson of
Harold Nicolson, he had recently bought Alderley Farm.
† The Hon. Sir Harold Nicolson, 1886–1968; diplomatist, writer, MP; m. 1913 The
Hon. Vita Sackville-West (d. 1962).
‡ Robin Fedden, 1909–77; writer and Secretary of Historic Buildings Committee,
National Trust, 1951–74.

faintest envy. Such honours mean very little to me, which sounds disingenuous, but truthfully isn't; also I *know* that Robin has done far more for the N. Trust than I ever did. I had my years of glory, a long time ago, twenty-five years or more, but did not sustain them. No, I am happy that Robin's services have been recognized. These are honest sentiments.

A. and I went to Leslie Hartley's[*] memorial service in Holy Trinity, Brompton. Congregation large, all old friends, most of them with one foot in the grave. The young seldom go to such services, and when they do their youth shines out like a good deed in a naughty world. We sang the first hymn, which had a phrase reminding us, the singers, how short a time we had to go. Not very tactful, I thought. Christabel Aberconway,[†] escorted by Ralph Dutton,[‡] sat beside me. She smelled of gin and talked throughout. Took one of my fingers and said loudly, 'Do you remember who I am?' Poor Norah Smallwood[§] felt faint and had to walk out, a long way down the nave all by herself. She sat under the tower with smelling salts and was taken home by Lennox and Freda.[¶]

Thursday, 11th January

Hugh Montgomery-Massingberd[**] lunched at Brooks's. Told me more news of the plans for Burke which he is fostering. Thinks that Weldon, the part owner of Bryant's index, may edit Burke's guide to country houses. Hugh definitely intends to tackle this formidable task, with the help of a committee of people like John Harris,[††], John Cornforth,[‡‡] me, etc. Is producing next month Burke's *Guide to the Royal Family* which won't interest me much. He

[*] L. P. Hartley, 1895–1972; novelist; author of *The Go-Between*, etc.
[†] Christabel, Lady Aberconway, widow of 2nd Baron (who d. 1953).
[‡] Ralph Dutton, FSA, 1898–1985; architectural historian and writer; s. cousin as 8th Baron Sherborne, 1982.
[§] Norah Smallwood, 1909–84; publisher; chairman of Chatto and Windus.
[¶] Lennox Berkeley, 1903–90; Kt 1974; composer; m. 1946 Freda Bernstein (b. 1923).
[**] Hugh Montgomery-Massingberd, b. 1946; genealogist, writer, and Obituary Editor of the *Daily Telegraph* 1986–94.
[††] Architectural historian; b. 1931.
[‡‡] Architectural historian, and writer, notably for *Country Life*.

had to see Mountbatten* who is writing the preface. Mountbatten told Hugh he must in the *Guide* call the royal family, i.e., the children of the Queen, Mountbatten-Windsor. So far there has been no call for a royal prince of this union to have a surname. Hugh said he supposed the name had already been settled by the College of Heralds when the Queen and Prince Philip were married, in the expectation of there being children. Mountbatten complained that Sir Winston, then Prime Minister, told the Queen the Cabinet would not allow this double name: but Windsor only. The Queen expostulated, saying her husband's name ought to be prefixed. Sir W. said the Queen must accept his Cabinet's ruling on the matter. Mountbatten said the Queen was so upset that she did not have another child for six years, and this was the cause.

Hugh M.-M. also told me a strange story of his great friend Mrs Lloyd, the stepmother of Sam Lloyd.† He met her somewhere, they became great friends and ultimately he lodged in her house. He thinks she is now about 70. He must be under 30 still. When he told her a year ago that he was engaged to be married she was furious, and would not speak to him. So he left. After an interval the new young wife asked Hugh to introduce her to the old friend of whom she had so often heard him speaking. Hugh thought he must do this and telephoned Mrs Lloyd, who in a sweet way consented to let him bring his wife to see her. He did so. Whereupon Mrs Lloyd made a scene, was extremely rude to the wife and said she had ruined her life. Hugh was appalled, and is greatly upset and embarrassed. The old woman must be mad.

To the V. & A. exhibition of one treasure lent by each of the nine Common Market countries, yesterday. Italy has lent Michelangelo's *Brutus*. It looked even more marvellous than in the Bargello where I have often worshipped it. The lighting splendid, and the bust against red velvet background. I was moved nearly to tears of emotion. This I seldom am by a work of marble. All the other exhibits left me unmoved, the Rembrandt of Titus dressed as a monk, the De la Tour of *The Card Sharper*, seemed flat compared with this speaking,

---

* Earl Mountbatten of Burma, 1900–79; uncle of HRH The Prince Philip, Duke of Edinburgh; killed by IRA bomb.
† Sampson Llewellyn Lloyd, b. 1907, and Margaret (Peggy) Parker, his wife; they lived at Bagpath Court, Gloucestershire.

tremendously powerful expression of strength and force. What a bust! I have always thought it the greatest in the world.

It is bad news Hugh told me, that there is not to be another Burke's *Peerage*. Finished, because of expense; they cannot be sold under £20 now. I don't understand about economics. Why, because wages rise, do goods have to stop being made? I mean, because higher wages are paid and incomes accordingly rise in proportion, why do businesses have to close down, and luxuries have to end?

In the British Museum reading room I asked the superintendent if I might be allowed to visit the shelves in order to search for an article in an obscure Italian journal of the 1850s and 60s, the reference to which was evidently wrongly given in the bibliography I have consulted. He looked at me and said, 'We are not supposed to, but you seem all right.' 'I hope I am, but I don't know how you can tell,' I said. He called a black assistant, who took me miles and miles upstairs past shelves and shelves and shelves, all beautifully stacked. We arrived at a little office amidst this forest of books.

The charming assistant took me to the shelves where the *Rivista Europea* volumes were stacked – about forty of them. He had them all taken out on a trolley and put on a table for me. I found my article and read it; it was of no use to me, but I was struck by the kindness and helpfulness of everyone concerned. When I came to leave my friend was nowhere to be found. It was terrifying being left alone in this deserted forest, no sound, only endless speechless books. Depressing, and frightening. Enough to make a humble author feel a worm.

Saturday, 13th January

At luncheon with Elspeth Huxley[*] sat next to Mrs Mackintosh. She and her husband (also present) had been hijacked in the plane flying from Ethiopia. I did not mean to embark upon this subject because I thought they must be sick of it. But we found ourselves discussing crises of one's life. And she said to me, 'When I had the dead body of a hijacker at my feet the other day, literally slumped across my feet, I was totally unmoved by his fate. I didn't mind a bit.'

---

[*] Elspeth Grant, b. 1907; m. 1931 Gervas Huxley (who d. 1971); writer of fiction and travel.

Ernst [Margery] set a mousetrap beside my bed and A. thought a mouse was in it because she noticed it upside down, having gone off. I got a shovel to scoop up the trap, and eyes averted threw it outside the back door. A. was very ashamed of me. I am ashamed of myself, but I cannot bear dead things, cannot even look at them, far less touch them. I wish I were less of a cissy, and also less ham-fisted. Spend hours trying to fit a new blade into the razor recently given me. Can't; have to abandon it and go back to my old razor until I can see the donor again and ask him how to do it. He will not be cross, but he will scold gently, for I *am* a fool. I am not pleased with myself.

Sunday, 14th January

Nancy [Mitford]* is still in the Nuffield Fitzroy nursing home. She has been there two to three months, perhaps more, since A. arranged for her to fly to London in September. I have long dreaded seeing her. However, having received messages that she would like to see me, and having tried several times and been put off owing to her relapses, I went last Tuesday. She received me sweetly, lying in bed, her head over the sheets like a tiny marmoset's. 'Jimminy, *do* sit down!' etc. She much brighter than I expected, but deaf and gets cross if she can't hear. So one has to enunciate clearly. But I was conscious that she barely took in what I said. I felt I was boring her. She says she reads all day, and since being in this home has read all Henry James and Trollope as well as every new book which is sent her. Only one book has 'gripped' her: *Lark Rise*, by Flora Thompson, about a village close to Swinbrook. 'And,' she added, 'Elizabeth Longford's† *Wellington.*' Nancy is still sharp and tart. Complained that Lady Monckton‡ came and 'beefed' continuously and told her about the ailments of their mutual friends, the last thing she wished to hear.

---

* The Hon. Nancy Mitford, 1904–73; eldest Mitford sister; novelist and biographer; m. 1933 The Hon. Peter Rodd.

† Countess of Longford (née Elizabeth Harman), b. 1906; m. 1931 Francis (Frank) Pakenham (who s. his brother as 7th Earl of Longford, 1961); public servant, and author of several biographies.

‡ The Dowager Viscountess Monckton of Brenchley, 1896–1982; widow of 1st Viscount (d. 1965; as Sir Walter Monckton he was Director-General of the Ministry of Information during the Second World War).

Helen Dashwood,[*] of all people, is the favourite. She brings her
food every day, never beefs, is always full of cheer and good news. I
felt most inadequate. The truth must be that when one is as ill as she
one only wants to see the same persons, and I suspect that seeing an
old friend like me, after intervals, is exhausting. She said how pleased
she was that Violet Trefusis[†] was dead. They had a row, and V.
wrote her an awful letter, 'such an awful letter'. A month or two
later V. telephoned N. and said, 'Did my letter give you offence?'
'No,' said N., 'only a glorious excuse,' and rang off. 'That was
the end of that. It is so seldom one is able to say the right thing at
the right time.' I made conversation like mad, as one does in the
company of royalty, because one fears possibly quite wrongly that
during a short, infrequent encounter, one should not permit silences.
Complaints there were, that Raymond [Mortimer][‡] was disloyal,
never came now. I said he was abroad.

Tuesday, 16th January

Talked with Sally Westminster[§] in her bedroom where she will be
for weeks, her leg in plaster from a severe kick out hunting. In the
course of conversation she came clean for the first time about her
origin. It began with talk about her sister Diana, who has been
staying with her reluctantly, because she is busily engaged on a book
about their mother. Sally told me that Diana has promised not to
mention her, Sally, by name. Perhaps this is the consequence of my
talk with Daphne Fielding.[¶] S. said they suffered terribly as children,
for their mother never allowed anyone to come to their house at
Barnes; her life was spent disguising her terrible circumstances,
terrible to her. The mother took to drink, and finally married a
drunken colonel who kept a pub. S.'s twin sister stole £60 from
their till, with which she and Sally went to the south of France, and
finally escaped from home. The sister went to Mr Ackerley, a banana
king in Covent Garden, and asked him direct if he was their father

---

[*] Widow of Sir John Dashwood, 10th Bt (1896–1966), of West Wycombe Park.
[†] Violet Trefusis, 1894–1972; d. of Colonel The Hon. George Keppel and his wife
Alice (Mrs Keppel); novelist; lover of Vita Sackville-West.
[‡] Raymond Mortimer, 1895–1980; literary reviewer.
[§] Sally Perry, 1911–91; widow of Gerald Grosvenor, 4th Duke of Westminster.
[¶] The Hon. Daphne Vivian; writer; m. 1st, 1927, Henry Thynne, 4th Marquess of
Bath; 2nd, 1953, Xan Fielding, war hero and author.

(he was always known to them as 'Uncle'). His reply was, in that
timorous way of men, 'You had better ask your mother.' They
never found out where their mother had come from. The mother
was very beautiful, and may have been a barmaid picked up by their
father in her teens. She had no relations, no educated friends, only
common people who would look up to her. Dreadful that only one
generation ago so much shame went with illegitimacy. Gerald
Westminster was very good to the mother and stepfather, having
them to stay at Saighton. It is a strange sequel that Sally from this
background should have married one of England's richest dukes, and
become in her own right one of the sweetest and least spoilt of
duchesses.

Friday, 19th January

A. and I drove on Monday to Wilderhope Manor in Shropshire, via
Kidderminster. What used to be unviolated Shropshire country
around Kinlet is now dotted with modern bungalows. Kidderminster is of course quite unrecognizable and has been bulldozed and
rebuilt, like Plymouth after the Blitz. Bridgnorth and Bewdley are
becoming a ghastly mess. The first, perched on its delightful acropolis, now overlooks an ocean of factories and horrors. The little
narrow Georgian street at its feet is about to come down. Bewdley's
outskirts are fringed with caravan sites along both ends of the river;
and houses are now to be seen on the crest of Blackstone Rock from
Ribbesford. Lax Lane, a street in Bewdley leading from the river
quay to the High Street, has every single house boarded up. These
are charming little two-storeyed artisan houses, which one might
suppose could serve instead of the caravans. But no. The house in
High Street in which Mr Baldwin was born – a plaque has been put
on the wall recently – has had the Georgian porch wrenched off by a
lorry. The conglomeration of wires, pylons, ill-placed factories and
execrable villas is so horrifying that I utterly despair of the landscape.
I know that people say there has always been change which is
resented by the old. But never, never has there been such devastating change as during my lifetime, change always for the worse
aesthetically, never for the better. The public *en bloc* are blind to
hideous surroundings. I prefer to stay at home in my ivory tower
and never go on expeditions rather than be affronted at every
familiar turn with a substitute architectural monstrosity.

Kinlet, a boys' school, once a sedate country house of red brick, is terribly down-at-heel. As children we used to go there with Granny when the Childe family lived in it. Exterior fire escapes, drains (in the wrong places), general disintegration and minimum mainten- ance. The Georgian trimmings as they fall off not replaced. Church- yard a wilderness, church empty and forlorn.

Monday, 22nd January

At my age dread of death governs all thought. Each fresh symptom of my decay, physical and mental, and the passing of contemporaries, all are clockwork reminders of annihilation. In reading biographies I always assess the span of life of others in relation to the span I have reached, the measurement permanently asserting itself. I don't believe any old people aren't frightened of death. All the ones I have talked to admit the fear.

Wednesday, 24th January

Reading Sir Walter Scott's *Journals*. Reviews of a new edition impelled me to take down the two vols which I stole from old Lady Muir's house, Deanston in Perthshire, when I was twenty-one; that must have been in 1929. Ever since then these volumes have followed me around, uncut. Scott certainly was a noble fellow, very honourable, courageous and kind. The journals include details of the dreadful financial disaster he went through, losing all his money – the folly of it – and then losing his wife three months later. Yet there lurks a vein of, not inhumanity, but rather insensitivity. I detect it in the passages where he mourns his wife. Does he really care? Was not Lady Scott, as he calls her – seldom 'my poor Charlotte' – a bit of an incubus? Had she not fulfilled her purpose, whatever that was – the begetting of his children, the housekeeping of her various dwellings? Was not this fat, placid, flaccid lady, which I imagine her to have been, and without the slightest learning, by now rather a bore, and a poor companion to a man of his wide erudition and renown? I don't think he was a man of deep feeling. The fact that he liked nearly everyone suggests it; suggests that he cared for no one much. What amazes me is the speed with which he wrote, a novel in a matter of months, and such long novels. Then they were published within months. Proofs were returned within days. He is generous about other authors, and gives a splendid passage of praise to Jane Austen.

Says she achieved in little as much as he in great. Or words to that effect. True, I think. He was no intellectual, had no fine feelings, or thoughts; yet nothing strictly speaking reprehensible passed through that clear mind, I am sure. A lovable man. But too facetious.

Friday, 26th January

Dear old Edward Hindle[*] has died at the age of 87. I said to A., 'Was it because he didn't want to come and stay with us because he was too old, or because he was too old, that we didn't invite him recently?' She said the last. Which bears out my certainty that people cannot be bothered with the very old. It is one of the saddest things in life. He was a man with the liveliest curiosity, full of theories and knowledge about a variety of subjects. An FRS, the inventor of anti-yellow fever vaccine and the introducer of the first pair of hamsters into this country, from which all hamsters are descended. He was merry, laughed a lot, talked incessantly, and yet was not quite boring; perhaps nearly so, verging. But one always left him with a new idea supplied, and he troubled to explain scientific data to us, which showed his patience and tolerance. He slushed good humouredly with ill-fitting false teeth. He was A.'s friend, not mine, and firstly Anthony's.[†]

Sunday, 28th January

Rather boldly, I thought, I wrote last Sunday to Lady De L'Isle,[‡] who was Lady Glanusk, asking if I might one day see the bust of my great-grandfather, Sir Joseph Bailey, which I understand she has at Glanusk. She telephoned last night, delighted. Apparently her daughter Shân is very keen on family history. They also have a good portrait of Sir J. by, she said, a pupil of Reynolds, which sounds improbable; dates don't fit. She was amused by my reference to him as a rough diamond and my quotation of Lady

---

[*] Edward Hindle, FRS (1942), 1886–1973; Scientific Director of the Zoological Society, London, 1941–54; researcher in tropical medicine.

[†] Anthony, 3rd Viscount Chaplin, 1906–82; zoologist and pianist; m. 1933 Alvilde Bridges (m. diss. 1950).

[‡] Margaret (Peggy), wife of 1st Viscount De L'Isle, VC, and formerly of 3rd Baron Glanusk (who d. 1948).

Charlotte Guest's reference to 'Mr Bailey's low-born, purse-proud cunning'. She said when she showed the passage to the aunts, then alive, including Gladys Bailey whom I knew, they were shocked and incredulous. Lady De L'I. has many family papers. Said Sir J. was obviously a brute, that he disinherited two of his sons and asked if my grandfather was one of them. Possibly he was, since my grandfather never had much money. At any rate she has asked us to lunch or to stay at Glanusk in the spring.

Saturday, 3rd February

Reading Edith Wharton's[*] autobiography. Too many famous people dragged in. But some amusing anecdotes of Henry James. She complains about her bad memory, except for people's telephone numbers; and says that everything she has once read must be stored somewhere in the depths of her memory. I agree with this notion. With me, old memories rise at quite unexpected moments, quite unsolicited, to explode on the surface like bubbles, sometimes years later.

Yesterday I met J[ohn] Betjeman[†] at Bath station at 12.20. He wanted to see the horrors perpetrated by Casson and Dr Stutchbury[‡]. I motored him round the city. He was appalled. Thought the worst offences were the new Balance Street blocks and the University. Agreed the latter was one's vision of hell. We lunched beautifully at the Hole in the Wall. Here the waitresses recognized him. So did Seager's book shop. So did the cashier in the Midland Bank, who at once informed the manager, who rushed out; so did the attendants in the Pump Room. In walking through Queen Square I saw a man turn round and stop before a house in the Square. John, hesitating on the pavement, said, 'In one of these houses there used to be the finest staircase in Bath.' Hardly were the words out of his mouth before the man rushed upon us, exclaiming, 'It was this house, Sir John. Come in.' We did, and admired the

---

[*] Edith Wharton, 1861–1937; American novelist, and friend of Henry James.
[†] Sir John Betjeman, 1906–84; poet, broadcaster, and writer on architecture; succeeded Cecil Day-Lewis as Poet Laureate in 1972.
[‡] Sir Hugh Casson, b. 1910; architect; President of the Royal Academy 1976–84; architectural adviser to Bath City Corporation in the 1960s and '70s when Dr Howard E. Stutchbury was the city's Planning Officer.

stairwell, all that is left, and the splendid stucco relief work on the walls. In an instant the manager of the firm, a gent with a purple face and breathing fumes of alcohol, ran from his office down the back stairs, eager to talk to the poet. Just as well I had not told the Bath Preservation committee that he was coming, for he would have been mobbed. J. says it is worse since he was made Laureate. That people all over the world send him their poems, seldom with addressed or stamped envelopes; and that people appear on his doorstep at eight in the morning asking to read their odes to him.

The other night The Widow Lloyd* had an accident. John had to take him to his room at Brooks's where he was staying, and put him to bed. The Widow Lloyd in writing to thank him afterwards said, 'This must be the first occasion of a Poet Laureate tucking a bachelor into bed since Tennyson did it to Arthur Hallam.'

J.B.'s humility is touching. To everyone who approaches him he speaks courteously; and when they leave him, he complains. After dinner last night he said to Burnet Pavitt,[†] 'After you, please. You are so distinguished. I am only a fraud who has got away with it.' A trifle disingenuous?

John B. said, apropos of changing values, that Dig Yorke[‡] refused to let him bring Bosie Douglas to her house. This was in the early Thirties. Nevertheless the Yorkes in those days were considered avant-garde young people, broad-minded and tolerant. Today one's grandmother would not refuse, if one had one.

Still reading Walter Scott's journal. He, the least valetudinarian of men, recorded the incipient signs of his old age: 'Terrible how they increase the last year.' He clearly had little strokes, yet was not sure whether they were strokes or not. Found he could not marshal his words, and thought it was fear or nerves which caused this; that he must pull himself together and snap out of it. Reminders of mortality are indeed painful.

---

* John D. K. Lloyd, 1900–78; conservationist and historian; known to friends as The Widow Lloyd from the peak of hair on his forehead.
† Burnet Pavitt, b. 1908; Managing Director of Roche, 1948–73, and Trustee of The Royal Opera House, Covent Garden for 25 years.
‡ The Hon. Adelaide (Dig) Biddulph, wife of Henry Yorke (the novelist Henry Green, 1905–73).

The young are odd, and extraordinarily casual. Nick my great-nephew,[*] having expressed the wish to be taken to Rome by me, repeated it on Xmas Eve. So I said I would consider taking him during his Easter holidays. I telephoned his mother a fortnight later, and suggested that Nick ring me up before he returned to Winchester. He never did. I wrote him ten days ago and put forward the offer as definite. Have had no reply. If I get none by Saturday I shall write and tell him I have changed my mind and the invitation is withdrawn. Or is it unwise for a great-uncle to treat the young as a governess treats delinquent children? On the other hand, how else can one inculcate manners into them? I suppose he really does not want to come. I am not sure how much I want to take him; certainly I don't if no one else will accompany me. The strain would be too great.

Thursday, 8th February

While in London this week went to Chatto's by appointment, to meet the publicity girl, I having been told she must see me. Got there. Girl very polite. Asks me what ideas I have. I say, None. Thought she might supply some. She said, It is difficult to boost a novel. I say, It must be. We part in a friendly way, having achieved – nothing, that I can see.

To my great surprise I find in *The Times* this morning the letter which I sent them ten days ago, and which they wrote declining to publish. I dispatched a private letter crossly on Sunday. I suppose this is the result. You must beat a horse if you wish to get anything out of it. I never wanted to write this particular letter in the first place, and only did it out of duty. What annoyed me was the familiar phrase, 'The Editor read your letter with much interest, took note, etc., but regrets...' I said in my retort that it was untruth.

Saturday, 10th February

Rosamond [Lehmann][†] was coming to stay this weekend, but put us off on the plea that she cannot leave London

---

[*] Nicholas and Henry Robinson, sons of J.L.-M.'s sister Audrey's daughter Prudence Arthur, 1932–76, who m. 1953 Major Edwin Winwood Robinson, of Moorwood, nr Cirencester.
[†] Rosamond Lehmann, 1901–90; novelist.

while Elizabeth Bowen[*] is dying, which seems to be the case, of lung cancer – she smoked like a chimney. I don't believe Ros was an intimate friend, but she designates herself death-bed watcher-in-chief. She cannot keep away, revelling in death scenes.

Did an impetuous thing. While lunching with Joan Drogheda[†] on Wednesday couldn't resist being persuaded to go to London next Friday night for *Don Pasquale* in the Royal Box. Took the 4.05 train from Chippenham. Arrived Brooks's just in time to change and taxi to Ros who wanted fetching. She had ordered a huge limousine to take us to Covent Garden. The performance was first-rate and I enjoyed that, the main thing after all, but hardly the social side. One interval only for a rushed dinner in the box. Couldn't get going with guests, couldn't make contact. Had nothing to say; dross. However, Ros and I left immediately the opera was over in our limousine and I talked to her in her flat. But I was *flat*. Felt that tickling in the left nostril which portends a cold, or worse. Today streaming, and headache.

A. and I met on the 8.45, hoping to get breakfast. But owing to a signal breakdown previous night no attendants able to reach Paddington, and breakfast (so-called) postponed till after Reading. We managed to snatch a piece of bread and butter and some nasty Nescafé. Lunched with Eliza [Wansbrough].[‡] The Eshers[§] and Eccleses[¶] there. Could not make much headway with the Eccleses. He is pomp. but jolly, forced. I don't believe a clever man at all. Whereas Lionel distinctly is. Christian Esher is sad. Says matrimony is a ghastly institution; and her children have the sense not to observe it. They have illegitimate children all over the place and come to her asking for congratulations. Honesty, their honesty is what is wonderful, she says. But weren't we honest? They must love without hurting others, she claims. I say,

[*] Elizabeth Bowen, 1899–1973; novelist.

[†] Joan Carr, pianist; m. 1935 Garrett, Viscount Moore, later 11th Earl of Drogheda; both d. 1989.

[‡] (Mrs) Elizabeth Wansbrough, d. of Sir George Lewis, Bt, well-known late Victorian solicitor.

[§] Lionel Brett, 4th Viscount Esher, b. 1913; architect and poet; m. 1935 Christian Pike, artist.

[¶] David Eccles, 1st Viscount, PC, b. 1904; statesman; m. 1st 1928 Sybil, e.d. of Viscount Dawson of Penn (who d. 1977).

we were taught that too. Yes, but we don't fulfil it. 'Do they?' I ask.
No answer.

Wednesday, 14th February

It snowed in the night, and having been freezingly cold yesterday,
is today warmer. Also still. The garden looked as though
sprinkled with icing sugar, the rich cake showing through, not by
any means deeply covered. Went for a walk with the dogs this afternoon around Badminton, from Shepherd's Cottage to Worcester
Lodge, and thought I could never leave this place, I am so fond of
it. A pale blue sky overhead, bright sun, and although a thaw, very
beautiful. Dogs did not much enjoy themselves. Nowadays they do
not like the wet, or the cold. They are dreadfully cissy. It is our fault,
we have made them so by treating them like humans.

I am reading Robin Maugham's[*] autobiography. Very readable,
and courageous. Yet I feel these homosexuals enjoy parading their
adventures. On every occasion he introduces some affair he has had,
with a boy at school, or in the tank regiment. All great fun, but
minorities become bores when they air their grievances. There is a
book out, I see, by a member of the Gay Club, indicating that the
government of England should be handed over to the queers. God
help us! Where would we be, for the temperament, the unreliabil-
ity? Maugham is also very severe with poor Willie.[†] I daresay what
he tells is true, but it certainly is unkind. Who am I to speak? If I
poke fun at my poor father, I don't, I hope, malign him.

I have finished putting down my chapter on the Countess of
Albany[‡] (not 'Lady Albany', as Master[§] would insist, for hers was a
foreign title), and am re-writing it, improving it. Soon shall be
typing out the whole book. I have still to begin, and finish, so to
speak – by which I mean, impart a consecutiveness to the whole, if I

---

[*] Robert Maugham, 2nd Viscount, 1916–1981; novelist (as Robin Maugham); nephew
of W. Somerset Maugham; his father, the 1st Viscount, was Lord Chancellor.
[†] W. Somerset Maugham, 1874–1965; orphaned at 10; qualified as a surgeon at St
Thomas's Hospital, London; novelist, playwright and short-story writer.
[‡] Louisa, Princess of Stolberg and Countess of Albany, 1753–1824; m. 1772 Prince
Charles Edward Stuart, 'The Young Pretender'.
[§] Henry Somerset, 10th Duke of Beaufort, 1900–84, of Badminton House, Gloucester-
shire; m. 1923 Lady Mary Cambridge, daughter of the 1st Marquess of Cambridge;
Master of the Horse and Master of Foxhounds.

can. Next week my novel comes out, a week tomorrow. The cover looks charming, and the feel of the thing is good. Chatto's have asked me to luncheon on the publishing day.

Thursday, 15th February

Robin Maugham is, I believe, a nice man, but he is vain. He is too pleased with his own writing. This is a feminine streak, *vide* Nancy M. and so many other women. He has descriptive ability. Tells a story well, and at times is very funny. But he compares himself with Willie. This should not be. Willie was a first-rate writer – I don't mean man – with an incisiveness which no one else possessed. A cold, steely, cruel style, but clean as a whistle. Robin is nothing to him. I only once met him, with Harold, who was fond of him. Robin had a friend whom he brought to see Harold in Albany. He made the boy take down his trousers and show Harold the size of his cock. H. somewhat puzzled, and displeased.

Friday, 16th February

Motored to Nottingham, 160 miles from here, to see the Lord Burlington Exhibition, the catalogue of which was sent me by a young don, Wilton-Ely,[*] very kindly making references to my *Earls of Creation*. A. accompanied me. We were given luncheon at the University; John Pope-Hennessy[†] had come from London too. I sat next to the Chancellor, a friendly old boy. I asked him why undergraduates of today, who were paid for by the state, were never sent down as were we (whose parents paid for us) if we misbehaved. 'Fear,' he said. 'Only fear.' Vice-Chancellors are frightened.

Tuesday, 20th February

David Somerset[‡] at dinner here said that the French papers have seriously reported that the Duke of Beaufort, having no children of

---

[*] Professor John Wilton-Ely, architectural historian and lecturer.

[†] Sir John Pope-Hennessy, 1913–94; Director of the Victoria and Albert Museum, 1967–73; Director of the British Museum, 1974–6; art historian; elder son of Dame Una Pope-Hennessy, author, d. 1949.

[‡] David Somerset, cousin and heir of 10th Duke of Beaufort; m. 1950 Lady Caroline Thynne, dau. of 6th Marquess of Bath (she d. 1995); living at The Cottage, Badminton, Gloucestershire.

his own, is going to adopt young Mark Phillips,[*] Princess Anne's young man, and make him Marquess of Worcester, in order to spare the Government the embarrassment of creating him a hereditary peer. It is amazing how ignorant foreigners are of our hereditary principles.

My self-confidence is struck down to the lowest bedrock, and the guts of it torn to shreds, by the review due to appear next month in *Books and Bookmen*, which the editor has sent me. Apparently there was an unfavourable review, or rather a short notice, in the *Observer* which I have not seen. It is absurd to feel so wounded. I do not mind disagreement, or disapproval. It is derision which I find hard to bear. Nothing so much hurts the pride. I feel I do not wish to see my friends, to listen to, 'I see your novel is out', or, 'What a horrid review you had yesterday', or, worse still, 'I am sorry. I am sure it is not deserved.' Nothing so exposes one as a novel, I think. Even an autobiography is less exposing because the reader can question whether the writer is telling the truth. In a novel the writer must be writing what he feels, or what he is capable of feeling, through the actions and words of his fictional characters, which amounts to the same thing.

Saturday, 24th February

Reading Flora Thompson's *Lark Rise*, written in the 1930s about life in an Oxfordshire hamlet in the 1880s, by the daughter of a cottager, reminds me of traditions which persisted even in the Twenties, in my childhood. Hopscotch, for instance, was played by all village children. I remember them drawing squares with chalk on the village street and jumping from one to the other. She calls to mind the callousness of country people. I too remember the dreadful killing of the pig in each cottage garden, how the poor animal would squeal piteously as it was bled to death. I too used to take birds' eggs, and blow them, for my collection, just as I put butterflies in killing-bottles. I would rather die than do such things today.

---

[*] Captain Mark Phillips, who m. 1973 The Princess Anne (now The Princess Royal); m. diss. 1992.

Thursday was publication date. No reviews. Only one review so far, in last Sunday's *Observer*, apparently very unfavourable. I lunched with Norah Smallwood and Hugo Brunner.[*] Iris Murdoch[†] was to have come too, but had influenza. Before arriving at the office I worked myself into a frenzy, and had to sit in St Martin's church trying to calm down before I could enter Chatto's office. In the London Library I skulked to avoid friends. Even so two came up to say, 'What about this novel?' I can't bear any reference to it. Luncheon was however enjoyable. Norah is a most sympathetic woman, calm too. Says I am not to worry for I am bound to get horrid reviews, and counsels me to not read them. I shall not in future. Even so, kind friends tell me about them. Someone wrote today condoling about the *Observer*'s. Norah surprised me by telling me how badly dear Ros behaved over the Day-Lewis[‡] break. Ros made terrible trouble with the wife, and abused the children of Day-Lewis. Norah said Day-Lewis had no alternative to bolting without warning. She was amused by Ros's assumption of intimate friendship with Elizabeth Bowen. They were never great friends, and years ago had a row over Goronwy Rees, the lover of both. Norah says the younger generation have no sense of humour whatever. It is extraordinary how she as a publisher takes the 'permissive' for granted nowadays; thinks a book without it lacking, like an egg without salt.

Monday, 26th February

Yesterday's *Sunday Times* had such an excellent, understanding review of *Heretics* that I was induced to read it. How dishonest one is. I vowed not to read any more reviews, because the unfavourable ones hurt so, and because I am assured one is favourable, I read it. Not without misgiving however. Weakness of course. Yet this review has restored my confidence a little. At last someone has recognized that the book is not contemptible, but is a serious effort. That is what I mind, that it should be dismissed for the wrong reasons, dismissed because it is about a vanished world which is realer than the present, hideous, squalid world we are living in.

---

[*] Hugo Brunner, b. 1935; publisher; Director of Chatto & Windus, 1967–76.
[†] Iris Murdoch (Mrs J. O. Bayley), cr. DBE 1987; academic and novelist.
[‡] Cecil Day-Lewis, 1904–72; Poet Laureate, 1967–72.

This morning a press cutting from the *Guardian* came. I put it in the file, unread. I am pleased because the *S. Times* is the paper read by the highbrows.

Derry Moore* is the dearest friend. He stayed this weekend. We went for long walks, and he talked openly, with no reservations. I no longer have this intimacy with either of his parents. Can't talk at all to Garrett who jumps like a cat on hot bricks from one subject to another, and Joan who is too affected, too intent on her wiles to operate her other talents until one has been with her at least twenty-four hours. Walking through the woods – and Derry is appreciative of everything, what the country has to offer, come sun, come rain – after a light fall of snow the trees were dappled with a smattering of down, which was not white at all, but blue. Extraordinary it was. We both remarked that it was more strange than beautiful, for the blue was the blue of American ladies' hair. Why was this? The sun was faintly shining, and the sky had become pale blue. We were looking down upon the trees from a height, not upwards.

I listened in bed to a second programme on Caruso, whose 100th birthday it is. I have always supposed his voice the purest tenor I have ever heard, on records I mean. He sustained notes without a tremor of effort. When I was at Eton I used to play over and over again in the holidays one record of him and Melba singing together, from? *Carmen* – can't remember; it was played last night and made me think that even in those remote days when I was more unmusical than I am now, and totally uneducated, I was not a philistine. It portended things to come. What pleased me inordinately in the *S. Times* article was being described as 'a distinguished aesthete'. Vanity.

Thursday 1st March

The crows, or rooks, for I never know one from the other, congregate upon the roads, picking at I suppose the grit from the surface. It must supply some strength they have need of. How beautifully sleek and glossy they look; and they are scavengers, feeding upon the nastiest offal. This the result. Yet I don't like these birds with their busy, sly and utterly unscrupulous cast in the eye.

---

* Dermot, Viscount Moore; s. father as 12th Earl of Drogheda, 1989; photographer.

Although I inveigh against motorways and the motorway means of transport, I confess to getting some satisfaction in buzzing along them in my little Morris. The car simply purrs and whizzes, and the country often is so clean and exciting as one slashes through it. There is no doubt that the sense of speed uninterrupted is stimulating, and arouses ruthless instincts.

Spent £5 on a Byron dinner in the House of Lords, thinking it would be fun. But not a single old friend; no one I knew, and the dinner filthy. Began with pale soup made of stickfast; dry fish in rolls, also in stickfast sauce; overcooked beef with stringy leeks; and what is called a sundae, i.e., a tinned peach covered with synthetic cream squatting on ice. Coffee undrinkable. This what the Lords and Commons have to endure, and most of them doubtless relish it. I sat next to a Dutch woman married to the Italian head of the Italian Institute in London, and a member of the Nottingham Council. Not inspiring. There was a top table with three lesser tables below the salt. At the top table lords – Lytton in the chair, Bessborough, Longford, Strabolgi, Abinger – and two commoners, Mrs Langley Moore* and Professor Somebody. The lords behaved impeccably. They were gracious to us poor everyday folk. They were courteous, slick and capable. They spoke well. I thought how these hereditary peers still count for something. But how snobbish the English still are. Bessborough read very well Byron's second of three speeches delivered in the Lords, advocating Catholic emancipation. An excellent sentiment behind it, but the speech of a dramatist. Then discussion. Tributes were paid to Byron as poet, prose writer, champion of the downtrodden. I meant to stand up, and then didn't because of my absurd shyness, to draw attention to Byron the sage, of whom his contemporaries – Scott, Moore, Rogers – spoke with awe, and whom Goethe who could not read English considered a prodigious intellect. For whereas Shelley was silly, and Keats adolescent, Byron however provocative never said a foolish thing, and his every utterance was noteworthy. He was a giant among men. This distinguishes him from his contemporaries.

---

* Mrs (Doris) Langley Moore, founder of the Museum of Costume, Assembly Rooms, Bath; designer of costumes for period films; writer.

Wednesday 14th March

Yesterday in London went to Graham Rust's[*] exhibition at Hazlitt Gallery of topographical wash drawings. Very high standard. I was amazed how competent and attractive. They resemble late eighteenth- or early nineteenth-century work, and are in the style of Labacco or one of those artists taken to Italy in the suite of Sir Richard Colt Hoare. Derivative undeniably, but delightful. Every single one was sold by the time I got there. Curious habit of leaving cloudless skies.

A. and I lunched with Nigel Nicolson[†] at the Café Royal by long invitation. I knew what he wanted to tell us. Sure enough it was that he has written a book, called *Portrait of a Marriage,* including Vita's autobiographical story of her elopement with Violet Trefusis, and amplified it with the story of her lesbianism and happy marriage with Harold. When he asked our opinion five years ago we said we thought this idea a mistake. Now we both feel that so much has been revealed since then about this subject and her, notably in Q. Bell's biography of V. Woolf, that it no longer matters. I said in fairness he ought therefore to say that Harold likewise led his own life, and was not an aggrieved but a complaisant husband. Nigel agreed, but said that his father never was *in love.* His affairs were like a quick visit to the National Gallery between catching trains. Both Eardley[‡] and John [Kenworthy-Browne][§] to whom I told this think Nigel ought not to cash in on his parents' love life, and that it is no one's business to know. Both strongly disapprove. I am not sure. I think the book, which is going to be *the* book of 1973, will enhance V.'s ultimate reputation, though not immediately.

Nigel is a ball of fire. He has his *Alex* book coming out now, having already been serialized. *Portrait* next year. He is going to the Himalayas in the autumn, to write about them; he has been commissioned to edit all Virginia W[oolf]'s letters, and the life of Lord

---

[*] Graham Rust, artist and painter of murals.
[†] Nigel Nicolson, b. 1917; yr s. of The Hon. (later Sir) Harold Nicolson and The Hon. Vita Sackville-West; writer.
[‡] Eardley Knollys, 1902–91; painter, and National Trust representative in south-west counties.
[§] John Kenworthy-Browne, b. 1931; on staff of National Trust and Christie's; expert on neo-classical sculpture.

Curzon which Philip Magnus is abandoning. He is a fearsome worker, just like Harold.

We got back from Morocco at three in the morning of last Monday, having stayed nine days with David Herbert[*] in Tangier. David's social existence appalled me, but I much enjoyed the three days we spent staying at Meknès and motoring into the Atlas and hinterland. A most beautiful country of infinite landscape variety, like England. Beautiful people, cheerful and sympathetic and picturesque, wearing their national dress, all the women veiled. Keen sense of colour in their clothes.

Sunday, 18th March

David is an engaging figure. He is adored by all and sundry. Wherever we went he was greeted with affection. Hall porters and waiters in hotels and restaurants kissed him on both cheeks. People on the road waved to him in his car. He is unguarded and cares not a fig who knows that he is homosexual; rather he revels in it. I was surprised to find on Sunday morning that he goes to church in time to show the congregation into their pews. He takes the offertory bag round, not like most of us discreetly looking away as he hands it to each member of the congregation, but peering in to see how much has been given, smiling, nodding and cracking jokes. At the airport we duly kissed each other goodbye on both cheeks.

Yesterday Midi[†] and Sally W[estminster] lunched. We told them that Joanie Harford[‡] was ill. Neither knew. Sally at once wished to rally; telephoned and was answered by Charlie Harford that Joanie could not talk to anyone on the telephone; felt too ill. So this morning Sally picked daffodils and collected foods which she thought Joanie would like, and again telephoned. Ben answered. Sally said breezily, 'I'm coming round now with some things for Joanie.' 'But, Sally...' Ben said. 'No, I am not going to be sent away. I insist on coming to see Joanie. I shan't speak, just sit with her.' 'But, Sally....' etc. 'No, no, no. I absolutely insist. I'm coming now.' Poor Ben, the son, had to say, sharply, 'Sally, I must insist on

---

[*] The Hon. David Herbert, 1908–95; yr s. of 15th Earl of Pembroke; resident in Tangier.
[†] The Hon. Mary O'Neill, wife of Derick Gascoigne, mother of Bamber Gascoigne; then living at The Mount House, Alderley; she d. 1990.
[‡] Joan Wylde, wife of Charles Harford of Ashcroft, Gloucestershire.

your listening to what I have got to say. Mother died this morning at 8.30.' Sally immediately rang us up, and could hardly get the words out. All day A. and I have been miserable. Yet we cannot cry. We ask each other why this is so. Is it because so many of our friends are going, one by one, Bob Gathorne-Hardy[*] the other day, Ralph Jarvis?[†] We agree that we mind more losing Joanie Harford than anyone else round here, even more than we would Diana W.[‡] who is old; and so our grief is in one sense selfish, because someone on whom we depend for company, at odd meals, with anyone or no one else, is taken from us. We mind not only because she was adorable, but because she was seemingly not cherished enough by those close to her. And caveat! strangers do not know how families inwardly feel.

I could not help seeing a short paragraph review of *Heretics* in the *Sunday Telegraph*. 'Silly', it said. The reviews have been, with the single exception of the *Sunday Times*, uniformly bad.

Monday, 19th March

On Friday I was taken by Tony Mitchell, the N.T. representative, to Charlecote to help put some finishing touches to the arrangement of the rooms for the forthcoming season. Alice [Fairfax-] Lucy[§] unable to come because Brian has had a heart attack. To think that I did this with Alice and Clifford Smith in 1947. I was appalled to find, in looking behind a picture which I had hung in the drawing-room then, that the strip of 1840 damask fabric was there a deep gold, whereas the rest of the hangings are now straw colour. Since this house has been in the Trust's care the light has faded these hangings. Found dear old Alianore[¶] wandering round the stables. She is 79, much

---

[*] The Hon. Robert Gathorne-Hardy, 1902–73, s. of 4th Earl of Cranbrook; writer and botanist.

[†] Colonel Ralph Jarvis, 1907–73, of Doddington Hall, Lincoln; Chairman of Banque de Paris et des Pays Bas.

[‡] Diana Lister, d. of 4th and last Baron Ribblesdale; m. 1923, as her 3rd husband, the 14th Earl of Westmorland; she d. 1983.

[§] Major Sir Brian Fairfax-Lucy, 5th Bt, 1898–1974; m. 1933 The Hon. Alice Buchan d. of 1st Viscount Tweedsmuir (the author John Buchan); she d. 1994.

[¶] Alianore Fairfax-Lucy, unmarried d. of Sir Henry Fairfax-Lucy, 4th Bt, who lived all her life at Charlecote.

changed. The new custodian apparently said, after I left, how much
he liked me, and how charming I was. 'Of course he is,' said
Alianore, who is simple but true blue. 'He was at Eton and in the
Brigade of Guards.' Brian rang me up to tell me this, with much
merriment.

Tuesday, 20th March

Poor Alianore looked stunted. Bent like a bow; a great cavity where
her chest should have been and a swollen stomach. Yet her face still
like a polished apple, though smaller, and her hair bright red in
wisps. Had she been a society woman I should have suspected it
tinted. She said she was suffering from the same trouble as Brian,
some form of arthritis, and takes that awful drug Cortisone.

A. came fully dressed into my bedroom at 7.30, assuring me it was
7.45 and that my clock was slow. Of course it was nothing of the
sort. Chuff bounding on to the bed and burying himself under the
eiderdown. A. will now get to Kemble station half an hour too early
and have to wait on the cold platform. Then before the train has
drawn up she will dash down the platform, throw herself into the
breakfast car and start agitating because she has to wait till Swindon
before they will serve her. Is always ahead of time, poor darling.

After breakfast I walk from the front door down the drive. It is a
beautifully still morning, crisp and cold, the slanting sun shining in
streaks like the haloes of saints. I watch the mist quickly rise from the
valley below our paddock. It gathers, rolls, creeps up the field and
within five minutes has gently lapped the house. Why does it decide
to do this at such an hour, at such a season, when with the gradual
warming of the earth one would suppose the mist would dissipate,
not increase? Such a smell of strong earth, almost autumnal. It is
dreadful how little I observe. The bunch of primroses on my writing
table, for instance: the centre of each flower is yellow, a star of five
rays, each having a pencilled dark green spoke. In the middle of the
star a minute detached pin-head, yellow likewise, not primrose. I
ought to spend a whole morning just looking into it, counting the
petals, five each − why always five? − the crinkly, corrugated leaves,
so stubby and inelegant, instead of thinking Hurray! the newspaper
van has just driven up and I can now read *The Times*. Ugh, the
world draws me, and yet I despise and hate it. Five more minutes
have gone, and outside there is a dense fog.

My figure has completely gone. My waist is non-existent. Two straight lines from the shoulders to the ankles. I remember noticing this sudden change of figure in my grandmother and, later, my father. Both had superb figures, as mine was. After this change both went very quickly. Mummy never lost hers. When I told A. this she reminded me that in Paris last year in trying on dresses she complained that none of them looked right on her. '*Alors, madame, vous êtes de pareille de haut en bas,*' the shop woman remarked in that charming French way.

Thursday, 22nd March

Yesterday I stopped and looked at Little Sodbury church. Three old country people were raking the graveyard. I asked them if Mark Harford* was buried here. He wasn't, but at Horton. One of the old ladies, wearing a bonnet with strings, said, 'I did so like Mr Harford. He was so natural. He kind of came down to one's level. By the look of him he mightn't have had a penny in's pocket. I wouldn't live in that there house (nodding towards the manor) for nothing. I once went inside, and I was hawestruck. I've never seen anything like it.' The old man said, 'Us gets Americans come to this church to see where 'e (meaning Tyndale) wrote the Bible.' He showed me a grave curb. 'It makes it difficult for we to mow the grass.' And he complained of the litter. ''E just chucked they 'ere.' 'E being the public, presumably.

Friday, 23rd March

At two o'clock we went to Joanie Harford's funeral at Kingscote. A most beautiful afternoon, clear fresh air, bright sunshine, warm and springlike. There were hundreds of people. This, I said to myself, is the consequence of being loved. All this attention, all these people standing in the churchyard, waiting and watching fearfully when the pall bearers carry in the little coffin, followed by two clergymen, Bishop Bill Llewellyn with episcopal crook, Charlie and Ben, the principal mourners. The grave-side a mass of brilliant wreaths. We had the committal service first, then trooped into the small church where Communion was held. This a new idea, but a good one, called a Communion of Thanksgiving. Both A. and I went to the altar. We left

---

* Of Little Sodbury Manor, Gloucestershire.

feeling very sad, for Joanie undoubtedly our most intimate friend round here, whom we would see without prearrangements, who had tea with us in the kitchen, or in summer on the lawn, who belonged, who knew everyone, and everything about everyone, who was kind and good.

Saturday, 24th March

On our way to Tetbury turned off the road to Kingscote church again, for A. wanted to see what the wreath we ordered for Joanie looked like. The weather has suddenly changed to a dank, drizzly, dripping afternoon. Where were crowds of loving friends yesterday was no one today. Utter loneliness and desertion. The wreaths already perishing, drenched. Since the cards had been collected, we never found ours. The desolation of the dead who are – rightly – forgotten in the twinkling of an eye.

Monday, 26th March

A. dropped me at the gate of Newark and I met a young man who has plans to make a flat out of part of the stables here. Went over the stables, which stink from the pigs next door, and looked at his plans, and said I would report on them to the Plans Committee. Walked home with the dogs down the wooded drive.

Wednesday, 28th March

Primroses out in abundance upon the steep bank in the village where the two lanes meet opposite the Gate House. So far the wretched machine to cut the verges has not come.

I find myself breathless these days for no apparent reason. This does not prevent me from taking fairly long walks – though I doubt if I would wish to walk more than ten miles now. Sometimes I feel as if a weight were on my chest. Some mornings rising from bed I feel stiff all over and frangible as though a loud noise might break me in two. Indeed, noises send me into great distress. Quiet is more and more necessary to keep me together.

I have lately been thinking that perhaps I shall never be able to cry again. Another emotion freezing up? But when this morning Schubert's Impromptu in G Flat was played on the wireless I was moved to tears. Glad of this.

Friday, 30th March

At 9.15 A. and I set out, without dogs, for Wareham. Lovely spring, sunny day, but oh the traffic! Lorries, lorries all the way. Object of journey threefold. First we took the typewriter I bought for Monica Baldwin[*] to Rethfelton House, where she now is living. A. dropped me at the entrance of the drive, where I sat reading *Country Life* on dead prickly leaves under an oak tree, while she delivered the type-writer. I have not yet seen Monica and feel it would be a mistake to do so. A. thinks this very foolish. Liked her enormously. Found her in bed for she has back trouble. Does not look 80, is extremely vital, talks much, is funny, very bright and intelligent. All that I knew. A. says I must see her. But should I? I fear the spell might break, she or I might find something in the other irritating, disappointing, so that we would no longer be able to correspond. We continued to Litton Cheney and lunched with Janet Stone,[†] deliciously off nursery food, kedgeree and wine, home-made brown bread, Jersey butter, Jersey cream cheese. Reynolds, alas, away in London for the day, a thing he rarely does. He seldom leaves the place. Object of this visit, to be photographed by Janet for her forthcoming exhibition of rogues. I cannot be natural when a lens is pointed at me. 'Don't smile!' she cries. Sensibly because of the inane grin people put on for studio portraits. So I endeavoured to look my usual, scowling self. 'Don't try!' Janet cried. I scowled more, gazing at the church tower in a soulful way, I fear. After luncheon, before we left the table Janet poured my half-empty glass of wine back into the bottle. I liked this. She is herself, yet contrived in that she wears fancy dress of an Edwardian lady – long, trailing, bouffé skirt of corduroy, frilled collar to her jersey, piled up, frizzy hair, and carries a sunshade. When smiling she shows gums. What a good-hearted, down to earth soul. I *do* love both Stones. As we left A. said we live the same sort of life as the Stones, and think along the same lines.

All this day I was feeling anxious and unhappy over the prospect of having to introduce David Cecil[‡] at this evening's reading at

---

[*] Monica Baldwin, cousin of the politician Stanley Baldwin, and one-time nun; author of *I Leap over the Wall*; d. 1976.

[†] Janet Woods, m. 1938 Reynolds Stone, 1909–79, designer, graphic engraver and printer.

[‡] Lord David Cecil, 1902–86; Professor of English Literature, Oxford University; biographer and man of letters; m. 1932 Rachel, dau. of Sir Desmond MacCarthy.

Coleridge Cottage in Nether Stowey. This the third objective. In all we covered nearly 300 miles. Drove over the Quantocks and being too early went to Alfoxton House, now an hotel, for tea. Arrived at the cottage to find David and Rachel also an hour early. David said he didn't want an introductory talk. I was delighted, and thought all this pain for nothing. But Ursula [Codrington]* wanted it recorded on her tape. So I spoke for five minutes to eighteen people in the tiny room. I knew my words by heart, and A. said afterwards that it was all right, but for one thing: I never mentioned David Cecil by name, which was inexcusable. Strange thought how once while at Oxford over forty years ago I, raw, excruciatingly shy, quite idiotic, found myself standing beside David after he had delivered a lecture. Out of sheer nerves I said, 'Did you write all that lecture yourself?' He turned and remarked tartly: 'I didn't get anybody else to do it for me.' I felt, as I deserved, shattered. And here last night was I introducing him to an audience, if you can call so small a gathering such. Amongst those present a delightful clergyman, Coleridge by name, the great-great-grandson of the poet. I don't think David a good reader of poetry; he gabbles and gobbles too fast. But he recites as poetry should be recited, with scansion and fervour. He is moved by what he reads. Like John Buxton, he said he could not read modern poetry when A. asked him if he liked Charles Tomlinson's verse. But, he said, one needn't read it; one needn't look at modern painting; one needn't listen to modern music. One cannot help seeing modern architecture. That is the worst offender.

Sunday, 1st April

Oh to be in hell! It is a cold, blustering day. Dear old Geoffrey Houghton-Brown† is staying. He is to be 70 next week, and suddenly looks it. His face is creased, and mottled, and very white. Has a frail skin. His hair is silver and he powders his head so that the scalp does not show pink where he is bald. He told us this, and then I noticed it. Geoffrey carefully read my first chapter on James II and made one or two corrections and suggestions, for he is a great

---

* Ursula Codrington, secretary and confidential friend of several well-known authors.
† Geoffrey Houghton-Brown, 1903–93; dilettante and painter.

authority on James II. I don't think anyone will take this book when
it is typed out. It will be very long.

I took against Betty Miller-Jones[*] (temporarily, of course)
when we lunched with Midi yesterday. She came round here this
morning and I talked to her about her forthcoming book on the
Lyttelton family. Charles Cobham[†] has sent her all the Hagley papers
to work on in her London house. She made no mention whatever
of my novel which she must either have read or read about.
Probably she was acting out of kindness because she couldn't praise.
And she said she didn't like Ivy Compton-Burnett's books, and that
Monica Baldwin's were puerile. She had such an opinion of herself,
was looking so hideous and spat when she talked, that I
positively disliked her. I was rude to her in the only way I
could be without being personal. When she said how much
she hated the country I told her how much I detested London.
Why? she asked. Firstly, I said, because I should have to meet
so many of my acquaintances. 'Oh,' she said, 'but as my
friends die off I want to see those that remain more and more.' So
I said, 'Betty, every friend I ever had is dead.' As she is an intelligent
woman she must have understood what I meant. (1996: How odious
of me.)

Thursday, 5th April

Yesterday I visited Ockwells in Berkshire. The first time I went
there was in 1936, the then owner being Sir Edward Barry.[‡] The
result was covenants over the house and estate, but no gift to the
National Trust. Sir Edward wanted to give, but could not afford to
do so. He had two married daughters, I remember, neither of whom
was rich. Even so, their agreement to their father giving away the
covenants was a generous concession. In those days Ockwells was
generally considered a very important house indeed. It was written
up in all architectural textbooks, as a mid fifteenth-century manor
house of the earliest non-fortified sort, of much importance. Sir
Edward extensively restored it before the First World War with the

---

[*] The Hon. Betty Askwith, b. 1909; d. of Baron Askwith; m. 1950 Keith Miller-Jones;
author.

[†] Charles Cobham, 10th Viscount, KG, 1909–77; of Hagley Hall, Stourbridge, Worcestershire.

[‡] Sir Edward Barry, 2nd Bt, 1858–1949; of Ockwells Manor, Berkshire.

help and advice of people like Lutyens,* Edward Hudson† and Avray Tipping.‡ No one disputed its merits. Yesterday however John Cornforth and Christopher Wall,§ who accompanied me, expressed the view that Ockwells was an over-restored fake, beastly in every way and not worthy to be held by the National Trust. Thus have I lived to see tastes change. Ockwells was never the sort of house I cared for, yet in the Thirties I did not dream of questioning its importance.

On my way home from Berkshire I called at Audrey's¶ for tea. Henry and Nick there to talk about our trip to Rome next week. I have a suspicion that Henry will be bored. Hope not. I look forward to becoming intimate with them both so that all shyness disappears. I do hope I can be natural with them and not pompous or trying too hard to please. Already Nick makes me feel that he and I are in conspiracy together. It is the rather mischievous way in which he smiles sidelong at things I say.

Saturday, 7th April

Yesterday long. Set forth in my tiny Morris by the motorway for Tabley House. Left here at nine and arrived Tabley dead on time at 11.45 a.m., getting off the motorway at Knutsford. Met Eardley and Merlin Waterson, the enthusiastic young representative. Object, to look once more at Tabley House and estate which John Leicester-Warren** intends to bequeath. He greeted us at the door. Reminded me that I last visited the place in September 1945 when his father and mother living there. He was at Eton with me, a ridiculous figure with absolutely no chin and a bewildered expression. Merlin says he looks like an old pheasant, with behind slightly sticking out, and nose like a pheasant's beak. At Eton he was cruelly mobbed. Now very old and rather less undistinguished, and with a gentle manner,

---

* Sir Edwin Lutyens, OM, 1869–1944; architect.
† Edward Hudson, d. 1936; founder, chairman and editor, *Country Life*; patron of Lutyens.
‡ H. Avray Tipping, 1855–1933; prolific author and contributor to *Country Life*; garden designer (laid out the gardens at Chequers, Buckinghamshire).
§ Christopher Wall, NT regional representative for Mercia.
¶ Audrey Lees-Milne, J.L.-M.'s sister, 1905–90; m., 1st, Matthew Arthur, 3rd Baron Glenarthur; 2nd, A. Stevens.
** Lieutenant-Colonel John Leicester-Warren, 1907–75; of Tabley Hall, Cheshire.

very courteous and good and poignant. He has a slight stammer. Has
turned Tabley into a school for what he calls slow developers – like
himself. Curious how men who themselves at school were bullied
cannot in after-life get away from the school aura. Obviously this a
good school, and the house very little injured by it. Full of interesting things, not least the Regency picture gallery built for the first
Lord de Tabley, all the pictures hanging as originally hung, on chains
from lion masks. These gold masks in most of the rooms. I stayed
here in 1945 but cannot remember in which bedroom. No rooms
arranged now and furniture merely dumped. House could be made
something very splendid, if we put back proper glazing bars,
removed outside stink pipes and tidied up generally. Yet not a
magical house, and a clumsy design. The great south front with
sweeping perron; the perron, instead of drawing the eye upwards to
the piano nobile as it should, drags the eye down the sweep – to
nothing. Perhaps a great statue between the claws would satisfy, in
providing the focus needed. From across the mere, with Turner's
tower on the water's edge, it makes a splendid scene. Oh, a good
place, and I truly hope we eventually get it. It nearly marches with
Tatton the other side of the motorway.

Eardley observed the curious, idiosyncratic manner in which
Leicester-Warren walks, with a slight lilt of the bottom, a walk of
great confidence and quiet authority. He said he has remarked that
only men owning more than 5,000 acres walk like this. The squire's
gait.

Then went to tea with the Sollys* at Congleton, in their villa on
the outskirts. A horrid little villa with barking dogs, on the road to
Biddulph. I like Solly, Doris Lees's husband, a sensible man. Told me
that each year he attends the Ypres dinner in London. Of 600
officers, sixty survived the battle. He was one of them. Today six
out of these sixty are alive. Said that a young person asked him why
he celebrated a disgraceful defeat for the British Army. He said he
did not celebrate, he merely commemorated the sacrifice made by
his companions on that dreadful occasion. I asked him if he was
haunted by it. No, he said. He has no nightmares and has forgotten
the horrors, and remembers the fun of the First War. But when in
1920 his uncle accompanied him to the battlefield he was so
disgusted by his uncle's attitude, which was that of a tourist, that

---

* Doris Lees, a cousin of J.L.-M., and her husband Joscelyn Norbury Solly.

he never felt the same towards him again. And couldn't explain why.

On the 12th I went to Rome with Nick and Henry Robinson for one week. A. joined us on the 15th. She had had a nasty experience the evening before. Went to dinner with the Chatwins* at Holwell Farm, returned at 10.45. On walking into the kitchen smelled cheap cigarette smoke. Saw the door into the garden open. Walked into passage and saw the dining-room upside-down, all drawers open and cupboards. Feared burglars might still be in the house. In fact they had been disturbed by her car lights on the drive, and had just bolted with all our china which hung on the walls, plus one of the pair of my Copenhagen fruit dishes. They had not set off the alarm or ventured beyond the dining-room. Strange thing that the keys of silver cupboard had been found by them and actually put in the lock, but the door not opened. Had it been, the alarm would have gone off. And it didn't. Until 1 a.m. A. was engaged with the police and CID men. Left next morning at ten to join me. We knew this was bound to happen sooner or later. Dining-room window smashed to pieces, one very small boy presumably having forced a way through the glass and cut himself in the process, for blood was found. Not enough blood unfortunately. They escaped over the garden wall. Two of our napkins found under the wall. All the rest and some table cloths were used for wrapping the china in A.'s shopping bag. China must have been broken in the wall climb, we suppose.

Rome was dreadful. My relations with Rome are love–hate. Love of the Rome I used to know just after the war. Hate of it today. The traffic, the crowds abominable. The Minerva Hotel filled no longer with cardinals, monsignors and old English governesses, but with hippies. Each evening a charabanc-load of students from everywhere, America, Europe, Asia, unloaded, and left next morning after breakfast, rendering the nights hideous with pop music and shouting.

The boys most strange. Sweet they were and polite, but never expressed enthusiasm for anything. Never read the guidebook I gave

* Bruce Chatwin, 1940–89; travel writer and novelist; his wife Elizabeth; then living at Holwell Farm in the Ozleworth valley, Gloucestershire.

them, seldom knew what they were looking at. Everything I told them was greeted with 'H'm!' Nick moderately interested in paintings, but Henry not apparently interested in anything. Neither used his eyes. Never looked at a building or discriminated between one church and another. Architecture quite out; ditto history, it seemed to me. No enthusiasm of any kind. At meals when well oiled with wine they unfolded a bit, but I did not get beyond polite terms, just like their buttoned-up mother in this respect. Their clothes ghastly, and they never changed in the evening, never once changed their shirts. Scruffiness unbelievable. Nick rather spotty, and teeth not clean. Henry the picture of cleanliness in his person, white teeth and rosy skin. Yet Nick's good looks are undeniable. Faultless features, eyes, and nose, and hair (unbrushed, the pity of it). Aged 18 only, he may improve. Can I tell his doting mother? Certainly I shall tell Audrey.

Don't want to return to Rome ever again. A. and I flew to Munich, from delicious cold sunshine to Siberian winter, snow blizzard which lasted two days; then Arctic sunshine. Stayed with Liz and Raimund Hofmannsthal[*] in their medieval castle of Prielau on the edge of Zell-am-See. Also were staying Loelia Lindsay,[†] Angus Menzies,[‡] Ali Forbes,[§] Diana Cooper.[¶] I did not enjoy this visit; too jet-settish for me, conversation about people, people; and Ali Forbes, though very bright and clever, loquacious, shouting every one down. Liz not easy to communicate with; the best Diana Cooper, who is very well educated, well-read. But I can't hear what she says in spite of her bell-like Edwardian voice with its beautiful pitch.

One evening at dinner Loelia and Raimund told Diana on my right that during this visit she was drinking less and they hoped she was drinking less elsewhere. No, she said, she was not. They said,

---

[*] Lady Elizabeth Paget, dau. of 6th Marquess of Anglesey, m. 1939 Raimund, s. of the librettist Hugo von Hofmannsthal.

[†] The Hon. Loelia Ponsonby, 1902–93, d. of 1st Baron Sysonby, Treasurer to HM King George V; wife of Sir Martin Lindsay, Bt, of Dowhill (m. 1969) and formerly (1930–47) of 2nd Duke of Westminster.

[‡] Angus Menzies, 1910–73; A.L.-M.'s first cousin.

[§] Alistair Forbes, journalist and book reviewer.

[¶] Lady Diana Manners, dau. of 8th Duke of Rutland; m. 1919 A. Duff Cooper, 1890–1954, cr. Viscount Norwich 1953, diplomatist, politician, ambassador, author; she d. 1986.

'Why on earth do you get drunk? You are so much nicer when you are sober.' 'Oh, but I am not.' 'Oh, but you are.' 'I have to,' she said, 'out of shyness.' 'Rot!' they shouted. 'It's not rot,' she said. Her reason is she fears, before appearing at a party or meal, that she will not be able to shine in the way expected of her. On others saying, 'But when you are drunk you don't shine at all', her reply was: 'I don't mind. I believe I am shining, and that is all that matters to me.' Loelia went on that it was absurd, because she (Diana) had been brought up to know she was the wittiest, most beautiful, most desirable person in England – which she is, or was – whereas she (Loelia) was brought up by her parents to believe she was stupid, hideous, hopeless and generally undesirable. 'So if I behaved like you there might be some excuse for me.'

Friday, 27th April

To lunch with Alex Moulton[*] in order to be photographed by Graham Rust who is to include me in Alex's conversation piece of old friends on the great frieze of the dining-room at The Hall. The whole background finished in a precise, detailed way, more like colour photography than art. Yet this boy such a good artist when he wishes, *vide* his exhibition of water-colours in London. I was photographed on the terrace, and since I am to be pointing out the beauties of The Hall to Ursula Codrington (already painted, and the resemblance striking), Alex engaged me in conversation, trying to make me cross by adversely criticizing my novel. Has read half-way through and considers it trivial; also criticizes the archaic setting, servants dropping h's, etc. Another criticism, that I jump from the present to the past tense all the time. Was unaware of this. Having been told to wear bright clothes today, I put on my mauvey tweed trousers, rather flared and bought in Marlborough, a striped blue and white shirt; over it my blue knitted jacket with collar and brass buttons; striped blue and white socks and my new red patent leather shoes with gold buckles. These last were a great success.

---

[*] Dr Alexander Moulton, b. 1920, of The Hall, Bradford-on-Avon, Wiltshire; innovating engineer and inventor of the Moulton bicycle and motor-car suspension.

Sunday, 29th April

While I was abroad my very old and once very dear friend Doreen Colston-Baynes[*] died. Her age given as 92. I would have thought she was more likely 102, for she was a contemporary of Dame Una [Pope-Hennessy]. It is dreadful that the very word *age* is pejorative. 'An old woman; she must be quite seventy. He can be of no use for he is a million', etc. Anyway I had not seen Doreen for about twenty years. Her memory gradually failed until she recognized and knew no one of her friends. It was not only painful for us to see her but painful for her trying to remember us. She was always a bit whimsy, and silly. 'Precious Baynes', Jamesey[†] used to call her. But she was infinitely affectionate and sensitive. She wrote several excellent biographies. When in Austria I mentioned her name to Ali Forbes. He called *The Regent and his Daughter* a first-class book, and said he would have liked to kiss her hands had he the opportunity. Oddly enough, while Peter Lubbock[‡] was staying the other weekend we spoke of her and wondered if she were still alive. I know I should have gone to her funeral at Golders Green last Wednesday, and it was disloyal not to. But I had only returned from abroad the previous evening and was confronted with the troubles and tribulations of our recent burglary. When I lived in Thurloe Square I visited Doreen at least one evening a fortnight for what she called 'a good pow-wow'.

Then on my return found a postcard from Kenneth Rae[§] that Newman, hall porter from Brooks's, had died of a heart attack, suddenly, and was being buried the same day as Doreen. He became a nuisance after he retired, by haunting the club and inviting one to give him drinks at the pub round the corner. Poor Newman, he had been my friend and many other members' for nearly forty years. Two nights before this news I dreamed of him, which was odd.

A. has heard the cuckoo and seen the first swallow. After lunching with the Somersets we went by invitation to the Saunderses[¶] at

---

[*] Doreen Colston-Baynes, 1881–1973, was the biographer Dormer Creston.
[†] James Pope–Hennessy, 1916–74; writer; younger son of Major-General Richard and Dame Una Pope-Hennessy.
[‡] Peter Lubbock ran a small and select travel agency.
[§] Secretary of the National Theatre.
[¶] Peter and Didi Saunders, of Easton Grey, Wiltshire.

Easton Grey to admire their daffodils. Drifts and drifts, almost too many and lavish. He buys bulbs by the ton each year.

A. has just come into the library with a dead thrush in her hand. She found it so on its nest, the head bitten and the blood sucked; clearly by a weasel. Hardly a bird's nest survives in this garden. Year after year the eggs are taken, and the mother birds are killed. It is dispiriting. Or cats?

Monday, 30th April

Walking up the church path yesterday morning at eight I noticed that all the graves were decked with flowers. Not only the new graves. I recall Kilvert's diary telling how the village children decorated the graves with wild flowers on Easter eve. Ours are not wild flowers, but cut flowers in pots. Not so good, yet someone has taken an infinite amount of trouble, and has observed the old custom which I thought was long ago extinct. Can only suppose it was that amusing monster, Bill Raines. If so, it shows that there is good stuff in him.

Tuesday, 1st May

'May is Mary's month and I / Muse at that and wonder why.' It is also the Feast day of SS Philip and James; and also Labour Day, which is not so good. Today is one of token strikes throughout the discontented country.

In the garden this evening I listened to a thrush on a post by the potting shed trilling with full-throated ease to a fellow. The other thrush, also presumably male, was a rival. He always began his canticle before the first had finished his. Just like my father and the vicar at Wickhamford in the old days during the reading of the psalms in church. Neither would wait for the other to finish before he began the next verse.

Sunday, 6th May

Complaining like mad I accompany A. to the Gloucestershire Society ceremony today. But it is really a charming affair, quite anachronistic and rather fun. This year Sally W. is President and she invites us, because I seem not to be a member. Church 11.30 at Wickwar. Procession up the nave. All very county, upper class and ducal. Sally [Westminster] reads the first lesson from Genesis, about the creation of the world. With her pretty voice she reads v. well. Then D. of Beaufort reads the second lesson. Increase and multiply the theme of the first lesson, which we thought unsuitable for these two. Duke and wrong Duchess – for Mary Beaufort conspicuously absented herself – walked arm in arm to their car and drove off. Master said, 'Didn't she read it beautifully?' Drinks in Sally's house and luncheon in a tent on the lawn. Bitterly cold day and I froze. My experience of tents being that they are usually boiling hot I wore my thick dark summer suit without vest. Sat with John Huntley* of Boxwell and his new wife, she very sweet and v. religious. Talked about Christianity. She thinks that instead of parsons taking three or four services each Sunday in a different church to which a handful of congregation attend, they should hold one service each Sunday in a different church in rotation. John Huntley and all the other ex-Presidents wear tails. At the end of the meal we drink the Queen's health, and finally sing the extraordinary colloquial song about Charles I composed when the Society was founded in 1657. It has been celebrated and this song sung every year since that date.

I feel my spirits raised to the skies because Elizabeth [Cavendish]† telephoned last night asking if she and John Betj. might stay on the 19th. How I love that dearest man, and dearest woman.

Friday, 11th May

Spent my first two days in London for weeks. Stayed with John [Kenworthy-Browne] who to my delight seems happy. He has a job from the British Council of organizing a big exhibition of National Trust works of art in Brussels, which keeps him busy and pays him. Would that he were always in this happy state. Went to Chiddingstone Castle with Don Nicholas‡ to see Denys Bower's collection of Stuartiana, and very fine they were. How on earth did this man acquire them? We saw at least two splendidly bound volumes from the Cardinal Duke's library. Did these come as loot from Frascati after the bombing of 1943 or when the library was

---

* The Huntleys of Boxwell Court, Leighterton have been Gloucestershire landowners since the Dissolution of the Monasteries in the sixteenth century, the Huntley of the time having been Steward to the Abbot of Gloucester.
† Lady Elizabeth Cavendish, b. 1926, dau. of 10th Duke of Devonshire.
‡ Donald Nicholas, author of *The Portraits of Bonnie Prince Charlie* (1974) and collector of Stuartiana.

salvaged and removed to the Vatican Library, where today it is still inaccessible?

Spent Tuesday evening with Rosamond [Lehmann]. She took me to a thanksgiving service in St Matthew's church of which the incumbent is that nice, slightly absurd, cultivated, popular Father Gerard Irvine. Service began at 7.30. We arrived at 7.20. One seat for Ros; none for me. I said I liked standing, which I always do in Papist masses of half an hour, expecting the same duration this evening. But the affair went on till 9.15. I was nearly dead. Never have I witnessed such triumphalism. Copes, bishops (who on earth?), the Dean of St Paul's, a Greek orthodox prelate, choir, sacristans, clergy, carrying silver crucifixes, swinging censers, the church billowing with incense. The full fig and liturgy all in English which sounds to my ears absurd and horrid; mixed with hymns too, beastly things. We were bidden to refreshments afterwards by Father Gerard, but finding that the entire congregation had been invited, could not face it. Ros was amazed by the crowd, the numbers of young, *jeunesse dorée* of boys and girls, all most fervent, falling on to their knees before the Host, singing most lustily. It suggested to me a club, a society of initiates, rather like the Oxford Movement of the 1850s. We slunk off and dined at an Italian restaurant near Victoria Station.

At Maggs's I was shown a lock of Byron's hair which I would have bought, if the authenticity were more certain. Belongs to someone called Caryll who claims he was given it by old Sir John Murray in 1962. I telephoned Jock Murray who said it was most improbable that his uncle would have given such a thing away. Like a fool I missed a splendid coronation medal of William and Mary at Whelan's. Couldn't make up my mind. Then made it up and telephoned Mr Whelan, who said he had since sold it to another client. One must never equivocate.

Sunday, 13th May

Margery, whom I now call Ernst, dearly loves animals and birds. He told me how fond he was of geese, but could never keep them. He had to on the farm where he worked. For to kill geese you must knock them on the head, stun them, and cut their throats so that they bleed to death, while alive. He cannot do this. He said that most farmers don't bother to stun the birds first. Ernst, the ex-Nazi, is the most soft-hearted man I know. Great scenes ensued over the

Margerys' colour television which Mrs ordered. When it arrived it
was installed and they found that it would not work without a huge,
unsightly aerial. Under cover of the Nat. Trust I would not allow
this, and protested that the aerial behind the parapet of our roof was
small and inconspicuous and perfectly adequate besides. Great distress caused to the family, so I felt obliged to take the matter up over
the telephone. No, the small aerial would not suit the cottage. I
made the firm in Gloucester come out and try the small aerial. They
came, it worked perfectly and is installed. It is exhausting having to
insist and fight for everything.

Last evening I caught the 5.15 train from Kemble for London,
dressed in dinner jacket; walked from Paddington to the Berkeleys'.
A. and I gave Lennox for his 70th birthday a very prettily-bound
almanac of poems, circa 1830, with a lyre engraved on the cover,
and also an autograph letter from Gounod to John Broadwood of
1871. Lennox delighted. We all went to dine at Helen Dashwood's
pretentious flat next door to the de Vere Hotel. Fourteen persons.
Stiff affair, too many, and it did not go with a swing. Only champagne to drink, before, during and after dinner. No wine. Only
alternative, orange juice. Patrick Kinross[*] was furious and called for
wine. I pointed out that we were Helen's guests and not in a
restaurant. I drank nothing. Sat between Freda Berkeley and Charlotte Bonham-Carter,[†] who is as bent as Sibyl Colefax[‡] used to be.
Had to lower my head into my soup plate, then skew it sideways in
order to be on a level with hers and make her hear. Most uncomfortable. She has however all her wits about her. Told me that
Elizabeth Bowen had the most fertile imagination of any novelist
she had known. E. Bowen once dined with Charlotte, having come
from Dorset in the train. C. asked her what she had read during the
journey. E.B. replied, nothing. 'What? Nothing?' 'No. I
formulated an entire plot for my next book.' Diana Cooper is an
exact contemporary of Charlotte, but whereas the latter is an old
woman, Diana is not. Looking splendid in a powder blue and gold
dress.

---

[*] 3rd Baron Kinross, 1904–76; author, journalist and broadcaster.

[†] Charlotte Ogilvy, m. 1926 Sir Edgar Bonham-Carter (1870–1956), jurist and colonial
administrator; a well-known and idiosyncratic social figure.

[‡] Sibyl Halsey, widow of Sir Arthur Colefax (d. 1936), barrister-at-law; she was a well-
known society hostess before and throughout the Second World War.

I do not like Helen Dashwood in spite of the years I have known her. Nor by all means dislike her. She is infinitely affected and brash. Said to A. 'I told the PM [Edward Heath]* yesterday that he must make Lennox a K.' When I remarked to her, concerning West Wycombe, that her taste was so good because she refrained from too much 'improvement', she said, 'Of course.' She still claims to know all important people, and to wield influence through them, which is patently absurd. She always has to do the posh thing, *vide* the champagne, regardless of most of her guests' preferences. For the old don't want to drink champagne exclusively.

Wednesday, 16th May

Two boys from Oriel, Oxford came by appointment to see the house. One an architectural student, pupil of Howard Colvin† whom he venerates but does not like. Says Howard is not popular because of his superciliousness; he never shows this to his elders. This boy with flaming red hair and beard looked like the young Swinburne; the other very handsome with nice, white teeth, looked like Desmond Guinness used to look, and rather affected, but charming. The last wrote me a letter of thanks and appreciation. The first called J. Martin Robinson, the second Colin McMordie.

Thursday, 17th May

To London for the day because my crowned dog-tooth came out yesterday. A vital tooth, to which my plate is harnessed one side. Plowman says the root is cracked and the whole stump must come out next week. Oh, dread! Lunched expensively with Eardley and was not in good form, which I think he sensed.

I dreamed last night that my late brother-in-law, of all unlikely people, telephoned me a message from Pam Jackson‡ that Nancy [Mitford] could not be expected to survive another twenty-four

---

* Rt Hon. Edward Heath (b. 1916; KG 1992); Prime Minister 1970–74.
† Howard Colvin, CVO, CBE, Kt 1995, b. 1919; Fellow (Emeritus since 1987) of St John's College, Oxford; Reader in Architectural History; compiler of (among other works) *A Biographical Dictionary of British Architects* 1600–1840 (1954, and now – 1996 – in its 3rd edition).
‡ The Hon. Pamela Mitford, 1907–94; second of the Mitford sisters; called 'Woman' by her intimates; m. 1936 Professor Derek Jackson.

hours. Next morning at breakfast I received a letter from her, complaining of her lot, poor thing, and asking for books. Did my best to choose four at Heywood's shop when in London. All the staff there gathered to advise, and all said that whatever was sent wd not meet with approval. Her letter written in remarkably neat, small script, although the content shows how drugged she must be. Dreadful indeed.

Sunday, 20th May

John Betj' and Feeble [Elizabeth Cavendish] came last night *en route* to London from Cornwall and left today. We looked at his film *Metroland* on the tele with Miss Barrett our wretched old housekeeper who was thrilled with the honour, and dined late afterwards. Rather shocked at how very old John has become, tho' worse on the film made some months ago than he looks now. Took them to lunch today at Cerney House with Quentin Craig. Never have I seen a Regency house more mauled within. No words can describe the horror of it. A. drove there with Elizabeth, John with me. He told me Penelope, although she had wanted to marry him, probably was never in love with him; that she is quite impossible to live with; that he does not know if his son is alive or dead, for his last letter was returned from the dead-letter office in New York. He is worried over lack of money. His secretary costs him £50 a week and he does not earn enough to cover this item of expense. The demands made on him now he is Laureate bring no financial return, and much work. Showed us a letter he has just received from the Duke of Kent who offers his services in preventing London being totally transformed. John must go and see him. Another letter, from Heath, asking him to translate a Portuguese poem into English to be put to music by Arthur Bliss and played to the Portuguese President on his visit to the Queen. And so it goes on. His poem published in Adam Fergusson's *Sack of Bath*, out tomorrow, has been written for nothing but love of Bath. As we drove past Malmesbury John said, nodding to a signpost, 'In that village I had my first experience of sex with the son of the Vicar. It was in a punt on the river. I was quite spent. That night the brother came into my room, but I was too shocked by what I had done with the other during the afternoon, and so lost a second opportunity.' He was then fifteen. We agreed that no subsequent escapades have eclipsed those early schoolday ones.

Tuesday, 22nd May

My article about Bath appeared in yesterday's *Guardian*. It looked very small among the several pages about Bath. I have never known any daily paper devote so much space to one threatened city. It shows that the tide has at last turned. But is it too late?

The cow parsley outside our lower gate on either side of the lane to Wotton is very prolific. I have never seen it so thick. Usually they cut it before it has time to flower properly. This year is an exception. One takes for granted this essentially English, slender, graceful and common weed. But what an object of beauty it is. In the evening I went to the Archdeacon's Visitation and was sworn in as church warden. Such a splendid old boy, so humorous, clever and holy, just what a high-up dignitary of the English Church should be, a true descendant of a Trollopean cleric. He gave the assembled wardens a little pep talk about their duties, and the importance of this ancient office. Not the least pi, yet serious and impressive. As I returned at 7.30 I passed A. in her car going to Chipping Sodbury (whence I was returning) for the synodical meeting, which lasted for two hours. She came back exhausted. Our assembly of church wardens was a musty, subfusc lot. While waiting for the Archdeacon I looked at them and wondered if there was one I would consent to go to bed with without being paid £50,000. I badly need £5,000.

Talking to Joan Lindsay about the Muirs in Perthshire* I said that in 1929 I stayed at Deanston with old Lady Muir, and could barely understand a word she said because her accent was so Glasgow. Joan replied instantly, 'It was not Glasgow. It was old Scots, which all the Scottish gentry spoke. It is now practically obsolete. You should cherish it. Not criticize.' Abashed I was.

Wednesday, 23rd May

In fear and trembling to the dentist this morning to have my crowned molar extracted. The crown finally broke off the other day, thus displacing the entire bridge, one side of which was attached to it. Plowman told me last week that the root embedded was split and must come out. So I went. He gave me two sharp injections of cocaine. Then poked the gum. Asked if it still hurt. Yes, I said, I

---

* Margaret Kay, widow of Sir John Muir, 1st Bt, of Deanston; her two sons, Sir Kay, 2nd Bt, of Blair Drummond, and James, of Braco Castle; all in Perthshire.

can feel it. My mouth rapidly freezing up and feeling swollen and paralysed. He gave me another which I did not feel. Then said, 'You must wait five minutes', during which interval I thought to myself I must concentrate on other things, and couldn't. Plowman returned and very breezily said, 'Nurse will hold your head', which she did. I thought then, 'I am sure my head must be very sweaty.' Plowman fiddled with my mouth, shook my head twice, and it was over. I felt nothing, and until I saw the blood did not realize that the tooth was out. Immediately he clapped the bridge back into my mouth with an additional false tooth. During the afternoon I felt slightly sore but by dinner time ate as usual. He does not pull, but shoves an instrument into the gum and out pops the tooth, I imagine. I said, 'It is like taking a plantain out of the lawn with a spud.'

Dined with the Beits[*] to celebrate Alfred's recent 70th birthday. Seventy people to dine at different tables in the Ambassador, a gloomy club off Park Lane. A poignant party yet I did not enjoy it. Talked before dinner with Mrs Henley[†] aged 91 and looking 60. She said she loved Randolph [Churchill] her cousin and treated him like a naughty schoolboy. I sat next to Helen Dashwood and Thelma Cazalet-Keir.[‡] Enjoyed talking to the last but not to the first. Helen told me that Oliver Esher[§] was in love with her before the war. I would not be inclined to believe her, had she not also told me that Oliver stopped her running away with someone just after the war. And this Oliver told me once. Then Helen said that during the war at West Wycombe Eardley [Knollys] went to Oliver and told him that I ought to leave the Trust and do war work so that he might become secretary of the Trust. Such a patent untruth and mischief that I turned on Helen and said that E. was one of my greatest friends, I did not believe it and if I did believe it I would not want to consider it. Made her change the subject. Helen said she had no wish to live and if God asked her to die this evening she would say Yes. No wonder.

---

[*] Sir Alfred Beit, 2nd Bt, 1903–94; Conservative MP 1929–45; art collector, of Co. Wicklow, Eire; m. 1939 Clementine Mitford.
[†] The Hon. Sylvia Stanley, dau. of 4th Baron Stanley of Alderley, m. 1906 Brigadier-General The Hon. A. M. Henley (d. 1925), s. of 3rd Baron Henley.
[‡] Thelma Cazalet, m. 1939 David Keir (he d. 1969); MP 1931–45, and public servant; she d. 1989.
[§] Oliver Sylvain Baliol Brett, 3rd Viscount Esher, 1881–1963; Chairman, General Purposes Committee of the NT.

Thelma Cazalet talked about Harold Nicolson. Said he cut no ice at all in the Commons and that he did something so dishonourable to her that she nearly sued him, and could never forget or forgive. Again I found myself protesting that I could not believe anything told against Harold, that I loved him dearly. I was rather too virtuous this evening.

Saturday, 26th May

The Lambton–Jellicoe scandal* makes me sick. It's a witch hunt. And what the hell does it matter to anyone on earth that these men have slept with whores. Thelma Cazalet said, 'I do not condone; and I do not condemn.' And she added, 'I do not understand.' That may be true. I do. Lord Lambton, interviewed on the tele by Robin Day last night, gave one of the most poignant and splendid performances of candour and guts. He was marvellous. Not that I hold him in high esteem as a public figure, from all I hear. I am far more sorry for Jellicoe, who is a quiet, un-raffish man. I wrote him a letter of condolence, in fact a second-class fan mail.

Wednesday, 30th May

Sally [Westminster] motored me in her comfortable old Rolls to Clearwell Castle, the far side of the Severn estuary, and close to the Wye. She thought it horrible. In a sense it is – a gloomy Gothick castle, but to me interesting archaeologically. For it dates from 1727, the architect having been Roger Morris. Unfortunately the people who now own it are what Sally calls 'lower class', and their furniture is beyond belief. Whole house stinks like a lodging-house. One could make it charming. It still retains some Baroque chimneypieces and compartmented ceilings. On the way back she took me to Bigsweir, a dear little Georgian house of the same date, but classical, on the Wye. Now an antique shop selling Welsh dressers.

Debo† and Woman came to dinner. Their news of Nancy dreadful. She knows she is dying, and they think she has about two

---

* Viscount Lambton, Conservative MP (son of 5th Earl of Durham) and the 2nd Earl Jellicoe (Lord Privy Seal) were involved in a scandal in 1973 in which they were discovered to have shared the favours of a prostitute in St John's Wood.
† The Hon. Deborah Mitford, youngest of the Mitford sisters; m. 1941 Lord Andrew Cavendish, who succeeded his father as 11th Duke of Devonshire in 1950.

months to live; her legs all swollen with water. Otherwise she is a
living skeleton and cannot move her body or even her head, and is
always in pain. Her pursuit is making her will with the sisters' help.
This gives her much pleasure and causes merriment. Sisters said I
would be receiving a letter from Nancy.

Debo asked to go round the garden before dinner. Torrents
of praise, and congratulation over the tidiness, the growth of everything, the blueness of the ceanothus in the north-east corner of the
first garden. 'Oh no, damn it. It's too much. Let's go home,
Woman. Don't look. I can't bear it. I've never seen anything like
it,' etc.

Thursday, 31st May

By this morning's post I receive a letter from Nancy, still in her firm
hand, but misspelt and shaky, and piteous. It begins, 'It's very
curious dying and would have many a drole amusing & charming
side were it not for the pain. We had screams over the Will. The
Dame's* share. "But she'll be furious if she only gets *that*."' Then she
says the doctors are so tiresome they will not give her a date for her
death. They merely say 'Have everything you want', meaning as
much morphia. I have been haunted by this letter all day. Extraordinary that someone on the threshold of death can write like this,
and still make jokes.

Saturday, 2nd June

Norah Smallwood and Patrick Kinross stay the weekend. She is a
most delightful woman, of very keen intellect. Knows the entire
literary world. A great talker, which Patrick is likewise. We watched
the Trooping the Colour on our colour television set, and were
agreed that it was the most splendid spectacle, which no other
country could stage with the same dignity and pageantry as ours.

Elspeth Huxley lunches; an old friend of Norah. Elspeth
always very gentle and sweet with us; yet she can be tart.
Has beautiful manners and writes little Collins poems after her
visits.

---

* 'The Dame' was Nancy Mitford's nickname for A.L.-M.

Monday, 4th June

Flaming June. David Herbert, his sister Patricia [Hambleden]* and
Michael Duff† lunched. The first time any one of them has been
here, which is amazing. All most appreciative and raving about the
garden and house. Whiffs of patrician fun. The overriding quality of
these people is a complete lack of seriousness, which is refreshing.
Conversation may lack depth but it scintillates with the ludicrous.

Tuesday, 5th June

Stuffy old Alec Clifton-Taylor‡ lunched with me at Brooks's. Very
affectionate as always. Said, 'You may appear to strangers to epitom-
ise the conventional; but you are thoroughly unconventional. This is
what your friends discover.' Tells me he has sold 40,000 copies of his
book on cathedrals. Yet has earned little therefrom. Whereas *The
Pattern of English Building* has made money. It deserves to do so.
Spoke disparagingly of 'the de Trafford man of Hill Court' as 'one of
those', the first time I have ever heard him acknowledge homosexuality as existing. De Trafford has withdrawn his offer of Hill
Court because, he alleges, the N.T. returned his loans of furniture
from Montacute damaged, and refused to pay for their repair. I
wonder if this is true.

J.K.-B. who dined with me at Brooks's has just lost his old aunt
aged 90. He has to arrange for the funeral, cope with undertakers,
obituaries, etc. with no help from his parents or brethren. Yet thinks
this quite in order, and acts as though it were the most natural thing
in the world.

Wednesday, 6th June

Properties Committee at Clandon. A lovely day. Meeting took place
in the saloon. Looking round I thought it the most hideous decoration I had seen, flesh pink (which John Fowler§ calls biscuit) and

---

* Lady Patricia Herbert, dau. of 15th Earl of Pembroke; m. 1928 3rd Viscount
Hambleden; she d. 1994.
† Sir Michael Duff, 3rd Bt, 1907–80.
‡ Alec Clifton-Taylor, 1907–85; architectural historian and broadcaster, specializing in
cathedrals and churches.
§ John Fowler, 1905–77; interior decorator of historic country houses and partner in
decorating firm Colefax and Fowler.

purple. John came up to me afterwards, took me aside to the chimneypiece and told me the doctors were worried about his heart on account of the Cortisone he has to take. Stopped it and sub-stituted some other drug. Within five days two more cancer growths appeared. Immediately the Cortisone was resumed. He says the worst effects are constant desire to pee, and his breasts are develop-ing. I said to encourage, 'Even if you are able to give suck, it is worth it. What does it matter how men look at our age.' He is full of merriment notwithstanding. Today A. went to Versailles for the day. Sat with Nancy who does not respond to talk, but lies quietly on her back, the tears trickling down her cheeks.

Monday, 11th June

Burnet [Pavitt] had A. and me to Covent Garden, *Trovatore*, and dinner during the intervals in the little closet, King Edward's smok-ing-room, below the Royal Box. It is minute and decorated in Edwardian Adam style, very *gemütlich*. Splendid cast and divine music. Yet throughout the witch's passionate arias I was steadily working out in my mind a theme for a novel: that of two sisters, one with young son who is a paragon of virtue; the unmarried sister was in love with the boy's father, now dead. Father would never look at spinster sister and married the other. So spinster sets out to corrupt the son, teaches him to smoke pot, drink, and finally tries to seduce him. Failing, resorts to drugging him, and then ravishes him. But having administered an overdose, she kills him. Is this plot too like that of *Heretics*? And shall I get the reputation of being obsessed with incest? Worse still, would I be identified with the spinster?

During the last interval we were summoned to the Royal Box by the Donaldsons.* Lord and Lady Carrington† present. She very beautiful. Introduced but I had no opportunity of speaking to her, sitting opposite. But she smiled at me constantly in the sweetest, friendliest way. How nice of her. I appreciate this because I am inclined to scowl at strangers, I fear. I said to Jack, 'Isn't it awful, Brooks's subscription going up to £70 a year?' 'Yes,' he said; 'never-theless I shall continue my membership. Don't tell Frankie. She

---

* John G. S. (Jack) Donaldson, b. 1907; cr. Baron Donaldson of Kingsbridge (life peerage) 1967; m. 1935 Frances Lonsdale (Frankie), b. 1907, writer and biographer.
† Peter Carington, 6th Baron Carrington, KG, b. 1919; m. 1942 Iona McClean; active member of the House of Lords (Foreign Secretary 1979–82).

thinks it absurdly extravagant. But in the awful event of her pre-deceasing me, Brooks's is all I would have left to me.' This is just what I feel.

Tuesday, 12th June

Embarrassing meeting of the MHA [Mutual Households Association], which Caroline Somerset attended for the first time. Jack Rathbone* to my intense surprise announced that he was no longer chairman, having been voted out. Nigel Nicolson and I asked why. Were told it was an unwritten rule that no one might be chairman longer than two years. We both expressed our disagreement with so foolish a rule. No matter. Mr Newell received the votes, and eagerly slipped into Jack's place. They are a dreadful lot of old men. Of course they imagined that Nigel and I were in the know, which indeed we were not. With such a second-rate person as Newell how can this organization expect to flourish?

Friday, 15th June

Having been badgered for months I finally motored to Nunney. Was taken by Robert Pomeroy† to see Marston House. While I should be sorry to see it demolished I do not think it very important. Handsome south front of symmetrical breaks and end conservatory wings like railway station roofs. Entrance front Edwardian and cumbersome. Whole house in terrible decay. Now flats of the slummiest description. Doomed I fear, and the owner, Bonham-Christie, longs to have it down.

Saturday, 16th June

John and Elizabeth to stay the night again from Cornwall. They arrive at seven o'clock, bringing a canary as present for A. and for me a book of London statues photographed by young Prince Richard of Gloucester. John met the Kents last week to discuss the saving of London. Found the Duchess physically attractive. Was amused to hear of Julian Hall's novel [*The Senior Commoner*] written

* John Francis Warre (Jack) Rathbone, 1909–95; Secretary of the National Trust 1949–68.
† The Hon. Robert Pomeroy, b. 1916.

forty years ago about Eton, with me figuring in it. Rather good as
portraits of boys and masters, but unco-ordinated and inconsequen-
tial. Well written none the less. While we were eating he said, 'Oh,
let's have a squint at it.' He always wants to look up a reference, read
a passage of verse immediately. This is what I like. So I fetched the
book, and read a letter tucked inside which Julian had written me in
1934 after the book had come out. 'Must be ninety per cent,' said
John. 'Yes, I can tell from that letter that he's queer,' Feeble said.
Then added, 'Tony Snowdon* says he always knows that when
people like you and me they're bound to be queer.'

Sunday, 17th June

John never misses Eucharist here, and Elizabeth accompanies him.
A. said when they had gone that E.'s love and solicitude for him
were boundless. In church she would not let him kneel on the altar
steps where the rails were not, but took that place herself so that he
would have a rail to rest his arms against.

Monday, 18th June

Reading in bed at 11.45 I heard the Bristol trains roaring down the
track. I rarely hear them, only in summer with the windows wide
open, on the stillest nights. Went and leant over the sill. As I did so
the electric lamp on the road went out. The air full of night noises,
quiet as could be, not a breath of wind. Dead silence, yet the silence
of life, and not of terrifying space. Or are there sounds there?
Terrifying gaseous screams? On the moon I fancy none. Last night
I felt the earth and all its little creatures were breathing in sleep.
Lately we have had wonderful days. Suddenly summer came with a
bang. The first spring green vanished, and the full blown, drowsy
brown-green took its place. The hedgerows thick with elder
flowers, those lovely creamy plates, smelling so acrid sweet, the cow
parsley suddenly gone, all together.
    Am reading Leslie Rowse's† *Shakespeare the Man*. Dreadfully good.

---

* Antony Armstrong-Jones, 1st Earl of Snowdon, b. 1930; son of R.O.L. Armstrong-
Jones, QC (d. 1966), and Anne Messel (who m., 2nd, the 6th Earl of Rosse); m. 1961
HRH The Princess Margaret (m. diss. 1978).
† A. L. Rowse, b. 1903; Fellow of All Souls College, Oxford; historian, poet and
Cornishman.

He may annoy with his pleased-with-himself certainty that he is always right. Reading this book I truly believe he must be. No one knows the Tudors better than he. And what a good writer. Such simplicity of style, conversational and intimate. Only occasionally I detect careless syntax. Another card from him, saying 'I am expecting your book of N.T. reminiscences.'

Wednesday, 20th June

Yesterday afternoon we went from London to the Queen's party at Windsor Castle. Was honoured to be asked, but reluctant to go. A. on other hand delighted, and looked forward to it like mad. Quite right she was. Why we were invited I could not guess. A. wore her diamond necklace and diamond bracelets and looked splendid in an Indian uncrushable dress. I, as 'commanded', in black tie. Although weather changed to rain it was a very hot day. We went to Robin Fedden's house where a hired car came to fetch the three of us at seven o'clock. Consequence was we reached Windsor too early and circled round the town and park. Then joined a stream of motors to the Castle. Drove through St George's Gate to the State Entrance Tower. Beautifully organized, polite policemen, and servants in scarlet livery. A. discarded her shawl downstairs. Up the Grand Staircase at the head of which a man and woman, may have been the Master of the Household and his wife, greeted us. Passed into the State Ante-Room where drinks handed round, and where we saw many friends, Ken Davidson, the Verneys of Claydon. Long talk with Ralph Verney who said my views on traffic control proved useful to his Traffic Commission. Admired the Gothic fan tracery ceiling of this apartment, by Wyatville. Then passed into the Waterloo Chamber.

We three sat in the third row; behind us a space and row for the royals, one armed chair for the Queen. An orchestra in front. A door from St George's Hall thrown open, and the Ascot house party trooped in and took their seats. After a pause the Queen entered, followed by the Queen Mother, Duke of Edinburgh, Princess Anne, Princess Margaret and Tony in Household dress, scarlet again and medals (he looking like a Ruritanian prince, like something from the *Desert Song*, rather stout I thought, and Robin thought exotic), beautiful Princess Alexandra, Ogilvy. Yehudi entered the platform, and 'God Save the Queen' played. Then a most suitable

and delightful concert ensued, Mozart, Schubert, Handel (all pieces
chosen by the Queen, Yehudi said afterwards), and one piece
specially composed for the Queen by a young man, who conducted,
Edwin Roxburgh, consisting of songs from Burns's verse set to
music, one Jacobite song. By now it was ten o'clock or later. We
walked out of the Waterloo Chamber – the best of the Lawrences
are of the two Popes, Pius VI and VII – through the King's State
Drawing Room, and there lined up to shake hands with Queen and
Duke. They were standing in the Guard Chamber. Our card was
taken by a liveried servant, names announced and we advanced. A.
curtseyed deep; I bowed, perhaps too deep, but my loyalty is deep.
The Queen smiled very sweetly, the Duke, wearing Household
uniform, Prussian blue Garter sash and star, said something like,
'Oh, yes, how are you?' We proceeded into St George's Gallery.
This really is a wonderful apartment and Fortune Grafton* was
shocked when I said I genuinely admired it. There were little tables
along the south side, and a long buffet table along the north-east
side. The royal party were eating in the adjacent Grand Reception
Room. John Sparrow,† when I asked him whether we were to be
placed or not, said, 'I don't know about you. I am sitting next to
Queen Elizabeth.'

A. pushed her way straight to a table where John Pope-Hennessy
was sitting with a tiny, little old lady dressed in white. I was made to
sit beside her and for ages had no idea who she was. She said when I
shook hands, 'Of course I remember you well.' Only half-way
through supper I realized she was Ava Waverley.‡ She must have
had a stroke. She whispered; I could barely hear. Delicious supper of
cold Vichyssoise soup in cups, cold meats and salads, chocolate
mousse or strawberries and cream. Champagne or red wine. I
drank, or rather sipped at, one glass of champagne (horrid drink)
throughout the evening. A regiment of attentive footmen in tailcoats
of scarlet. Looking down the great length of this room I was
reminded of one of those coloured lithographs in Pyne's *Royal
Residences.*

---

* Fortune FitzRoy, Duchess of Grafton; Mistress of The Robes to HM The Queen
since 1967.
† John Sparrow, 1906–92; Warden of All Souls College, Oxford 1952–77; man of letters
and bibliophile.
‡ Ava, Viscountess Waverley, widow of John Anderson, 1st Viscount Waverley, who d.
1958.

Supper was finished after midnight, when we supposed we were
to go home. But no. The royals came out of their room into the
Gallery. I avoided Tony Snowdon and Princess Margaret. In passing
close to her I overheard her say to Angus Ogilvy who happened to
brush her arm in passing, 'Oh, must you do that?' in her snappish
voice. I didn't want to get into conversation. Hugh Grafton* said,
'Well, fancy you being here. You are getting on' – a snide little jab I
thought.

We were conducted by the Queen round the staterooms which
are not usually open to the public, beginning with the Queen's
Presence Chamber and ending with the Rubens room. It was
difficult to look at all the treasures on account of talking. Celia
McKenna† kept running up to me asking, 'What was that?' as
though I could possibly know. But I did recognize the two cabinets
made for Henrietta Maria. Wonderful silver-on-ebony furniture.
The wall hangings nothing like as pretty as they were in George
IV's time, and some carpets very unworthy. The Vermeer had been
brought from London specially for us. A. rushed up to me in
the Queen's State Drawing Room to say, 'You must come and see
the Cardinal Duke's canteen in the Library.' As we walked through
the door the Queen was standing in the doorway talking. So we
flattened ourselves against the wall. Until she passed on everyone
stopped stock still. I remarked how obsequious most people look on
talking to royalty, bowing and scraping ingratiatingly. How
impossible to be natural. I am sure one must try to be. Yet when
it came to saying goodbye to the Queen at the head of the Staircase,
all I could murmur was, 'It has been the greatest treat,
Ma'am.' Really, how could I? She smiled wanly. It was 1.30. We
got back to London in pouring rain at 2.15. I stayed the night at
Brooks's.

I wanted to take in everything I saw, but could not. The salt on
our table was gilt, of a putto and shell, as though it were by Cellini;
the sugar caster of silver weighed a ton. Pair of gold mandarin jars on
the chimneypiece, portrait by Honthorst of Charles I as a boy,
Canaletto of Murano unlike anything else by Canaletto I have seen;
the Wyatville ceilings, the would-be Grinling Gibbons work

---

* Hugh FitzRoy, 11th Duke of Grafton; b. 1919; m. 1946 Fortune Smith.
† Lady Cecilia Keppel, d. of 9th Earl of Albemarle; m. 1934 David McKenna.

reminding me of what the 6th Duke of Devonshire did at Chatsworth. While waiting for our car to come under the *porte-cochère* I talked to Michael Hornby's[*] wife, an Austrian, who said, 'Only England does this sort of thing now. It is wonderful. It makes me cry.' 'Yes,' I said, 'may it go on for ever.' Several people told me they had enjoyed *Heretics*, and Lady Sekers[†] said she wanted her son, a film producer, to make a film of *Another Self*. Would that he would.

Saturday, 23rd June

A. tells me that the Queen was dining in our room, i.e., St George's Hall. I had my back to her so did not see. Her table was decorated with floral sprays. A. had a full view. Q. had a special footman in royal blue livery behind her chair, at a decent distance so that he could not overhear conversation. He waited upon her only. Every now and then she turned and gave him a message, or a note.

Met the builder Stanley Durn in the churchyard to discuss whether he could restore the table tomb next to the one on which the PCC has spent nearly £300. Yes, Stanley said with the great modesty which distinguishes him, he could do it for between £60 and £80 he felt sure. He pointed out how the expensive one, done by the pleased-with-himself diocesan architect, lacked the proper rain-mould under the ledge to keep the water from trickling down the sides and rotting them. Stanley with his nice, open face, gentle manner and real knowledge of the old Cotswold craftsmen, gave me many interesting tips about stonework, why certain stone from the same quarry spalls, and other doesn't, and so on. He was taught by Scrapy – he had no other known name – and I remember him as a lad scrambling about the roof here with Scrapy who taught him all the unwritten lore he knew. Scrapy finally had a stroke while on somebody's roof, and died almost at once.

I have decided that the reason why one keeps a diary is the compulsion to write something, anything. Secondly, all intending writers are well advised to keep diaries, for practice, like doing

[*] Michael Hornby, 1899–1987; m. 1928 Nicole(tte) Ward; Vice-Chairman, W. H. Smith & Son, 1944–65.
[†] Agota, wife of Sir Nicholas (Miki) Sekers, 1910–72, textile weaver and entrepreneur immigrant from Hungary, and patron of the arts.

scales. Mine are absolutely unstudied. I never pause an instant to consider whether I write grammatically, or not. No doubt diary-keeping is also a kind of vanity. One has the sauce to believe that every thought which comes into one's head merits recording.

Yesterday I went with Bloggs Baldwin[*] to Ribbesford church-yard. I noticed on the way that the elder is more splendid than I ever remember it. Round here the hedges are crammed with plates of cream. In Worcestershire there is far less elder. Round Apperley the elm disease is terrible. Every elm, great and small, is dead. It is most depressing.

We went into the church, Bloggs with a pair of binoculars in order to read the inscription in small letters at the bottom of the Burne-Jones west window to his great-grandparents. We looked at the tablet to my grandfather and the over-varnished pews which he constructed for himself in 1905. Then we advanced in search of the graves of Bloggs's great-grandparents and my grandparents. He donned a pair of waders, although it was a fine day and the grass dry, and a pair of thick leather gloves, and took up a billhook, and I a scythe. By chance our two graves were practically adjacent at the top of the hill in this huge churchyard. We hacked away and revealed the inscriptions on the stones; mine were quite obliterated by moss, the graves choked by long grasses. Bloggs very cross because his grave is endowed and he had written to the Vicar who never answered his letter. Instead they have spent money on plant-ing hideous plots of lobelias and geraniums round the church. I told Bloggs they ought to scrap all this nonsense and put the sheep in the graveyard.

We lunched at a buffet at The Hundred House, Abberley. Bloggs talked a lot about his father whom he worships. While Prime Minister he used to walk from Astley to Rock church, some ten miles apart. He walked everywhere, talking to yokels as he went. Nothing he liked more in Downing Street than to hear Bloggs tell him stories in broad Worcestershire, which he speaks fluently. He said that his father in old age steeled himself by means of his implicit religious faith, his love of literature and art, against the ferocious criticism of his neglect to re-arm between the First and Second World Wars. But what wounded him most was accusations against

---

[*] A. W. Baldwin, 3rd Earl Baldwin of Bewdley, 1904–76; biographer; m. 1936 Elspeth Tomes.

his honour: the worst, that he had let down Austen Chamberlain. This story, quite untrue, emanated from Ava Waverley who, Bloggs said, never could speak the truth. I said how curious that I was sitting next to her at Windsor two nights before.

He told me a story about his grandmother, Mrs Ridsdale, who was an earthy, middle-class woman, but psychic. The Ridsdale family lived in the Tower of London, for the grandfather was Master of the Mint. One day Mrs Ridsdale took Bloggs's mother, Lucy Baldwin-to-be, aged seven, shopping in the West End. They got into a horse-drawn bus. Half-way there, in the Strand, Mrs Ridsdale said, 'We must get out.' She dragged Lucy out of the bus and they took another bus going north. After an hour's drive they got out, and ran down streets to a cemetery. Into the cemetery they ran, down paths to a grave. There they saw a grave-digger, who had that moment dug up the small coffin of Mrs Ridsdale's baby which had died before Lucy (Baldwin) was born.

Sunday, 24th June

We had Diana Cooper to stay the weekend. I met her at Chippenham station. Saw her at the far end of the platform struggling with a suitcase and a large basket. Embraced her, took the suitcase and would have taken the basket, but no. She insisted on carrying it, because inside was her Doglet, under a coat. A dog's ticket is as much as a child's, and she won't pay for one. We got through the barrier all right. In the car chat about this and that. Easy. It is when others are present that I find her less sympathetic. For she must be, no, *is* the centre and she will talk so much. I find her constant drinking merely a bore. Fill up, fill up with gin, vodka, anything it seems. The garden was open this afternoon and she sat with me at the gate, taking the money because it amused her to talk to the people. Some recognized her under her large hat, those unmistakable, God-given features. Who would guess she was over eighty? And Doglet on her lap was an object of attention. She has little balance and wobbles perilously. With the least prompting she spouts scenes of Shakespeare. She eats nothing; pecks at a spoonful on her plate, and leaves most of that. She is indifferent to comfort and possessions. Doesn't mind what happens, whom she sees, so long as it is somebody interesting.

Wednesday, 27th June

Caught the 8.08 from Gloucester, where A. drove me, to Crewe. There a charabanc took us, those members of the Arts Panel come from London, to Erddig,[*] where we spent the rest of the morning looking over the house. At 2 o'clock we lunched, and returned to London. What an astonishing house, nothing touched since the mid nineteenth century, and by untouched I mean uncleaned, uncared-for. The house itself is barely interesting. Ralph Dutton does not think the place acceptable. But the furniture startling, the early Georgian mirrors in the saloon, the bric-à-brac. I was interested to see that the three small panels of tapestry are precisely the same as mine, by which I mean the same figures are recognizable, same ugly women's faces, and one youth wearing the same hat with feathers. This makes me wonder whether my panel came from Emral and not from Camphill, as I always supposed. Because Emral was next door to Erddig and the Yorkes and Pulestons intermarried. The present Yorke's father's first wife was a Puleston, just as my grandfather's first wife was also.[†] The Erddig tapestries are Soho, and the bills survive.

Friday, 29th June

To a concert this evening at Badminton in aid of the Conservatives. When I see a heap of Conservatives, tradesmen from Bristol and hunting people, all affluent and with mouthy, greedy faces, I feel I do not conform to their standards. Moura Lympany[‡] at the piano in the large room. I stared at the decoration of this room, which must be Wyatville I guess. Splendid portraits in this house. Again the Duchess took me and A. to see the charming little portrait of the Countess of Albany at the top of the stairs. Buffet supper in the north hall. Nothing but one éclair with custard inside and champagne which I hate. We took Angus [Menzies] who is staying and Pam Jackson who motored over. Woman looking more beautiful than words can say. Her face radiates light.

---

[*] Erddig, Denbighshire (Clwyd), seat of Yorke family; given to the NT by Philip Yorke in 1973.
[†] Emral Hall, Flintshire (Clwyd), seat of the Puleston family; disposed of by Crawshay Puleston, J.L.-M.'s half-uncle, and demolished in 1936.
[‡] Dame Moura Lympany, concert pianist, b. 1916.

Saturday, 30th June

After breakfast Pam telephoned to say that Nancy is in a coma and sinking fast. This evening before dinner she telephoned again that N. died at ·1.30. She is to be cremated and her ashes buried in Swinbrook churchyard next Saturday. Difficult to imagine that bright spirit silenced.

Sunday, 1st July

Nance must have died during the total eclipse of the sun yesterday. Her *Sun King* is by coincidence to be serialized on the radio this week. She told A. only a few months ago that she intended to be buried in France and had bought herself a plot in Père Lachaise for the purpose. Within the last few weeks she changed her mind. It is a fact that towards the end people usually wish to go home. It is at Swinbrook that Tom's[*] memorial tablet is to be found and where Lady Redesdale's ashes were buried. And poor Bobo's[†] too, I'm almost sure.

Moura Lympany came yesterday accompanied by a nephew whom she had staying with her at Badminton. He is a young man, hippyish and bearded, with abominable manners. He came into our house and before waiting to be introduced went straight to look at the pictures and books. Then remarked, 'I always judge people by their books rather than their conversation.' Threw himself down on an armchair, cocking his leg over the arm. Brash and conceited. Probably concealed insecurity, and a chip, for he said on departure for Cirencester Park, 'That is not the sort of place which suits me.' Has some job at the Tate; talked of a life of John Martin he is writing, yet is totally ignorant of art. Strange youth. Eardley told me that last weekend Mattei[‡] had a young friend to stay. He was very nice but behaved as though he owned the house; took what he wanted without by-your-leave, even driving off in Eardley's car without permission or request.

---

[*] The Hon. Thomas Mitford, 1909–45; brother of the Mitford sisters and only son of 2nd Baron Redesdale; killed in the Second World War; Lord Redesdale was succeeded by two brothers, then a nephew.
[†] The Hon. Unity Mitford, 1914–1948.
[‡] Mattei Radev, Bulgarian immigrant; picture-frame gilder.

Wednesday, 4th July

I wonder what Nancy has left to A., and also I wonder just a little if she has left me some small thing. I try hard not to think anything of the sort, but do not succeed.

Cecil Beaton* who came to tea here on Monday said that Jamesey [Pope-Hennessy] ought to be set up now, for he has two commissions for books which are money-spinners. One is the life of Noël Coward, whom James admired; the other the life of the Duchess of Windsor. I said I did not envy him the last one. 'Oh, but just think of the poor little Cinderella who made good,' Cecil said. C. looks immensely distinguished. We all went to Claverton to listen to Desmond Guinness† lecture on Jefferson. He did it thoroughly well, with much confidence, all the jokes, the grimaces, the flirtatious mannerisms carefully rehearsed. Cecil said afterwards that Desmond is beautiful, but not nice. He certainly is handsome and attractive with piercing, clear, cold blue eyes. Reminds me very much indeed of Tom [Mitford] without the straightforwardness.

I went to see Joan Evans‡ yesterday evening. I said to her that I had been proposed for the [Society of] Antiquaries and would probably be blackballed. To my surprise she said, 'Yes, you might be.' 'Why?' I asked. 'Because you don't care much about digging, do you? And you have made it known. But I will support you, if asked.' Decent of her. She showed me the gold medal which the Society has given her. It feels really solid.

Saturday, 7th July

Have received a snub from the Librarian of Windsor Castle to whom I wrote asking permission to see the Stuart papers. Was given to understand from Don Nicholas that anyone reputable was given permission. But no. R. Mackworth-Young replied that unless I was an accredited biographer of a Stuart I could not visit the library. To my questions about the Cardinal King's jewels I got no answer at all.

---

* Sir Cecil Beaton, 1904–80; artist, stage designer, photographer and society figure.
† The Hon. Desmond Guinness, b. 1931; s. of Bryan Guinness, 2nd Baron Moyne, and The Hon. Diana Mitford; author and Irish conservationist.
‡ Dame Joan Evans, dau. of Sir Arthur Evans; writer on art, and first woman President of Society of Antiquaries; she d. 1977.

Are all handsome men narcissistic? During these hot dog days all the young and not so young doff their shirts and work naked to the waist; and solicitous they look. They love exposing their bodies. The other day I met Mervyn the Badminton keeper in his jeep, naked to the navel. Had a chat with him. All the time he was caressing his torso, running his hands soothingly, affectionately across his breasts and navel, and under his arm pits, like a lover with his mistress. Does this mean that he is in love with himself, or what? I have often noticed this behaviour by men who are not at all homosexual, the moment they are naked. They do not make love to themselves when they are clad. Perhaps it is shyness because they are naked in public. But I think not. Men are more interested in titillating themselves than women are.

Dale and James Sutton* dined on Tuesday. They are both so unread that it is difficult to converse with them, sweet though they be. A. asked Dale what was the colour of her child's hair. The reply was 'Teeshion'. Every sentence is punctuated with the adverb 'ackshally'.

To the Gala at Covent Garden on Wednesday, *Carmen*, not my favourite opera. But the negress Verret was a very good actress, beguiling, seductive and beautiful, with an excellent figure. Heat overpowering. We only survived by fanning ourselves with our programmes throughout the performance. The next day I had to return home by the 3.45 train because I could not walk the streets for the heat. Meant to attend the ceremony of the Cardinal giving Lennox [Berkeley] the Order of St Gregory at the Archbishop's House, at 6.30. But could not face it.

The Kiftsgate rose on the fir tree outside my bedroom window is today at its fullest bloom of loveliness. It irradiates my bedroom, and when I enter it from the bathroom I see the rose framed in the window like a glorious aura of purity and godliness. I am distressed by the knowledge that flowers are the sexual organs of plants. This is puritanical. Instead of being put out I should be pleased. On the contrary I am shocked. The greatest glory God and nature provide, their most aesthetic, spiritual manifestation is therefore sex.

---

* Dale, dau of J.L.-M.'s sister Audrey Stevens, wife of James, s. of Sir Robert Sutton, 8th Bt.

Monday, 9th July

On Saturday A., Helen Dashwood (who had invited herself for the night) and I motored to Nance's funeral. We were bidden to lunch by Rosemary Bailey[*] at Westwell at 12.30. It was a family affair. The Beits, the Gladwyns[†], the young Redesdales gathered. All dressed in black, I in a dark blue suit for I no longer have a black suit, and morning dress is no longer worn. Lord Redesdale[‡] who was chief usher *was* so dressed. We motored to Swinbrook church. It was a most lovely day, sunny with clouds which rendered the Windrush landscape blue. Greeted at the church door by Peregrine Harting-ton.[§] I wore dark spectacles to conceal the tears. We were put, with Geoffrey Gilmour[¶] who had come from Paris, in a front pew. In front of us were only Rosemary Bailey and Clementine [Beit] who wore a black straw hat perched becomingly on the top of her head, tilted over the nose. C. kept turning round watching who came in. Before us on the chancel steps, raised on a small blue velvet cover-ing, a tiny, common little wooden box, one foot by one foot, containing all that is left of Nance. The utter nullity of existence and fame overwhelmed me as I gazed at this piteous object. Such a beautiful church, with the fine Fettiplace monuments and Tom's tablet, and the clear windows with the sun filtering through, the west window framing the great fountain of green trees beyond the churchyard. Lord Redesdale carried the box on its little cushion down the aisle. We all followed. Close to the tower a tiny, shallow hole was surrounded by wreaths and bunches of flowers. The tiny box was lowered, not very far. Then Lord Redesdale beckoned the three sisters to file past. Diana,[**] Debo, Pam, all three wearing black scarves over their heads like three Classical graces. Tom Mosley bowed to the grave in passing. We were all directed to file past. A. was so upset by the cards to Nancy from the sisters, and the

---

[*] Rosemary Mitford, b. 1911; m. 1932 Commander Richard Bailey, RN.

[†] Cynthia Noble, m. 1929 Gladwyn Jebb, later 1st Baron Gladwyn; ambassadress in Paris, 1954–60; memoirs published 1995; d. 1990.

[‡] Clement Mitford, 5th Baron Redesdale, 1932–95.

[§] Peregrine Cavendish, Marquess of Hartington, b. 1944; s. of present Duke and Duchess of Devonshire.

[¶] Geoffrey Gilmour, 1907–81; collector of *objets d'art* and resident in rue de Bac, Paris.

[**] The Hon. Diana Mitford, b. 1910; third of the Mitford sisters; m., 1st, The Hon. Bryan Guinness; 2nd, Sir Oswald (Tom) Mosley, 6th Bt, politician and author.

inscriptions with their pet names for her and from them, that she burst into tears. I wanted to escape by the back gate but we were obliged to stop and chat. I merely kissed Diana and Debo and Woman, and avoided Tom Mosley out of shyness – no other reason. He looks like an old, old Rabbi. A very harrowing experience.

Saturday evening to Cheltenham for Lennox [Berkeley]'s symphony and his short piece specially commissioned for this festival. Might have liked the last if I could have heard it repeated. I think contemporary music should be played at least twice running, for once only it is impossible to take in, there being no tunes. If I heard the piece played today, and was not told by whom it was composed, I would not recognize it. And who, apart from a handful of musicologists, would?

Helen looked a figure of fun, wearing long, black artificial eyelashes which dripped jet inkstains down her cheeks. Throughout the visit A. who dislikes her pricked her several times I fear. Of course she shouldn't have done it. Yesterday morning Helen asked me what was the matter with A? She said she never used to be like that. I refrained from comment. Embarrassing. At luncheon we had Andy Garnett.* Talk was about the National Trust, and I said jokingly to Andy, 'You had better be careful what you say about the National Trust in front of Lady Dashwood who does not care for it.' 'I should think not,' Helen yelled furiously. 'We had better change the subject,' A. said, tactful, with that deadly calm habitual to her. There was a heaving silence of simmering antipathies. I talked to Helen with calculated sweetness. After coffee on the terrace she went upstairs to pack, and left at three. We kissed all round and waved her off.

The Berkeleys stayed from Friday till Wednesday. I went for two longish walks with Lennox in Westridge Wood and through Foxholes. We talked about his father's illegitimacy. Although the father died when Lennox was thirty he never touched upon the subject, because he was very fond of L.'s grandmother and was very defensive of her. She came from a grand French family, called de Melfort Drummond, actually of Scottish descent. I was able to find out that she was directly descended from the Drummond Duke of Melfort who was Secretary of State to James II. The late Earl of Berkeley

---

* Andrew Garnett, entrepreneur; husband of Polly Devlin, journalist and author.

quarrelled with Lennox's father, who was his eldest brother. So it
was not specifically on account of the illegitimacy that he disinherited Lennox. We talked too of L.'s work. He said he was so afraid of
boring his listeners that he kept most of his compositions short. We
went to two concerts in all at Cheltenham at which his works were
performed, and I fear all but one left me tepid. The exception was
the piece for the piano, violin and horn, which I found deeply
moving. In it I detected greatness. L. is perpetually in the clouds,
from which he descends with an effort, the most modest of men,
and the sweetest.

Sunday, 15th July

Helen is quite unabashed, which is what I do rather like about her.
Precious little else. I received a letter saying she has heard I have
written a novel which is riveting, and will I give her an inscribed, a
lovingly inscribed copy for Christmas.

A county weekend! Yesterday we lunched at Sezincote with the
Kleinworts;* and today with cousin Cheethams† at Eyford. Sezincote has been repaired and done up, and saved by these nice people;
yet it has lost something of the arcane since the Dugdales owned it
when it was falling down so romantically. After Eyford today we
went to Bourton House and were shown round by its new owner,
Alan Tillotson. This dear old Queen Anne house has utterly lost its
soul. Fitted carpets throughout. The dark and dusky panelling
stripped, and now drag painted; pretentious wallpapers, orange stair
carpet; entrance hall panelling painted sealing-wax red. Bathrooms
everywhere; fashionable pleated lampshades. Garden over-laid-out;
tasteless planting. All tarted up like an old bedizened madam. I liked
the Kleinworts: sympathetic, intelligent, unpretentious, and so rich
withal. Cheethams unrelaxed, he difficult to talk to. Shy? Enough
county society. Sat next to a friendly woman today who imagined
she broke the ice with, 'Did you ever find out who the woman
was?' I knew she referred to *Another Self*. 'No,' I said. She then
launched upon the *Earls*. I wished she wouldn't. I can't talk to
strangers about my books.

---

* Sir Cyril (1905–80) and Lady Kleinwort (Elisabeth Forde).
† Sir Nicolas (John) Cheetham, b. 1910; Ambassador to Mexico, 1964–8; m. 1st, Jean
Corfe (diss. 1960); 2nd, 1960, Lady Mabel Brooke.

Thursday, 19th July

The young poplar outside my bedroom window against the garden
wall already has yellow leaves. This season plants have flowered and
faded quickly. All our roses wilted as soon as they bloomed. Has
been a short-flowering summer.

Grievously disappointed, in that summoned to sit on a jury at
Bristol I spent the whole of yesterday and the better part of today
waiting in the Guildhall, expecting to be called. Finally at three this
afternoon we were informed that the defendant had failed to turn
up, and a warrant for his arrest had been issued. So we were
dismissed. Twenty-four of us had sat in a room like a doctor's
waiting-room for twenty-four hours altogether I guess. From time
to time were told we might go out and must return at ten, twelve,
two-fifteen. I wandered round the centre of this strange, exciting
city. Saw a number of churches and the Cathedral. Some of the
happiest hours of my life have been spent in cathedrals. Their
antiquity and sanctity compel prayer, and identification with God.
Can't make out whether the motive is good, or bad: bad because
prayer ought to be stimulated by ugly modernity just as much. In the
waiting-room I was the only person to read a book. A few
read newspapers while groaning, several chatted; most gazed into
space.

After dismissal we queued up before the cashier's office where we
were given our expenses for these abortive days. I got over £8 for
my mileage and food allowance. All the others who were of
working age must have got much more in compensation for
lost earning hours. I should think this incident has cost the
taxpayer over £500. The cashier, a nice woman, said to me as I
entered the room and before she saw my name on the form, 'Have
your roses been good this summer?' She had visited the garden last
year.

Am reading Sachie Sitwell's latest book [*For Want of the Golden
City*] which he sent us. I think it a work of near genius, although
discursive.

Sunday, 22nd July

What we have dreaded for months, no years, has now happened.
One of the dogs, Chuff, died yesterday evening. We had to take him
to the vet, whose advice was that we should let him go. I suppose

we did right. Neither of us could face watching him die, for which I feel guilty. Vet said in an extremely kind way, 'Wait in the car and I will tell you when it is over.' We managed to get out of the surgery, both sobbing, and in the car gave way completely. Suddenly I laughed at the spectacle of two elderly people sobbing together in a small car. But tears keep returning and have flowed ever since.

We are so unhappy that we are driving to Scotland tomorrow, to stay at Haliburton for three days.

Friday, 27th July

On Monday we drove, taking Fop, to Scotland. Over 570 miles by motorway, and we reached Haliburton by seven o'clock. Had two full days there and three nights. What a grim and dreary house it is. Yet interesting to both of us in that it was built for A.'s grandfather, and for the first time she was able to look at all the pictures, the portraits of her grandparents and great-grandmother (hers by the same artist, the Scot, Watson Gordon, who painted my great-grandfather here [i.e., at Alderley] upstairs on the landing). Joan and Mick Lindsay[*] very kind but oh, their limited interest, and that an intense one, the four legs of a horse. Went to Glamis Castle, and Guthrie Castle for tea with Eve Gregory[†] who looks fragile but handsome. Glamis not as I supposed perched on a cliff, and lacking the magic I associated with it. This driven away perhaps by the hordes. Until lately it was an exclusive place. Still is beautiful outside though disappointing within. On return we lunched with the dear Fulfords[‡] at Barbon. Roger's library is at one corner of the house with round bay window, and views across the valley into infinity. A sort of eyrie. They send up my spirits, and arouse my interests in life. We both agreed over this.

Back to the Chuff-less home A. said this morning she did not think she could go on living here without him. I said we must in the autumn get another and call him Chuff and lavish our love upon the successor. To this A. replied 'How like a man!'

---

[*] Of Haliburton, Perthshire, the home of A.L.-M.'s mother.
[†] Eve Hill, wife of Vice-Admiral Sir David Gregory; they both d. 1975.
[‡] Sir Roger Fulford, 1902–83; biographer and editor; m. 1937 Sibell Lyttelton (née Adeane).

Sunday, 29th July

Roger Fulford talked of Evelyn [Waugh]'s diaries in which he is mentioned as one of Evelyn's oldest and most intimate friends since Lancing school days. He said that as a boy Evelyn had immense, uncanny power over his schoolfellows. He was determined to make his company win the prize for the best-disciplined in the corps, in order to make mock of the corps when they had won it. By sheer pertinacity and determination he made the company win, and then to their surprise lay back and laughed at their success. Roger's father was referred to by Evelyn as 'a genial fool', whereas, R. says, his father was neither genial nor a fool. Already young students approach R. in search of data for their boring theses on E.'s generation. Roger says it is terrifying how wrong they are, the gross errors they make about his friends long dead. I said how little truth there must be in all history. 'Yes,' he said, 'the people we write about who are long dead, must be turning in their graves.'

At Sally [Westminster]'s last night Clare Crossley said what a splendid, gallant old woman Mrs Fleetwood-Hesketh* had been. She had tremendous influence upon her sons' characters. During the war while crossing the Atlantic to visit her daughter in America, her ship was torpedoed. Mrs Hesketh found herself in a lifeboat full of children and young people. There was no room for further survivors. So she said quite calmly, 'I have had a good life. I am near the end of it. Goodbye.' And walked into the sea.

Saturday, 4th August

How sad to be incontinent without being aware of it. Long may it be before the valves give out, for the absolute necessity of the old is to be clean. Otherwise they have no right to expect anyone to come near them. And too many old people are unclean.

On Thursday we went to picnic with Penelope [Betjeman][†] in her tumbledown hovel near Cusop on the Brecon–Herefordshire border. She told us that John's shuffling was not a trick he had subsided into, but was caused by hardening of the arteries. She is

* Anne Brocklebank, mother of Peter Fleetwood Fleetwood-Hesketh, architect, author, and Hon. District Representative for National Trust 1947–58.
† Lady Betjeman, wife of Sir John Betjeman; author, as Penelope Chetwode, of *Two Middle-Aged Ladies in Andalusia* (1963); dau. of Field Marshal Lord Chetwode, 1st Baron.

having to build a shower in her cottage because he can no longer get into and out of a bath. She deplores the amount he drinks. Told A. she was hugely grateful to Elizabeth for looking after him. Penelope has no running water, no electric light, no telephone. Water has to be fetched from a neighbour – God knows where there is one – and the lavatory tank must be filled before the plug can be pulled. This operation is restricted to once a day. P. doesn't mind these deficiencies the least bit. She is fearfully bossy. 'Now Jim, you are to put the horses in the field. When you have done that I want you to put up an old door so as to prevent the puppies escaping from the stable. Alvilde, get the cider from the barrel in the woodshed.' At first one thinks one cannot stand it. But one falls into her ways. She is so good-hearted. When she laughs, which she does at all jokes against herself, she roars. Over coffee I was handed a bowl of sugar, brown mixed with white. I said, 'Darling, are you quite certain this mixture is not worm powder for the horses?' Penelope looks much older, lined and yellow. This is 'Inja' for you.

We visited Moccas in the afternoon, now open once a week. House practically empty and what furniture and rugs put in, are all wrong. What's called out-of-keeping.

It is too easy to be impatient with and censorious of sex when one is 65: the squalor of it, the repetition, the inanity. Yet there's ground for disagreement that to be in communion with God all carnal appetites should be eschewed because the very actions of fornicating, over-eating, over-drinking are ephemeral, finite. Lusts being mortal are in consequence negative, without injury to man's immortal gnosis. Whereas cerebration, devotional exercise, worship being perdurable and victorious remain unaffected by them. I daresay the old Fathers would dispute this ratiocination.

Monday, 6th August

Today I become an old age pensioner. If I wished to get a job I couldn't. Henceforth I receive a pension from the state. A. gave me a new radio, very small, chic and pretty with an excellent tone. The old one which was Aunt Dorothy's still works but is becoming a trifle senile.

Last night reading in bed I thought I must have cancer of the chest. A tightness, a restriction, a hesitancy in breathing. Today I have forgotten all about it.

Jack Rathbone said yesterday that he has read Nigel's book on his
parents; that Vita does not come out of it in an attractive light,
which I feared. He, Jack, said of course he was not shocked, but the
Gibbses (they were also lunching with us) will be. Thinks it a
mistake of Nigel. He has sold the rights for serialization at £1 a
word. The book is expected to sell nearly a million copies. Jack says
he doesn't like Nigel better for this. Raymond [Mortimer] also told
me on Sunday at Eliza's that he had read it. It was very well done,
but he wished Nigel had waited a bit longer.

Raymond apropos Antonia Fraser's book on Oliver Cromwell
which I am wading through says if she can use seven words when
one will do, she does. I am impressed by her vast industry, and
research, and architecture of this stupendous work, 700 pages. But I
am not enjoying it a bit. Far too long and O. Cromwell a most
antipathetic person.

I see a new book on the Kingsleys by Elspeth [Huxley] is favour-
ably reviewed. When we lunched with her last Sunday she never
mentioned it. She is a very modest woman, who always depreciates
her own writing. Agreed with me that only idiots could be optimists
today. Her literary agent, a nice old Jewish man, staying. Van der
Tyll? [van Thal] Spoke most appreciatively of *Another Self* and asked
if *Heretics* was making large sums of money. I laughed, and disabused
him.

I have finished typing and correcting my last chapter on the
Countess of Albany. I still have to incorporate Don Nicholas's
corrections of Prince Charles's section and write my explanatory
foreword, before submitting the finished thing to David Higham.*

Friday, 10th August

A maddening time in London endeavouring to look at portraits of
the Pretenders in the National Portrait Gallery, by appointment
made weeks ago. Had to go to an annexe I knew nothing about,
in Carlton House Gardens; and when there, two portraits could not
be found. In old days the walls were crammed with portraits which
was as it should now be, for one uses the Nat. Port. Gall. as one uses
the *DNB*, not for aesthetic enjoyment of its rooms but for icono-
graphical purposes.

---

* Literary agent, David Higham Associates.

Dined by long pre-arrangement with Rosamond [Lehmann] and Hester Chapman.[*] The latter is brimming with energy, enthusiasms, information, ideas, eager curiosity, and is life enhancing. Ros ready to be immolated as the poor hostess who does all the work and gets an occasional word chucked like a bone her way. So I had to see that she was not left out of the conversation. There is a sort of love-hate between these two old friends, and a weeny flavour of jealousy. Talked of the Empress Eugénie, Hester full of reminiscences, and anecdotes. Said that when the young Prince Imperial was killed the mother insisted on procuring the weapons which had killed him. She made a pilgrimage to the site and knelt on the spot where he was slain. The Zulus who had killed him were found and interrogated. Asked why they had not stripped the corpse and looted his possessions as was their custom, they replied that they dared not. He had fought with such gallantry they supposed he must be a god. Jean Cocteau came to know the Empress well in her old age. One day when nearly ninety she handed him a flower, saying, 'This is the best thing I can give a poet.' At that moment her face was transformed with a radiance and she appeared in a flash a beautiful young woman. In 1918 someone said to her, 'Wouldn't the Emperor and the Prince Imperial have rejoiced to know that the Germans are defeated?' The Empress rejoined: 'Do you suppose that I have not already informed them?' She had a habit of communicating with them in the chapel at all times of the day. Such is faith.

On Wednesday A. telephoned me in London that she had seen her doctor, Allison, about the throbbing in her head. He told her she had come to him just in time. She was suffering from temporal arteritis; he has given her Cortisone and performed a slight operation. Had this not been done she might have been struck blind in both eyes. This upset me greatly. I immediately telephoned the Sitwells with whom we were to stay this weekend. Told Sachie calmly. Even talked about his book. I said, 'It contains all the wisdom of the ages,' which I think is true. Said I knew he disliked discussing his books, but I wanted to talk with him about it. He seemed pleased, and said there were few indeed with whom he could bear to talk over his writings. 'I think it is quite funny in parts,' he said. Said he was very exhausted by it. Then Georgia came

_____

[*] Hester Chapman (Mrs R. L. Griffin), 1899–1976; novelist, biographer, historian.

on the line and commiserated about A., which reduced me to tears.
I wish I were not so uncontrollably melted.

Saturday, 11th August

A. has had a small fragment of the artery wall removed under local
anaesthetic. She takes it very philosophically. Yesterday I lunched
with Joan Altrincham[*] and the John Griggs[†] to meet Iris Murdoch
and her husband, a gnome-like sprite, bald, plain with bad teeth, an
impediment in speech, quick and very clever. Iris Murdoch and I sat
together. The party was clearly given for us to meet, and because I
was aware of this I had nothing to say to her. When introduced she
said, 'I am so glad to meet you. I have looked forward to doing so
ever since our novels came out together in February and I had
influenza and could not join you and Norah Smallwood.' Now all
would have been well if only general conversation had been per-
mitted; and it might have been had Joanie not been present. She at
once engaged me in *sotto voce* conversation. I could not hear a word
she said; but guessed that it consisted of complaints. Then turned to
I.M. She is a little forbidding. Has short cropped hair *à la* Penelope
Betjeman, whom she somewhat resembles. Is stocky, wearing a
maternity gown of flowered muslin, and trousers. She made a few
trivial remarks of politeness about my novel which she intended to
read, and *Another Self* which she heard was so entertaining. At least I
was able to riposte by saying I *had* read and enormously admired *The
Black Prince*. Asked if she ever wondered what her hero was now
doing and thinking in prison. She said once a novel was finished she
never dwelt on the characters again. 'Of course.' The asinine things
one says because of one's upbringing not to allow silences when in
the company of strangers. Enjoyed talking to John Grigg after
luncheon. He has splendid manners, is attentive to fools, very
intelligent, and the quintessence of a gent., which I suppose
he would not care to be thought. But he could never fail to be
just that. We talked of Baldwin and Lloyd George. I told him of my
one and only meeting with Lloyd George in a committee room
of the House of Commons. He was offhand, autocratic and

---

[*] Joan Dickson-Poynder, Lady Altrincham, widow of 1st Baron Altrincham.
[†] John Grigg, b. 1924; political journalist and writer; succeeded his father as 2nd Baron
Altrincham in 1955, but disclaimed title 1963.

unsympathetic. A fussy, florid little man with an over-endowment of white hair.

John agrees with Philip Magnus[*] that verbal recollections and anecdotes of the subject of a biography one is engaged on are practically valueless. People's memories are coloured by what they think the listener wants to know; and usually faulty. I asked because that morning, yesterday, I received a letter from Jamie Hamilton[†] pressing me to write a biography of Nancy Mitford. Me of all people. Diana Mosley is her sole literary executor and apparently wants me to. I am amazed. First impulse to say No, No. But on re-think am not sure. Anyway am to lunch with Jamie and Roger Machell[‡] week after next. 'I want to make the announcement without delay,' Jamie says. Oh God, what a perplexity. I really want to try and write my eccentric country house owners book.

Tuesday, 14th August

The Filipina is quite clearly not going to be any good. She forgets things one has told her five minutes before. And is unreliable. In other words we shall never be able to go away and leave the house in her care. That I foresee. I suppose all coloured people are like this. They have to be watched over. We shall never get her to understand the intricacies of our burglar alarm. When she let it off by mistake she thought it a huge joke, and has no understanding why we have the thing at all.

The two great-nephews dined; and we invited the Barlows' elder daughter Alexandra, aged 20, and her Austrian female friend to meet them. They were all very sweet. When we asked the father, Basil Barlow, next day to tell us honestly whether the girls enjoyed the dinner, he said they did; we were agreeably surprised. We did not suppose that they could enjoy themselves, because we are so old. Anyone over thirty must be hopelessly uninteresting to them. I daresay the nephews think the same and are too polite to let us see it.

---

[*] Sir Philip Magnus-Allcroft, 2nd Bt, 1906–88; biographer; m. 1943 Jewell Allcroft, of Stokesay Court, Shropshire.
[†] Hamish Hamilton, 1900–88; publisher; m. 1940 Countess Yvonne Pallavicino; she d. 1993.
[‡] Eton school friend of J.L.-M. and backbone of Hamish Hamilton Ltd, publishers.

Wednesday, 15th August

Met John Cornforth in Bath and drove him to Beckford's Tower. He agrees it is worthy of an article in *Country Life*, if we include the coloured lithographs of the rooms as Beckford had them. There is always enough material where Beckford is concerned. We lunched at Batheaston House and admired the river front. Preferred Mrs Hilliard to the Doctor.[*] J.C., sharp as a needle, saw at once that he was the follower and she had the nous. We both marvelled that two people who liked Georgian houses so genuinely could have such non-Georgian taste. Then we motored to Upton-on-Severn.

Had tea with the Lechmeres.[†] One of the hottest days I ever experienced. Tieless and in shirt-sleeves we dripped. Lechmeres most friendly, typical squire and squiress, good, dutiful, decent and ignorant. No children and the heir to the baronetcy a distant cousin. So this is another country house reaching the end of its family tenure no doubt. I was surprised that my memory of the house was so faulty, for nearly the whole of it was rebuilt in the 1890s; all the central part in half-timber, but well done, with care and good craftsmanship. Several family portraits and the diary of the builder, Judge Lechmere of the seventeenth century. Garden layout interesting. John, captivated, agreed that this was likewise worthy of an article in *Country Life*.

Thursday, 16th August

Another stifling day, but glorious, such as one likes to remember – erroneously, of course – every summer day of one's childhood to have been. Motored in a great rush to Plowden Hall near Lydbury North and got there quarter of an hour later than arranged, viz., 11.45. Expected the owner, William Plowden,[‡] who wrote me a fussy letter, to be in a rage. But he too turned out a very charming man. The Plowdens have lived here since the Conquest, he supposes. This is an untidy muddly little Elizabethan house which his grandfather exposed so that it is now

---

[*] Dr Leslie and Mrs (Elizabeth) Hilliard, conservationists of historic buildings.
[†] Sir Berwick Lechmere, 6th Bt, b. 1917; m. 1954 Norah Elkington.
[‡] William F.G. Plowden, b. 1925.

half-timbered. The plaster fillings have had artificial key marks cut which look absurd. The owner has added an unsightly conservatory lean-to, removed some Queen Anne fireplaces with coloured Delft tiles in the grate, and done other questionable things. Indoor panelling much Victorianized and floors all up and down steps. Most interesting contents the splendid family portraits and the Chapel in which the Blessed Sacrament has been reserved since pre-Reformation times. He is devout, and we are told the family keep to themselves. He farms all day, and has reverted to yeoman status one might say. The house I found less interesting than Severn End, but the family no less fascinating in its wonderfully ancient, dim way.

A. and I dined on the terrace, a thing we seldom do, and sometimes never do a whole summer long. Listened to the tired bees buzzing.

Friday, 17th August

Much to our surprise we were invited to lunch at Badminton in order to meet Horatia Durant, an ancient cousin of the Somersets, and a great-great-granddaughter of Nelson. Only us and the Duchess, four in all, Master mercifully away fishing in Scotland. Duchess as always friendly, simple and child-like. Took A. and me round the downstairs once again and said exactly the same things I have now heard her repeat four times, some good little jokes too. Occasional touching remarks like, 'When I was little I was a Teck.' And 'Queen [never 'Aunt'] Mary insisted on buying that Garter ribbon when it came into the market and put it into Windsor, although it was really ours.' Showed us the travelling George [the jewel of the Order of the Garter] which is said to have belonged to Prince Charlie, and dozens of Garter ribbons and seventeenth-century Georges which didn't, and William IV's hair, 'cut off his head and given by Queen Ad'lid to my grandmother.' Mrs Durant evidently bores them stiff with her interminable stories of Somersets. 'I say, "What about my family for a change?" But it might not exist for all she cares. Let's be on Christian-name terms.'

Saturday, 18th August

Reynolds Stones stay the night *en route* to a family wedding at Worcester Cathedral. Each will talk either to A. or me singly, just

like the Sitwells, and will not allow general converse, which
when there are only four persons is even worse than when
there are six. So A. deliberately interrupted my and Janet's tête-à-
tête, which I had reluctantly been persuaded into, with questions to
bring us to heel. It is a struggle and desperately awkward.
Both Stones down to breakfast before 8.30, dressed, he in tail-
coat with coloured waistcoat, she in cartwheel hat with ostrich
feathers, and tight-waisted coat and skirt down to the ankles, of
corduroy (in this heat), plus white lace sunshade. White lace
collar (whaleboned) and cuffs. In this get-up she photographed
me in different attitudes in the garden, to the surprise of
the Margerys who were peeping from behind rosebushes and
windows.

Dined with Caroline and David [Somerset] which was relaxing
and delightful for we all talked together in full spate.

Thursday, 23rd August

Cannot get over the appearance of Philip Magnus on
whom John Cornforth and I called last week. He is but 2 years
older than I am; but is bent with a hump behind and in front, a very
unsightly old object indeed. Eyes look bad too, much filmed. Says
he must have an operation by Pat (Trevor-Roper)[*] for cataract.
Thinks the world of Pat who does not send him in a bill. Told
me, not for the first time, that he gave Pat a set of Piranesi prints
for his services. Lady Magnus (Jewell) enormous like an over-
ripe pear, yet with a distinguished face, once pretty I daresay.
She has more dignity than Philip who darlings her and fusses round
her in that way which husbands who have not consummated are apt
to do. I fancied it irritated her. Stokesay Court is a fascinating
example of an untouched house of the 1880s built by a self-
made businessman. She told me that her grandfather was self-
made. Philip added that he hadn't an aitch to his name; but
Lady Magnus's mother was somebody grand, a Russell of
whom she is proud. I much like the great marble relief by
Adams Acton of her three boy uncles with their pets included, birds,
shells, dogs.

---

[*] Patrick Trevor-Roper, b. 1916; ophthalmic surgeon and lecturer, of Long Crichel
House, Dorset; brother of historian Hugh Trevor-Roper.

Went to Mells Manor on Monday, spending the afternoon, three hours or more, reading manuscript letters to Sir John Coxe Hippisley from the Cardinal Duke, the Countess of Albany and others. Most interesting and rewarding. Came upon a few new facts and confirmation of facts hitherto uncertain. Rather tiresome this discovery coming after I have typed out the sections on Cardinal and Albany, but Lord Oxford* took two months to answer my letter. Mells is a wonderful old Elizabethan house with pointed gables, superbly set in relation to the parish church tower, which is one of the very best Decorated buildings in Somerset, and the West country. The house is gloriously filled with family portraits, miniatures dreadfully fading (I pointed this out), being hung unprotected in the reveals of a window, and that air of William Morris, also faded, and the Souls† of which doubtless Lady Horner was one. Moated Grange sort of garden surrounded by high grey walls, with apple trees, much ragged grass, a raised terrace which he assured me his mother Katharine Asquith remembers having two mounts, one at either end, when she was a child. I told him these mounts were usual in the seventeenth century. A most sympathetic place, reminding me of Westwood, délabré, full of memories hovering in the air, masses of books and treasures all left helter-skelter. Large family of young, all intelligent and dusty. Lord Oxford I liked this time. Clever, indolent man, very non-soigné.

Yesterday went to London re the proposition of the book on Nancy. Talked first to Eardley who said, 'I hope you won't do it; but I am sure you will.' He evidently thinks I would bungle it and get fussed and the result would disappoint all Nancy's admirers. Then went to Albany where I lunched with Roger Machell and Jamie Hamilton.

They were very friendly and talked politenesses. Asked what book I had finished. I said the Stuarts, 'which you turned down'. No response. No mention of the novel which they also turned down. Just as well. Half-way through luncheon I raised the matter which I

---

* Julian Asquith, 2nd Earl of Oxford and Asquith, b. 1916; his mother Katharine, d. of Sir John and Lady (Frances) Horner of The Manor House, Mells, m. 1907 Raymond Asquith, s. of the Prime Minister and 1st Earl.
† The Souls were a self-named group of intellectually-minded aristocrats of whom A. J. Balfour (Prime Minister 1902–5) was the cynosure.

had come about. They asked what were my reservations. I said the chief one was that I did not admire Nancy's prose style; never had. They took this badly and were, I could see, amazed. Anyway Jamie had received that morning a letter from Diana saying that on no account must mention of Palewski be made. I said then no book could be written because he was the inspiration behind N.'s writing and the cause of her going to live in France and her pro-French, anti-British outlook. He need not be mentioned by name but this great and only affair of her life could not be omitted. Diana also now favours a symposium, not a straightforward biography. I said these sorts of commemoration were seldom satisfactory. I suggested that her letters should be published. Oh, said Jamie, Diana has asked Joy Law to edit these. Rather unsatisfactory meeting. I told them Raymond [Mortimer] was dining with me and they gave me permission to discuss the matter with him, and let Jamie know.

Raymond came to dinner at Brooks's. We ate grouse, deliciously cooked. Raymond said nothing would induce him to write N.'s life; that there was little life to write about. Said N. might be classed with E. F. Benson by future generations. He did say that the best thing would be to publish a selection of her letters, carefully edited with connecting passages, and a longish introduction about her. I entirely agreed, and after he left me, telephoned Jamie and told him this. I said that if Joy L. had not already been asked I would be prepared to undertake this gladly. Pointed out what Raymond said, that it was necessary that the editor could write, and asked if J.L. could write. He said he thought not. I did not tell him that Raymond said he would hand over to me all his letters from N. but would be reluctant to do so to J.L. whom he didn't know. I think I shall hear no more of this proposition.

Friday, 24th August

The IRA activities now spreading alarmingly to London must I fear make most Englishmen detest the Irish with deadly loathing. Why the hell do we not send every Irish citizen back to Eire, impose passports and ban suspects from entering this country?

Yesterday we went to visit the Haineses* at Wickhamford. They very much aged. Haines has had another stroke since I last saw him

---

* Mr and Mrs Norris Haines; Haines was J.L.-M.'s parents' chauffeur for sixty years.

around Christmas time. Is very shaky on his legs. Does not listen and talks ceaselessly about his own interests, which seem to be exclusively the old man who lives opposite; never about the family any more, ours or his. Yet he calls me 'Master Jim'. Can there be any other old age pensioner who today is called Master? I think this makes me unique.

Went to Ragley: much improved since my last visit and largely redecorated by John Fowler. I like the Gibbs hall, but A. thinks the pink walls too pink. Both of us agree that the huge red carpet in the hall is a mistake. The colour clashes with the walls; there should be no carpet in this room, but the noble stone flags left bare; and thereby the unsightly posts and ropes done away with.

The elm disease hereabouts is terrible. Every elm tree large and small, old and young, is a dead skeleton. Poor Simon (L.-M.) who bought his new house two months ago was delighted with four fine old elms then flourishing. Today all four are stone dead. Simon says the cause of this devastation is the elimination by insecticides of some sort of wasp which used to prey upon the elm bug. I don't think enough fuss is made about this disease, which is changing the entire character of the Midlands.

Simon and Lois[*] are delighted with their quite nice, formless (central portion Regency) house which is fairly large, with one vast billiard room and vast table, score board and cues, all bought by Simon for £25. He told the vendor that he must remove these things since he (Simon) had bought the house with vacant possession – knowing it would cost the vendor £200 to remove the table which weighs two tons. In actual fact the table is just what S. wanted. He is not a businessman for nothing. We derived the impression that he is flourishing. They are decorating the house themselves; he lays the wallpapers, she makes the curtains. Nice to see them so happy and so busy. Choice of all things *quelconque*; lampshades, the usual give-away (about which I am not one to boast) are a cause of universal concern.

Graham Rust's *trompe-l'oeil* mural and ceiling decoration of Ragley staircase does not accord with the surroundings, to put it mildly. He is a *faux* Rex Whistler: gaudy butterflies painted between the Gibbsian stucco work. Conversation piece of Lord Hertford and wife mere. Indeed Ld H. made to look nicely pleased with himself

---

[*] Simon Lees-Milne, nephew of J.L.-M., and his first wife, Lois Jane.

and his enviable nobility enhanced to the skies. One senses this as one perambulates. I suppose that patricians who qualify for and fail to acquire Garters and GCVOs can only redeem themselves by visible display of their illustrious rank. And they must exercise great care not to appear vainglorious these days.

Wednesday, 29th August

My mama's birthday. She would be 89 if alive. Shall I see her again? I much doubt it; but because she is fresh in my memory she must still be alive while I am. When the last person who has known her dies, then she must fade away forever.

My strictures about Ld Hertford* (if they are strictures) are met by a charming postcard from him this morning thanking us for signing his petition against a new road through his park, and wishing he had been at home to receive us. I wish he had.

Twice now an American, Craig Smythe or some such name, has telephoned me about my painting of the interior of St Peter's which was used as an illustration in my book. He sounded as though speaking from Wotton-under-Edge. Asked innumerable questions: what is the colour of the nave walls? are the capitals of the pilasters gilded? is the apse of travertine? what is the pattern of the floor? I dashed from the telephone to the picture, and back. Conversation lasted twenty minutes before I learnt that he was speaking from Rome. It appears that my picture is the only record of the interior of the basilica at this date. I can hardly believe this. Nice man; he tells me he is taking up post of Director of I Tatti in December.

Having read through my transcript word by word for the second, or is it the third, time I put it aside as finished. This was months ago. I decided I need not look at it before submitting it to David Higham in September. Then yesterday morning I take from my drawer a sheet of paper on which I had begun to retype page 329. For some reason I must, after typing four lines, have jettisoned it; must have read the first two lines and noticed that I had repeated the same phrase twice. Very ugly sentence. Thought to myself: 'This is the reason why I scrapped it. But I had better look at the finished thing to be sure.' Now to my horror I find that I had done no such

---

* Hugh Seymour, 8th Marquess of Hertford, b. 1930, of Ragley Park, Warwickshire.

thing. There is the clumsy passage undetected! This makes me exceedingly lacking in self-confidence. Indeed I am appalled that I can overlook such dreadful mistakes. I do not observe enough. Or my ear does not function when re-reading.

Thursday, 30th August

On the point of leaving for Scotland at eleven when the telephone rang. It was Jamie Hamilton to tell me that he saw Diana [Mosley] in Paris yesterday, and explained my reluctance to write Nance's Life; and he and she agreed to ask Harold Acton.* Jamie hoped I would agree also. I do, and I am sure Harold will be far more suitable than me, for he belonged to N.'s sophisticated, scratchy young Twenties generation. Besides I am sure Nancy would not have wanted me to write her life. In a way disappointed, although the decision has been mine. Had I not turned the offer down I might have written the one best-seller of my lifetime, or at least had the chance of doing so. Yet I feel relieved. Am certain my decision has been the right one. Poor A. disappointed however.

Reached Barbon for tea, and went for a stroll on the fells with Roger [Fulford] before dinner. Delicious talks with these two heavenly friends. Sibell is so funny, and full of interests. They have asked me to return on Monday.

Friday, 31st August

An extremely exhausting day which I survived unscathed. The Fulfords had produced an electric kettle, tea and biscuits which I partook of at seven. At 7.30 left in my car. Terrible weather, blowing a hurricane and rain. Much angst in finding the way to the Glasgow airport, and foolishly motored slap through the city. Caught the plane for Benbecula at one. Should have reached Benbecula at 1.45 to be met by Gilbert Wheat. While in the air the pilot announced that the weather was too bad to land on Benbecula, and we must continue to Stornoway on Lewis. Assured us that travellers for Benbecula would be given alternative transport. What sort? Two choices faced me. Either to stay in Stornoway for one or possibly two nights because no seats available in tomorrow's plane, or go by ferry boat to North Uist at once. Chose the second. Telephoned

---

* Sir Harold Acton, 1904–95; writer and aesthete, resident in Florence.

Gilbert Wheat awaiting me at Benbecula. Our party then herded in a small bus crammed with luggage and driven in blinding rain to Tarbert. I was so desperately cramped that I developed agonizing back trouble next morning. At Tarbert bundled on to the ferry boat bound for Skye and back again to Lochmaddy on North Uist. By great good luck managed to get a cabin to myself where I lay flat, and was not sick, though the sea extremely rough. Arrived Lochmaddy at midnight and given a room in an annexe to the only hotel. Slept fairly well.

Saturday, 1st September

Walked along the road in the morning in clear sunshine. Weather changes from one extreme to another within hours. All tiny lochs and bogs around me and distant hills. At eleven took the mail mini-bus to Benbecula airport where met by Gilbert Wheat and an assistant master at Rosehill, John Storr, young, twenty-seven, with Maoist moustache ridiculous to look at, but nice, with definite views about life and bitterly opposed to big companies financing and fashioning politics. I liked him.

The three islands composing the Long Isle quite treeless, and spoilt by a plethora of wire; wire fencing, telephone and low tension wires following the road, drooping, dangling, beastly. A perpetual wind it seems. Strong, invigorating smell of seaweed. Hired a motor boat to take us to Eriskay and wandered along the beach on which Prince Charlie landed, looking for the *Convolvulus major* without success. A few of the old crofts left, but none inhabited now. They are thatched with reed and covered with net; stones are attached to ropes which dangle from the eaves, to keep the roof on presumably against the prevailing wind. Many sea birds, but oh how desolate! From the house on the southernmost tip of South Uist we look across at Eriskay and to Barra beyond where Monty [Compton] Mackenzie* lies buried

Tuesday, 4th September

Uneventful journey back yesterday. Through the clouds recognized Connel bridge. Only thirty-five minutes in the air. Easy exit from

---

* Sir Compton (Monty) Mackenzie, 1883–1972; prolific author.

Glasgow and stopped at Carlisle. Within one hour I had left the motorway, visited Mr Dodd's shop, been directed by him to another antique shop where he said there was a delightful portrait of Prince Charlie, bought it for £135, and was back on the motorway. I suppose I have been sensible. It is a primitive affair, showing the Prince full face wearing bonnet with white Jacobite rose; is colourful and I imagine to be eighteenth-century. When I get Don Nicholas's published iconography I shall doubtless discover of which well known portrait it is a version. Stayed again with the Fulfords. A little distressed to hear Sibell repeat all the stories she told me only three evenings ago. Roger never once pointed this out to her. They are a devoted, divine couple. Long talk at dinner about Princess Beatriz of Spain ('Baby B') who was the last grandchild of Queen Victoria and with whom the Fulfords stayed in Spain. She married to an Infante who is still alive, the Infanta now dead. She gave Roger a locket which the Prince Consort had given to his daughter-in-law the Duchess of Edinburgh; or was it to the Duke his son? When Roger expostulated, 'Oh, Ma'am, I am sure you ought not to part with this treasure. Oughtn't it to pass to your children?' she replied, 'No, they are all beatniks.'

In a great rush, leaving Barbon at 9.15 managed to arrive at Leominster just after one for the Poës'* diamond wedding party. A good thing I went. On arrival was informed that I was expected to propose the couple's toast. But I got out of this in saying that I knew no one there, and it was unsuitable for me to undertake the privilege. I suppose Frida regards me as the senior representative of the Lees family. But there were far more Poë cousins. Anyway their son John did it. He read out several telegrams, the first from the Queen. Can it be that the Queen sends telegrams to all Diamond Wedding couples? Or was it because Jack held some military post at Court? Crowds there. I only knew the Wrigleys,† Edith and Alice (Witts), and the Sollys. Rather agonizing affair, but glad I went. Jack Poë is 94 and Frida rising 90. She was at a finishing-off school, I think in Dresden, with Mama. Through her Mama met my father, Frida's first cousin. Hence me.

---

* Frida Lees, m. 1913 Colonel John Hugh Lovett Poë, DSO.
† A gaggle of female cousins through their mother Ailsie Lees.

Sweet letter from Diana [Mosley] quite understanding my reluctance to write N.'s memoir. Agrees it is really too soon. Points out the great difficulties which must arise in publishing any of her letters, for she wrote the most dreadful things about loved ones. Every letter contains a barb, Debo says. That I well knew, and it is that side of Nancy which makes her unsympathetic to me.

Thursday, 6th September

I really have done with the Stuart manuscript – for the time being, that is to say until David Higham has read it and told me it is no good, or far too long. Yesterday I added a few pieces arising from my visit to the Outer Hebrides; and this morning I wrote a short Preface explaining the purpose of the book.

Glorious weather again, long shadows and golden harvest sun. Yesterday was the hottest day in London since 1940; but here it was not merely bearable, but divine. A. and I cut dead branches off the cherry tree which grows beside the terrace.

Sunday, 9th September

And glorious harvest moon too, like a silver-gilt porringer by Paul Lamerie. I never remember a more beautiful summer than this has been. September and October are always the best months.

Yesterday the telephone bell rang and a voice said, 'I am Dorothy Hobhouse, Christopher's sister. May I come and see you?' I invited her to tea today. A charming, tall, distinguished, un-smart typical English spinster which is what I expected. Christopher* used to be ashamed of her. She reminded me that they were brought up in Gloucester Cathedral Close, their father being a Canon. In 1920 he lost his mind, their mother died, and they were passed on to an uncle parson who could not make head or tail of Xtopher, Kit she calls him. She is immensely proud of him. Said on shaking hands, 'You will see at once that I am unlike Kit. I am neither good looking, nor brilliant.' This drew me to her at the start. She wanted to know what I could tell about him in his young days – he never reached middle-age days. I said that we all admired without revering

---

* Christopher Hobhouse, b. 1910; author of a Life of Charles James Fox; killed while serving with the Royal Marines, 1940.

him; that we laughed not at, but about him. We would say to one another, 'Have you heard this outrageous thing Hobvilla has said or done?' That he showed incipient signs of greatness in his keen curiosity, his determination to try everything at least once. I said if he had lived and stuck to the Bar he might have been Lord Chancellor today. That he was no romantic; was a realist. Was sarcastic, and his pomposity was assumed. We found it funny. He was arrogant, and would speak in slow, measured terms with his head thrown back and a contemptuous curl on his lips. He was paradoxical, brilliant, absurd, amusing and conspicuous. I see him very clearly with his handsome face and lithe figure. He must live like a prince without a penny; must be an MP at the age of twenty-one; that he might well have made, and lost several fortunes. She said her cousin Sir Charles warned her never in any circumstances to lend him money from her slender capital. Sure enough he asked her to. She had the strength to resist, and refuse. I showed her the copy of his *Fox* which he gave me, with his immature, terse inscription, and told her I somewhere had a photograph of him. This I could not find. A nice, touching woman. She left me to visit Joan Evans. What I did not tell her was that Christopher had little use for me; and that I did not really love him. Nor did I tell her that Harold [Nicolson] did love him very dearly. She made no mention of his tiresome wife and the child. Jock Murray was extremely kind to them after C. was killed.

I am amazed more and more by the brilliance of so many of my contemporaries. Cyril [Connolly]* gets unstinted praise from K. Clark† in today's *Sunday Times*.

Thursday, 13th September

In the train on my way back from Paddington I drafted a letter to *The Times* on the IRA outrages. Posted it yesterday, but of course they will not publish it. I notice a complete absence of letters on this subject. Perhaps the editor thinks the subject too delicate to risk a correspondence. In so many words I said ordinary people were fed up with the government taking no retaliatory measures against the

---

* Cyril Connolly, 1903–74; author, journalist, and literary reviewer.
† Baron Clark of Saltwood (Life Peer, 1969), 1903–83; best remembered as Sir Kenneth Clark; art historian; m. 1st, 1927, Elizabeth (Jane) Martin (d. 1976); 2nd, 1977, Mme Nolwen de Janzé-Rice.

IRA, who claim to be 'at war' with us, and suggested that all Irish citizens be expelled, all captured IRA activists be shot and a form of martial law be introduced.

Saturday, 15th September

Yesterday A. and I went to Raglan to meet and have tea (which we did in the custodian's cottage and pretty beastly it was, of stale rock cakes and sandwiches which people of our age don't want, especially at 3.30) with poor old Horatia Durant whom we met at Badminton. One of those engagements which made far ahead we imagine will never take place, and lo, they are upon us, and it is too late to get out of them. There the old lady was, crippled, on sticks and ready to bore us with interminable stories of the Somersets. I warned A. what to expect and suggested she did not come, but she wanted to. And inevitably she was restless before she had sat down, and wandered off when Mrs D. began holding forth. Mrs D. kept turning round and complaining, 'But she has disappeared.' I said she always disappeared and she, Mrs D., must pay no attention, all the while making fierce faces at A. to come back and pay attention. But no good at all.

Mrs Durant's great-great-grandparents were Nelson and Emma Hamilton. Horatia was her great-grandmother. Her mother knew and remembered her well, but would never speak about her because of the impropriety of the illegitimacy. She merely referred to 'Granny' as some remote, impersonal being. I said, 'What a lost opportunity. Do you mean you never asked your mother what her grandmother looked like, or what she was like?' 'NO,' she said, 'never. I simply did not dare. It was a closed book.' 'And when did your mother die?' A. asked. 'Only the other day; in 1929,' was the answer. Only the other day.

When A. finally waltzed off, with Fop on a lead, and I was left on a bench on the bowling green, the old lady went on talking, as old ladies always do with me, intimately. I tried to parry some of the intimacies about the Beauforts. Sally Westminster's name came up as usual; how disgracefully she was behaving, etc. I said I never discussed this subject since we were fond of Sally and both parties were neighbours. Mrs Durant told me how humourless Master was. No jokes. He gets things wrong. She bites her nails every time she hears him tell visitors how a cannon ball came through the Raglan panelling – here, and he points to a hole – during the Civil War; whereas of course she knows that the panelling had been removed to Troy House long before the Civil War started.

Mrs D. is shrewd, but stupid, and she has a deep chuckle. Much on the offensive about the Somerset lineage, and pulls one up. A. was indignant at being supposed to know all about the family. Why on earth should she? she complained.

The Luke[*] family have decided on the spur of the moment to go to South Africa with the four children for the winter, leaving next week. Reason being that they can no longer endure the noise of aeroplanes over their new house at Barnes. I sympathize; but why didn't they discover the noise before buying and decorating the house?

Like so many old ladies Mrs Durant exuded that sour smell of unwashed clothes. I notice that in this respect upper-class old ladies are worse offenders these days than lower. Explanation presumably is that they have been accustomed to maids washing their clothes for them, and now they have none.

Monday, 17th September

Last night to a piano recital given at Bad. House by Christopher Osborn[†] to an audience packed with friends, always a tiresome 'house'. Talked in the interval with Julian Fane,[‡] uncle, who much doubts if Christopher will make the grade, and deplores that he now has no teacher. I am unable to judge but thought that his playing of romantic music preferable to classical. Thought his Mozart not too good, but then he began with Mozart, and the piano being abominable was more noticeably so at the beginning than towards the end of the recital when I had grown accustomed to its badness.

I was asking Julian, 'When does a pianist reach that terrible watershed, faced with deciding whether he is good enough to go on, or should stop and adopt another profession?' Julian said the lot of writers was worse if they were not first-rate. We agreed that

---

[*] A.L.-M.'s dau. Clarissa Chaplin, m. 1958 Michael Luke.

[†] Son of Franz Osborn, concert pianist, and June Capel (now wife of Lord Hutchinson of Lullington).

[‡] The Hon. Julian Fane, b. 1927; novelist; younger son of Diana, Countess of Westmorland.

neither he nor I were quite bad enough to meet with success from the untutored herd.

We took the two Tomlinson girls.* The younger has just got a music scholarship at Westonbirt school. I asked, 'Are Mummy and Daddy musical?' 'No,' she said, 'I do not know where I inherit my genius from.' She is 11.

Midi asked me to walk with her this evening down the lane. She said she was in a quandary. Brian her younger son announced a month ago that he had an illegitimate son, aged three years, by a black girl. He is no longer living with the black girl, who has another lover. The two parents are now merely friends. The way the bombshell fell on Midi was aptly chosen. She was tending Derick's grave in the churchyard here, with Brian. In a moment of happy recollection she remarked to Brian, 'Father loved this place. He was so happy during his last years. He had come to understand and tolerate his sons, and was so proud of you and Bamber and Veronica. I think his only disappointment was there being no Gascoigne grandson. He passionately wanted a Gascoigne grandson.' 'Well, he had one. There is one,' came the reply. 'He's black.'

Wednesday, 19th September

Eardley and I lunched. I think I shocked him by saying airily I would quite like to die now; that I hated the world which had left me by, and had no future to look forward to. And future was all that mattered to a man. I did not go into particulars, the millstone dragging me into the abyss of annihilation. It is the certainty that I have been a failure as a son, brother, lover, husband, conservationist, committee member, friend, writer, and what else? Everything really. I suppose most people have a similar millstone tied to the neck.

Sunday, 23rd September

Had a disagreeable little parish meeting summoned last Friday at the RDC's request to ascertain the parish's views on the potato factory installed opposite The Mount House by the wretched Hale son-in-

---

* The daughters of Charles Tomlinson, b. 1927; Professor of English, University of Bristol, 1982–; poet, writer and translator; and his wife Brenda Raybould.

law. There was much feeling. All the oldies were against the project out-and-out; the younger ones in favour. After some acrimonious discussion I put an alternative before the meeting and they voted. I remained neutral and didn't vote. Luckily by two the votes were for total objection. The oldies were of course quite right because once an industry is established in this hamlet it will grow and grow, and will never be dislodged. The young *know* they are always right; they seldom are. The oldies *think* they are right, and usually are.

It is absurd how worried I get over taking the chair at this potty little meeting. I waffle and am hesitant; and I think A. thinks so too. But I know I was fair and impartial. Received a note of compassion from Midi. It makes me laugh in retrospect.

Joan Evans lunched and the Vereys[*] came to meet her. Truly she is a horrid old thing. She spat the meat into her fingers and on to the table without using a fork. She gurked, and farted. In speaking to me at luncheon she let fly an enormous piece of artichoke. I saw it coming and ducked. She saw me duck and rise again and resume the conversation as though nothing had happened. How absurd social conventions are when you do not know people well enough to laugh over these incidents. Neither of us betrayed by one muscle of the face what both had noticed.

Joan Evans, asked by the Wotton people to suggest someone to open some exhibition or other, suggested me. The reply was, 'Oh, but we see him at least once a week in the town, paying his bills like anyone else.' I said, 'I am glad my reputation for payment is so good.'

I am saddened by the sudden death of William Plomer.[†] I met him only a few times, and he stayed here once, or at most twice when on a Kilvert 'do'. But he hated staying away and would not come when I pressed him this spring. He then wrote ominously that he had to take care of himself 'these days'. So I suppose heart failure carried him off. Our introduction was brought about by Richard Rumbold's death, for he was very fond of Richard, and edited his diary. William was one of those rare people whom I saw but little, yet felt I knew intimately. For I could talk to him with utmost ease on any subject. He was quite uncensorious, had a delicious gentle

---

[*] David Verey, 1913–84, architectural historian, and his wife Rosemary, garden designer and writer.
[†] William Plomer, 1903–73; writer, poet, and editor of the Kilvert Diaries.

irony, was self-deprecatory, yet knew perfectly well his worth in the world's esteem, which was considerable, and had a quiet dignity. He was tall, distinguished, and looked wisely and owl-ly through thick-ish-lensed spectacles. He had a deep, soft voice with a distinctive timbre, rather musical, and sympathetic. Humour pervaded every-thing he said, and wrote. He felt deeply, was far too intelligent to be anything but pessimistic about the future of the world. He thought rightly about all fundamental issues. A most charming, sweet, lovely man.

Thursday, 11th October

On 25th Sept. we flew to Pisa, with Hugh and Fortune Grafton and Christopher Chancellor.* Told to keep on our seat belts for our own comfort, mark the word. Always an ominous warning. At one moment over the Alps the huge machine took hold of the reins like an obstreperous horse which bolts; it shook, then plunged, then righted itself, and tossed up and down. I have never experienced this in a large aeroplane before. It is far more frightening than being on the sea, for on the sea one can rely upon the regularity of the tossing. In the air you do not know what to expect next. I sweated with fear. Then the captain announced that owing to the bad weather we might not land at Pisa where, he said, the air strip was defective at this moment. We would continue to Rome. But we did descend at Pisa, and were alarmed at the prospect of touching down on a defective air strip. However all went well. It was unlike the cus-tomary British phlegm and stiff upper lip attitude, we thought; and silently we condemned our captain's propagation of panic among the passengers.

Left England on the most settled and beautiful, sunny autumn day imaginable. Pisa on the contrary horrid, storm raging, and dense rain. On arrival at the Chancellors' villa Butari, 8 miles from Lucca, the lights went out as we crossed the threshold, and remained out for 24 hours. The water was cut off; also the telephone. A gloomy villa, decorated in Twenties' browns. The first night we were woken by a tremendous thunderstorm. Water poured through the roof. We

* Sir Christopher Chancellor, 1904–89; General Manager of Reuters Ltd, 1944–59; Chairman of Bowaters, 1962–9; brother of Robert Chancellor of Stoke Bruerne Park, Northants.

guests searched for basins and buckets. Christopher completely lost his head. Panicked and dashed around, holding out a teacup.

Met Vernon Bartlett* who lives permanently near Lucca, two miles from the Chancellors' villa. He is rising 80, a dear, modest, wise man like a comfortable owl. His small eyes notice everything and twinkle. He and his second wife, a dull lady, but benign – Christopher says she is like a pig, which is unkind – invited A. and me to dinner our last evening. We remarked how much we dreamt here, presumably on account of the mountains. He told us of a dream he had lately. He was in the jungle, lost. For hours, days he desperately was cutting his way through impenetrable bush. At last he came to a clearing. To his joy he saw ahead a notice-board on a pole. It contained two lines of writing. Hurray! he thought, now I have found directions how to get out of this impasse. He read the first line. The words were, 'What did Mr Gladstone say in 1888?' The second line said, 'Fuck off!'

While he was *Times* correspondent in Rome he frequently met Mussolini. M. was always grotesque and vain. Bartlett gave the oft-quoted description of being announced into Musso's office, a long, empty room with the dictator seated writing at a large desk at the far end. The visitor clattered over the echoing marble floor. Musso never would look up, and when the visitor reached the desk he continued writing. On Vernon Bartlett's third visit Musso condescended to meet him a quarter of the way from his desk; and on his fourth visit, half-way. Whereas Musso was a show-off, and something of a music hall joke, Hitler was from the first deadly serious. Bartlett said he could never make out what was the colour of Hitler's eyes.

We were away a fortnight in Tuscany. Alas! Italy has lost some of its magic for me. Several reasons contribute to this. Chief are the overwhelming number of tourists, and the declension of the Italians' image of themselves from picturesque to portentous. Florence has become a nightmare city. To manoeuvre oneself along the pavements is like pushing a motor car out of a swamp. The churches have become museums and for the most part are no longer places of worship. Gone are the incense, the holy water, the lighted candles, the *bondieuseries*, the continuous Masses and chaunting in the larger churches. Gone too are the peasants on their knees with baskets of

---

* Vernon Bartlett, 1894–1983; publicist, author and broadcaster.

produce, vegetables and chickens alongside. The churches seem
emptied of the Holy Spirit, and secular. The Italians have become
hippies, I mean the Italian young. Whereas immediately after the war
they were the cleanest and best-dressed young, as well as the best-
looking of Europeans, now they wear Anglo-Saxon tatters, albeit
cleaner than our young's tatters, and their physical beauty seems
somehow to have faded. At intervals however one sees Venuses and
Adonises who take the breath away.

Sunday, 14th October

Today was an occasion which might have happened forty years ago
– no, a hundred and forty years ago. The Bishop of Gloucester
visited our church and gave a sermon. Afterwards, escorted by the
Rector, he came to luncheon here. To meet him we had
Gilbert Wheat, our friend the headmaster of Rosehill School,
Rachel Savory[*] the good woman of the village, Midi and her
brother Terence [O'Neill][†] who was staying with her. The Bishop,
charming to talk to, human and understanding, looks and behaves
like a Prince of the Church, which is a nice change. In church he
wore a splendid scarlet chasuble with gold tassel hanging over his
surplice at the back. When he came to us he wore a purple soutane
with double-breasted top-piece of embroidered buttons, a fine silver
cross suspended on a chain around his neck, and snow-white
starched dog-collar. We filed into the dining-room and, when we
reached our places, A. said, 'And now my Lord Bishop, will you
please say Grace.' He told A. that lunching at Badminton last Sunday
Mrs Durant was present. An interesting old woman, he said. Mary
Beaufort complained to him, just as she did to us, that Mrs D. was
interested only in the Somersets, and her own family might not
exist for all Mrs D. cared. In fact she said to the Bishop, 'I was only a
Teck girl.' The Bishop told us he was one of those in the House of
Lords who had pressed for the amendment that Alderley and
Berkeley villages should remain in Gloucestershire, and not go to
Avon.

---

[*] Wife of John Savory; friends living in Alderley.
[†] Terence O'Neill, Baron O'Neill of the Maine (Life Peer, 1970), 1914–90; Prime
Minister of Northern Ireland, 1963–9.

Terence hates Faulkner[*] whom I rather respect. He said he was the Wilson of Ulster. Terence agreeably relaxed and giggly; less tense and political.

Nigel [Nicolson] has sent us a copy of *Portrait of a Marriage*. I have read it. It is very well done and will I am sure eventually enhance Vita's repute in so far as she was a vindicator of extra-marital liberties of the Lesbian kind. Vita loved with passion. She was a passionate woman. I think Nigel exaggerates in making Harold out to be a saint. He makes no reference to H.'s peccadilloes which, in contrast to V.'s, were casual, little fly-by-nights. Vita's affairs were all love ones. She was monogamous, not promiscuous. She loved, not merely lusted. There is barely a mention of Harold's minor-key infatuations. Of course the starry section of the book is Vita's autobiography on the elopement with Violet. I find something a trifle comical about the elopement; and something almost disingenuous about the endless expressions of her and Harold's mutual adoration. As Frankie Donaldson said last night, surely married couples do not keep on reiterating their deep devotion to one another after 40 years. There is no need to do so. Were H. and V. writing with an eye cocked on posterity? In thanking Nigel I somewhat impertinently put to him these points, all but the last one. I did not want to suggest that the letters had been intended for future publication, like Horace Walpole's, lest he might suppose I questioned their sincerity, which I don't. But I did say Harold was not an immaculate saint.

Monday, 15th October

The Bishop made one remark at luncheon which I found poignant. He said no clergyman of the Church of England could claim spiritual success. Discounting presumably his own political success in reaching the See of Gloucester, which in a worldly sense is something. He was referring to the empty churches. He said that in his city 80 per cent of the inhabitants had never heard of him and didn't care tuppence for his office. Told A. that as a young man his first cure was in Cornwall. At his first service one person attended, at the second two, and at the third three. At the fourth, none. The

---

[*] Rt Hon. Brian Faulkner, 1921–77; MP (NI) 1949–73; cr. Baron Faulkner of Downpatrick, 1977.

loneliness and depression of spirit of the sincere priest were devastating today.

Last night reading in bed I looked up and gazed at the Mortlake tapestry beyond the foot of the bed on the wall opposite. In a flash, so quick that it occupied the fraction of a second, I understood the whole meaning of existence. It had gone before I had time to grasp what this visitation was, or implicated, or portended. Vainly I endeavoured to recall what it was, why it came, what provoked it. I had been reading a passage from Anthony Rhodes's excellent book on papal policy in the era of the dictators [*The Vatican in the Age of the Cold War*, 1973]. I presume something he wrote induced this visitation, but on re-reading the actual passage on which I was concentrated at the time I found nothing to suggest it, or explain it. Strange. This has happened to me before.

Wednesday, 17th October

It was a great relief to get a letter from David Higham that he thought my Stuart book 'excellent' and had already sent the typescript to Chatto's. Norah Smallwood has also written that she is beginning it and hopes she will like it. So do I too. Unfortunately a second life of Prince Charlie has just come out and I fear this may prejudice Chatto's against producing yet another Stuart book. I live in much apprehension.

Lunched with the old Matley Moores[*] in Worcester yesterday at the Greyfriars. Asked how they liked their new bishop, 'Royal Robin'.[†] Answer was not at all. That no one did. Neither the county nor the clergy. He high-hats them all, and says how much he dislikes Worcestershire. He has incensed the citizens of Worcester by appealing to them for money for the support of the well-endowed cathedral. Matley has put about the fiction that, whereas Robin Hood robbed the rich in order to support the poor, Robin Woods robs the poor to support the rich. Very unfair, really.

This morning I motored Filipina Susanna and her nephew to Wotton for them to catch the Bath-to-Bristol bus. Came out of the front door to see Polly, the nephew, holding something in his hands

---

[*] Matley Moore, Worcestershire historian and conservationist; his sister Elsie, leading restorer of mural paintings.

[†] Rt Revd Robert Woods; Dean of Windsor and Domestic Chaplain to HM The Queen, 1962–70; Bishop of Worcester 1970–81.

and laughing with glee, showing it to his aunt. I asked what it was. It was a large leaf frozen stiff from the slight frost we had last night, and curled and hard. He had never seen effects of frost before. Such a thing is unknown in the Philippines.

Midi with whom I lunched today gave advice about the publication of my diaries. I had told her I felt bound to edit before submitting them. She approved but earnestly begged me not to omit references to my own love life of the past for fear of wounding A. Curious assumption and advice of Midi's, which I don't take to. She then asked me if men ever criticized their wives to each other in their clubs, or when together. I said Never. We agreed that men were just as bad gossips as women, but as regards their wives they never discussed them. This I am sure, from my experience, is true; whereas M. says women constantly discuss together their husbands' prowess or failure in the bed. The notion horrifies me.

Thursday, 18th October

Wishing to buy another odd pair of trousers I went to what used to be called The Trouser Shop next to the Café Royal in Regent Street. The entrance looked different. A young man dressed in velvet, although in the middle of the day, approached me. Hesitantly I asked if this establishment still sold trousers. His greeting was 'Hullo!' which took me aback. I replied 'Hullo!' Then asked if he had any trousers that would suit me. With bland surprise he said regretfully, 'We can only cater for clients with a waist of less than 36,' and gave me a snide look. 'Besides, all our legs are much flared.' Oh dear, I found myself apologizing for being so old and untrendy. But on reflection, why the hell should a man apologize for no longer being young, as though he was thereby an inferior being?

A. took me to Britten's *Death in Venice* at Covent Garden. Before the first act and in the interval we drank and ate sandwiches in Burnet's sitting-room, King Edward VII's smoking-room, under the Royal Box. Opera totally devoid of tunes. Not one aria in the whole long performance. For four hours Peter Pears crooned a wailing monody about beauty and his reactions to carnal temptation. I concede that the orchestral music is full of original percussions which illustrate the mood of the story's theme. But the vocal music is atonal. The boy had a beautiful face but his body was beefy, and non-innocent. Lustful, but not celestial.

Friday, 19th October

I waited a horribly long time at Earls Court station for a train to Paddington. Asked a man waiting on the platform whether he thought a Paddington train was coming, and got into conversation. Was he Scotch? No, he came from Belfast. He told me that all the Ulster troubles were caused and fomented by Communists. That religion had nothing whatever to do with the issue. While we waited, he talked and talked and talked, until I could no longer bear it. This seems to be a common propensity of Irishmen.

Sunday, 21st October

Two days staying at Rhossili walking with Robin [Fedden] and Eardley on the Gower Peninsula. At breakfast on Saturday morning Robin worked himself into a rage and because he was not given toast was very rude to the waiter. E. and I were embarrassed and upset. For a time we sat eating in silence. Then Robin, having recovered, asked us, 'Did I behave very badly?' 'Yes,' we replied in duet. For the rest of the day Robin was much distressed, and on our return late in the afternoon soaked to the skin he went up to the waiter, proffered his hand and apologized. This was handsome of him.

While motoring Eardley from Bath to the motorway we drove up Lansdown Hill. He said, 'Don't take me near Richmond Terrace [where his mother had lived]. I don't want to see the horrors that have been committed to her garden.' Approaching Lansdown Tower he asked to stop in order to look at his parents' grave. I said we would look at Beckford's grave afterwards. Perhaps I was insensitive because I accompanied him to his parents' grave, and removed some litter from it. Then I said airily, 'Now let's go to Beckford's.' E. said, 'I am sorry. I am going back to the car,' and I noticed a tear trickling down his cheek. Yes. I certainly was insensitive.

Anthony Rhodes's book about the Vatican is splendid. Impartial and wise. He gives a favourable character to Pius XI and is very fair about Pius XII. The latter was clearly not quite courageous or outspoken enough in condemnation of the Nazis' behaviour; but what terrible perplexities confronted him. And I earnestly believe he feared lest strong denunciations from the Vatican might bring further harm rather than relief to those Catholics suffering under those bestial persecutors.

Thursday, 25th October

Nigel [Nicolson] has replied that he did not think his father was a *maculate* saint, and seems a little surprised. I am now a little disconcerted and have written again that I hope he did not consider me censorious, for that was my very last intention. Said I felt rather like what his grandmother, Lady Sackville, ought to have felt after disclosing to Ben his parents' homosexuality.

Received a letter from Norah [Smallwood] yesterday which should have rejoiced my soul. To my amazement she says that the foremost American publishers of paperbacks have taken my *Heretics* for issue in the USA in paperback, mentioning the possibility of sales at 150,000 and dollars galore. Now hopes that perhaps a British firm will follow suit. This astonishes me for I imagined the book had been a complete flop here. Moreover before it came out Higham told me that America had refused to touch it with a barge pole. What odd fortunes one's books do have. But she continues in a postscript to say that because of the recent publication by some woman of a second book on Prince Charlie this year and because of the great length of mine she fears, etc., but before giving a final verdict is handing the manuscript to one of her historian colleagues. Clearly does not like the book much. This information has depressed me far more than the other gist of her letter has impressed me. I have replied that once my books have been launched I take little further interest in them. Before they are born I am extremely sensitive and solicitous about them. After three years of sweat, blood and tears over the Stuarts I shall be in despair if it is rejected. I make a great mistake in telling people what I am writing about. It invites bad luck.

Saturday, 27th October

Drove to meet the 6.20 train at Kemble this evening, to pick up Pat Trevor-Roper. As I turned off the Cirencester road the sun was setting on my right. The glowing ball had retreated below a bank of rising mist, throwing upon the twilit sky a pinky primrose light which was translucent and pure. Against this backcloth a row of elms, their feet in the swirling river of mist, their arms drooping against their sides, looked tranquil and serene as though they must endure for ever in this setting, a kind of promise that England would remain as I had best loved it. Whereas of course it is a miracle that the row of elms has survived, and doubtless by next year these divine trees will be dead. The disease has not yet exterminated every single elm in this part of Gloucestershire, as it already has in Worcestershire. This morning Alastair Finlinson* showed me what happens to the elm. On Fry's land by Wotton he tore off the bark from a dead elm. It came off like parchment. Underneath the bole was covered with a film of sticky white foam, like castor sugar. This is the fungus which the beetle brings. The fungus throttles the tree so that it cannot breathe.

Monday, 29th October

David Somerset told A. that Georgia [Sitwell] walked into the Marlborough Galleries, while he was out, and asked to see the finished portrait of Sachie which she had commissioned Graham Sutherland to paint at £15,000 to £20,000. A young man in the shop took her upstairs and indicated the portrait, framed. Georgia looked at it a long time, turned on her heel, muttering, 'It is awful. It is a travesty; a caricature. I won't pay for it.' Later she rang up David. He said he could not understand because Sachie's portrait was not in the shop. It was away, being framed. It turned out that the one Georgia had seen was of Adenauer.

A discussion at dinner on Saturday on the differences between a bounder, a cad and a shit. Pat Trevor-Roper professed not to know the differences. The older ones among us explained that the first two terms were common in our youth, whereas shit was a term we did not use, and it approximated to the second term, cad. Caroline in her outspoken, absolutely candid manner said, 'I know what a shit is,' and turning to David said, 'David's one.' She thought it was a complimentary term. Since David has frequently been called one, we were amused. I don't think he was.

---

* National Trust Agent for Severn Region.

Tuesday, 30th October

Walked away from Eny [Strutt]'s* luncheon while A. stayed and talked – Eny to be 90 next Sunday – to be picked up by A. after half an hour. Walking along Eny's drive at Hodges, there on my right across the field I noticed the church. I have never before admired the tower as much as this afternoon. It is by T. H. Wyatt, built in the 1860s, and a beautiful thing. The sun was low on the horizon, crossing the end of the village at an oblique angle and striking the tower sharply, clearly, throwing the buttress at the west end and the angle turret at the east end into detached masses of white and black, a most impressive spectacle. Wyatt must have had this late autumnal effect in mind when he so contrived the design. It was perfect, and makes a noble piece of architecture. Yet how many people today in passing by this church ever look upon it as it was meant to be seen, and assess its merit?

Mr Bray, husband of the lady who delivers our newspapers, called this evening to attend to my feet. He is a chiropodist by training, although now working at Lister's factory in Dursley. Took my feet in both hands and said that, were it not for my two ghastly big toes, which horses trampled on forty years ago or more, my feet were perfect. Kept stroking them as though they were bronzes. An interesting man. Was in the Consular Police for 20 years, has lived in 22 countries and seen every degree of vice and virtue. In the war in the RAF. Only abandoned chiropody as a living because of the number of clients who chucked appointments, thereby causing him to lose fees. Always wanted to become a doctor but his father was a poor man, so in his youth such an aspiration was beyond the realms of fulfilment. This was dreadful. He still does occasional chiropody 'in order to keep my hand in, sir'. Has one old client friend whose foot was damaged during the war. It is like a hoof, all horn, the toes crushed into one stump.

Sunday, 4th November

Eny Strutt's 90th birthday party. We were greatly flattered to be invited by the Hornbys; and at first declined because we were to stay with the Sitwells this weekend. They put us off. We motored Diana

---

* Baroness Irene de Brienen; m., 1st, Capt. The Hon. C.A. Ward, who d. 1930; 2nd, Vice-Admiral The Hon. Arthur Strutt; she d. 1974.

Westmorland to Pusey. This John Wood house is disappointing. The entrance front with projecting half-octagon wings is imposing. It sits well in its park; but the garden side is ponderous and dull. From what I could see of the rooms they were not exciting. One long room, or gallery, with two fireplaces, has large over-mantel landscapes framed in stucco.

We sat down fifty in the dining-room, at five tables of ten each. I next to Mary, Duchess of D. and Lady Ward, wife of Geordie Ward, a difficult, uninspired female. Sally Duchess also at my table which was the host, Michael Hornby's. A. at Eny's table, A. sitting next to George Gage[*] and Tom Goff,[†] and Eny having on her right the Duke of Westminster. Master also there. Otherwise chiefly family, and masses of beautiful great-grandchildren, some of these adults, like Blandford, an extraordinary pretty boy, and some of the girls, notably Peter Münster's daughter, ravishing. Michael Hornby made an excellent speech of teasing affection, with anecdotes of Eny's eccentricities, her generosities ('You may well wonder where your beautiful presents to her will be tomorrow'), her little savings (telling her children to pick stone copings from her host's park wall for the rockery at home). Her health drunk while a cake was handed round. After luncheon a helicopter landed on the lawn and she was whisked into the sky for a half an hour. This arranged by her grandson, Münster. She adored it and told us she now wanted to marry a pilot.

Thursday, 8th November

Have read Siegfried Sassoon's[‡] *A Poet's Pilgrimage* with the interest and sympathy with which I always approach these sorts of confidences from poets I admire; they are apt to contain all the secrets I want to know. And I accept poets, true poets, as Shelley's unacknowledged legislators of the world. And yet, attractive though Sassoon's poetry is to me, plus his principles and his prejudices, there is something about his personality which... In fact I have slight reservations about him after reading this book. I cannot put my finger on them. Are they his underlying vanity, his sense of

---

[*] Henry Rainald Gage, 6th Viscount Gage, 1895–1982, of Firle Place, Sussex; m. 1st The Hon. Imogen Grenfell, d. of 1st Baron Desborough; 2nd, Diana (née Cavendish), The Hon. Mrs Campbell-Gray.

[†] Maker of harpsichords.

[‡] Siegfried Sassoon, 1886–1967; poet and prose writer.

superiority beneath the ostensible humility, or merely the fact that he has not much brain? I cannot be sure.

Yesterday I spent at Uppark with the NT Arts Panel. What is certain is that nearly everyone connected with the Trust is 'decent'. Sitting round the dining-room table, on which incongruously Emma Hart once danced, there were some twenty of the most understanding, cultivated, earnest men of good sense and taste it were possible to find – Robin Fedden, Brinsley Ford,[*] Johnny Walker from the Metropolitan Museum, Roddy Thesiger,[†] Lord Plunket,[‡] not to mention the staff: Bobby Gore,[§] young Martin Drury,[¶] Gervase Jackson-Stops[**] and Merlin Waterson. Could they be a bettered lot? No.

A horrid thing happened last night as I was driving back from the station. Beyond Little Badminton and Shepherd's cottage, not going very fast before a corner, in the headlights I saw rushing sideways from the verge an enormous fox. Before I could stop there was a bang against the front wheel, and a bump, and I had run over it. What was I to do? One cannot kill a fox without a large stick or an instrument. One cannot touch it with bare hands. I hoped it might be dead. However I turned in a gateway and anxiously and with dread drove back. There in the middle of the road in the distance I saw reflected from my head lamps two, huge eyes which moved slightly, pitiably. I was so stricken, so revolted by myself, so at a loss, that I backed away, turned and drove on. I am sure the poor thing must have been nearly dead, and must now be dead. Ought I to have run over it again? Oh, the horror! And the shame! A real countryman like the D. of Beaufort would have known what to do immediately. Not so a cissy from the suburbs.

I daresay what irritated me just a little about Sassoon was – and this is the tenor of the book – his acceptance of, swallowing of,

[*] Brinsley Ford, b. 1908; a Trustee of the National Gallery; Chairman of the National Art Collections Fund, 1974.

[†] Roderic Thesiger, b. 1915; Director, Colnaghi's; member of NT Historic Buildings Committee.

[‡] 7th Baron Plunket, 1923–75; Equerry to HM The Queen; a trustee of the Wallace Collection.

[§] F. St John Gore, b. 1921; m. 1st Priscilla, dau. of Cecil Harmsworth King ; 2nd, Lady Mary Strachey; NT Adviser on Pictures, 1956–86.

[¶] Martin Drury, b. 1938; NT Historic Buildings representative (now Director-General).

[**] Gervase Jackson-Stops, 1947–95; architectural historian and adviser to NT.

hook, line and sinker the tenets of the Catholic Church and his almost emotional correspondence with the (doubtless) worthy, saintly, Dame what's-her-name* of Stanbrook Nunnery. When a man who all his life has been a free-thinker becomes in the eve of it a blind accepter of the Church's doctrine, I feel that this signifies weakness, a voluntary surrender of mind to spirit, no, to spiritualism, with a dash of hocus-pocus thrown in. Had he been all his life a devout believer in Christian tenets, then I should not feel suspicious of his old-age digestion of everything; I would merely think, here is a religious man who with one foot in the grave has quite properly and sensibly decided to devote all thought and energy to what throughout his life has been his dormant, but fundamental, creed, hitherto not always observed. In fact I am suspicious of 'enthusiasm', especially in the elderly convert.

I am in an unhappy state at present – waiting for Chatto's verdict on my Stuarts, and meanwhile not being able to develop a theme for my next book, and indeed wondering if there is to be a next book, if the mind is capable of such a thing, for my mind becomes woollier and woollier. I find myself havering, moving in circles like a demented hen. A lot of people distract me; my mind becomes suspended in vacuum.

Friday 16th November

Passing St James's Palace I was surprised to see, instead of the red-uniformed guardsmen in the sentry boxes, a pair of oriental soldiers, small and wearing funny, square caps. Who on earth can these Chinks be? Midget Gurkhas?

The morning of Princess Anne's wedding I walked from Eardley's flat in West Halkin Street through the Green Park. It was a fine, brisk November morning, the sun out. There was an unusual atmosphere of festivity and expectation. Crowds of women were scurrying from Hyde Park Corner down Constitution Hill towards the Palace to catch a glimpse. They were carrying curious ugly yellow cardboard signs with small mirrors at one end, home-made periscopes I presume. The newspaper posters on the other hand contained the gloomiest portents in their headings, fuel crises, more strikes, the Bank Rate rising to unprecedented heights, the Stock

---

* Dame Felicitas Corrigan.

Exchange falling to the plumbiest depths. Yet the public were determined to enjoy the spectacle of this Princess, who is ugly, marrying a handsome boy who is barely a gentleman. It seems to me that royalty forfeits its mystique, its pointfulness when it becomes like you and me. It should remain aloof, absurd, clever or cretinous maybe, but it should marry only other royalties, and not nice, healthy, sporting, silly commoners, who are common. I meant not to view the wedding, but at Brooks's saw members and staff gathering round the television set brought downstairs into the bar room. Curiosity impelled me to look; the sheer beauty of the glass coach, the scarlet trappings, the baroque pageantry, the beauty of Princess Anne's white dress and the slimness of her waist; and the beauty of the bridegroom's uniform and the back of his well-shaped head and young, glossy chestnut hair, riveted me for one hour.

All the way to Brooks's there were black plastic bags containing offal outside the houses on the pavement. Before the dustmen's strike two years ago one was never offended by this squalid spectacle.

Harry Horsfield* lunched and I asked him if marriage to my Mama had been unadulterated hell for him. He said, not unadulterated. He contradicted my surmise that drink was the cause of her tiresomeness. He said she did not drink so very much, but her illness, her moods were the principal cause. At times she became possessed of demons, would not allow things to remain in a happy state, simply had to throw a spanner in every wheel. He said her rages were often dreadful to witness. When finally he told her that he thought it best for him to leave her, she brightened and said she agreed absolutely. 'And then, Harry,' she said, 'we can go back to being the friends we were before we married.' But he told me they never did. It was too late. The truth is that Mama was not made to live with others. She could not bear having the same person about her for more than a few hours. Like me she was a recluse, or more accurately a solitary.

Eardley will *never* say a nice word about my writing, will never commend, or even concede that he has derived one word of pleasure from my books. Is this grudging attitude induced by my

---

* In Royal Army Flying Corps in First World War; for a brief spell (1953) m. to J.L.-M.'s widowed mother.

not being able to admire his paintings? When I told him that the USA were taking *Heretics* in paperback, he merely grunted.

Yesterday morning I was walking across Belgrave Square, thinking my own thoughts. A small car was jerking away from the pavement, going forwards and then backwards. I noticed that the driver was waving. I went up to the car. Charlotte Bonham-Carter was at the wheel. She opened the passenger door. At once the strong wind blew clouds of papers stacked on the passenger seat into the Square. I chased and retrieved them. One flew under the car. I asked if it was important. Charlotte said, 'Yes, my dear, very.' So while she reversed, accelerated, and jiggled about I managed to retrieve this single paper. At much risk of being run over by her I picked it out of the gutter. It was a sheet with no writing of any kind on it.

I had a strange sensation while holding in my left hand the remains of the heart of James II. This relic belongs to Felix Hope-Nicholson.* It is a small very light piece of gristle. A puff would blow it away. To think that once it beat inside the body, kept alive the body, of the last Stuart sovereign of Great Britain, France and Ireland.

Harold Acton lunched with me at Brooks's yesterday. The first time I have had him alone for years. Undeniably his charm is limit-less and his wit contagious. We talked much of Nancy. I have offered him all her letters to me, and felt sure A. would let him have hers which are far more numerous. He said he didn't ask Raymond [Mortimer], who he knew disliked him, for his. I said I would ask Raymond, which I have done. R. said it involved labour on his part searching through trunks, sorting and re-reading. But he told me to convey to Harold that he would let him have some letters, if not all. Harold is mischievous without being malicious.

Saturday, 17th November

A stag in the park at Charlecote mauled the administrator, who was badly wounded. The stag had to be shot. The keeper thought it had passed the rutting stage. Evidently he was wrong. This particular stag had been reared by hand-feeding so as to become tame. Therefore it

---

* Of Tite Street, Chelsea; collector.

had no fear of humans. I have been told it is a dangerous thing to hand-rear these animals. Perhaps by mauling they mean to show affection.

Friday, 23rd November

The Osbert Lancasters* stayed last weekend. Osbert, whom I nowadays see once every two years at most, remains the same as he was at Oxford, only he – unlike another unchanged Oxford convivial, Johnnie Churchill† – was highly sophisticated at the university. A little greyer, Osbert is no whit less plain, or rugged, or facetious. That is his pity, he is more facetious than funny. And the text of his latest book which he brought for us, *The Littlehampton Bequest*, bears this out. The incomparable illustrations (and they are marvellous) are far more amusing than the text. It was strange to be reminded by Osbert that he stayed with me at Wickhamford with my parents and brother Dick, in I suppose 1930. Very few of my friends were invited to the manor. The idea of them bored my parents. Anne Lancaster is extremely tall, with a splendid lissom figure, very pretty face, dresses admirably and is elegant. Is the exact opposite to Osbert in looks, demeanour and behaviour, although O. is always neatly dressed, too neatly for the country. She told me that Osbert is not the least bit interested in individuals, only in people in the mass. He knows nothing, she asseverated, whatever about the heart, a piece of anatomy which bores him stiff. Talking of novels Osbert said he enjoyed all Anthony Powell's and looked forward eagerly to the next. We three said, although we admired them, they left us rather colder than warmer. Why? Because they are about people without hearts, or insides.

Poor Angus [Menzies] was run over last weekend while walking down a country lane near Basingstoke on one of his rambles, by a learner motor-bicyclist. A. and I were told by telephone and on Sunday drove to Basingstoke hospital to see him. He has broken both legs and his head is badly battered.

---

* Sir Osbert Lancaster, 1908–86; cartoonist, painter, theatrical designer, writer; m. 2nd, 1967, Anne Scott-James, journalist and gardener.
† J. G. Spencer Churchill, 1909–94; nephew of Sir Winston Churchill; artist and old friend of J.L.-M.

I have again read Denton Welch's[*] diaries. A small genius truly, with acute observation and a gift for making trivial incidents fascinating.

On Wednesday received a letter from Norah Smallwood, very kindly expressed, turning down my Stuart book on the grounds that the Stuarts were boring people all but the two last characters and asking if I would scrap the first three altogether, and write a book on the cardinal and the countess only. I was very distressed and hastened to David Higham yesterday. He reassured me somewhat, disagreed with Norah, deeming the book as it stands good. Anyway he is going to send it to Weidenfeld. If he rejects it, then I shall perforce fall in with Norah's proposition.

Monday, 26th November

At a meeting of the Byron Exhibition committee, John Pope-Hennessy in the chair read a letter he had received from the present Lord Elgin[†] in reply to a request for the loan of an exhibit. Lord Elgin wrote that at first his inclination was to refuse in view of Byron's diatribes against his ancestor for removing the Elgin marbles from the Parthenon to London; but on reflection he had decided to turn the other cheek and be accommodating. This a splendid example of family feeling persisting for well over a century and a half.

The taxi driver who took me to Paddington talked to me through the partition, as drivers so often do regardless of the fact that their passenger is obliged to perch precariously on the edge of the back seat straining his ears. I seldom if ever meet a driver who is disagreeable, or is not loquacious. This one launched into politics and was almost incoherent. He expressed the view that the division between rich and poor was more sharply drawn than ever before. I told him this was rot, for I remembered how in the 1930s and even 1920s the division was far more apparent and actual. 'Believe me,' I said in an elder statesman manner, 'I was alive then and can vouch for it. Today there are not the same

---

[*] Denton Welch, 1915–48; writer and painter.
[†] 11th Earl of Elgin, whose ancestor the 7th Earl arranged for sculptures from the Parthenon in Athens to be brought to Britain.

number of poor, and no one goes about literally in rags.' I mentioned that I was an old age pensioner. When I got out to pay he said, 'Well, guv'nor, time has treated you kindly.'

Tuesday, 27th November

Walking this afternoon with Fop down the old drive from Newark to Lower Lodge I saw through the bare trees on my left a rushing torrent below. It was a rapidly flowing, silvery river in spate, of regular width, at the bottom of the valley. I was amazed because I could not understand how it so suddenly came. There never was such a river before; and it couldn't be flood water. Then I realized it was a bank of hoar frost in the field where the sun had not penetrated all the morning. The moving wavelets I thought water were tussocks of grass bent forward by the north wind in the direction of the fall of the valley from north to south, and the sun sparkling on them added to the illusion of water breaking over boulders.

Saturday, 1st December

When I was a boy in the 1920s old photographs of my father and mother, their relations and friends taken in the 1890s at the age I then was, looked to me incredibly archaic, with their antediluvian clothes and fusty fashions. Whereas today when I look at photographs of myself and family taken in the 1920s they look slightly different, but by no means archaic. In fact were I now to see people in the street wearing these clothes I should pass them by without astonishment, merely thinking them rather square. Yet the difference in time is forty years compared with thirty when I was a boy. Can it be that the change in men's and women's dress style during the last forty years has been less momentous than during the first period?

Monday, 3rd December

Denys Sutton[*] has long talks on the telephone about the difficult conditions in which he edits *Apollo*. Cannot find printers, and hawks

---

[*] Denys Sutton, 1917–91; Editor of *Apollo*, 1962–87; art historian and dilettante.

his texts around the continent, not just around England. Consequently his issues get later and later each month. This annoys and upsets the advertisers on whom the paper depends for its existence. Furthermore art paper is getting scarcer and scarcer, because it is partly manufactured out of oil. Denys complains that he tried six haberdashers in London before he was able to buy the pants he always wears. They are made of a substance, also partly oil. At last he found a consignment, and bought two dozen pants – 'under-pants' he calls them – hoping they may last his lifetime.

He says it is a great pity that Derry Moore does not keep a diary. Derry complains that he cannot write, I don't mean compose, but manipulate his hand. Denys says he is too idle. Derry has met all the most distinguished persons of three generations, beginning with Kokoschka, under whom he learned to paint.

Last night Simon and Lois [L.-M.] dined. Midi also came, and was very interested in what Simon had to say about his work. His company is fairly small, with about 100 workers. Is booming at the moment. It has no industrial troubles because it is *small*. The men have free access to see the managing director at all times, either singly or in groups. The firm's problems are explained to them. They are shown the company's accounts. Are told that always one-third of annual profits is ploughed back into the business, one-third is paid to shareholders, and the last third goes to the workers. They have no strikes, for the workers will not allow Union officials to visit them. These officials, not the shop stewards, are, Simon says, the agitators. They foment trouble and discontent in the minds of the shop stewards. They even intimidate the wives and children of the workers. A minority of these people hold thousands to ransom, for their weapon is fear. Simon explained to us that inflation was caused basically by acute shortage of materials. For instance, steel is so scarce that the price of it has increased 100 per cent in one and a half years. The earth's resources are becoming exhausted. At last the terrible fact is being recognized. This morning's *Times* stresses the fact. The prospects are grim indeed. The masses, who have been indoctrinated by successive governmental exhortations to spend, and produce more and more goods, now classed as 'necessities', are not going to forgo these things. When the supply dries up, and only a few goods will be procurable, at outrageous prices, they are not going to submit. They will revolt, and seize what they want from those who have.

Saddened this morning to see announcements of the death of Raymond Erith,[*] whom I did not know but regarded as the very best architect alive in England, and of Don Nicholas, my new friend, the great collector of Stuartiana. I thought when I last saw Don he looked doomed – purple and grey in the face, glazed and watery eyes, drinking too much, having to pee constantly when we went by train to Chiddingstone Castle in the summer, all the signs which formerly I was unaware of, but which now I recognize as the fingers of death.

Charles Tomlinson asked me in a bewildered sort of way how Tolstoy, who like Shakespeare understood everything about human nature, who penetrated the recesses of the human soul, could have been so silly in his own conduct? I said I had always wondered too, and now wondered if Shakespeare had also made a muddle of his human relationships. How I wish we knew. Tolstoy's example bears out the fact that a man can be a great sage *and* a great fool.

Tuesday, 4th December

We were lunching with Audrey today, ostensibly to meet the Wingfields of Barrington, a long previous arrangement by poor Audrey, in the hope that they might let me see Barrington Park; but they never turned up, or even sent a message of excuse. Theirs is the most inaccessible house in England, and all attempts at entry fail. All the art historian boys who write, like John Harris, Gervase Jackson-Stops, have received a flea in their ear, if any acknowledgement of their requests. Prue and Ted [Robinson] however also lunched, and just before leaving at three we talked about Angus's accident, for Prue knew him. On our return to Alderley the telephone rang and Angus's niece, in a great state, informed A. that Angus had suddenly died an hour ago. Presumably from a clot, or the wrong drug, for he was being treated with anti-pneumonia biotics. Angus who was so healthy, vital, and beloved, almost a brother to me (as he certainly was to A.) for I had grown to love him dearly. He was the only one of our relations, of our age, who was on our beam, with similar interests, similar friends, similar horse sense and understanding.

---

[*] Raymond Erith, RA, FRIBA, 1904–73; architect in Classical Revival style.

Wednesday, 5th December

Went for a short walk with Fop through Foxholes Wood, with a
note pad and pencil, and before I reached home had jotted down an
appreciation of Angus. While I thought, and jotted, the tears rose
and welled, but not the sobs. I posted it to *The Times* in the evening.

Thursday, 6th December

While I was in Bath at a Preservation Trust meeting the obituary
editor telephoned to thank me for my words about Angus, which he is
going to publish, with one necessary alteration. I had written that
he had been 'run over'. This has to be deleted for it might be
actionable.

Midi talking to me about Brian's child who again stayed with her,
says that she does not mind about its illegitimacy, but does mind
about its colour. It is black with crinkly, negroid hair. She says
Derick would have minded dreadfully about the illegitimacy but
not about the colour.

Sunday, 9th December

The Times published my appreciation of Angus the very day after
they received it.

Why do owls hoot during nights of frost? I have noticed it lately
during the heavy frosts we have been having. One sits on a tree in
the garden and hoots for hours. During mild winter nights I never
hear him. Does he hoot for fun, to keep himself warm, to invite the
little birds and mice to leave their lairs, to mesmerize them, intoxi-
cate so that he can find easy prey? Does it mean he is hungry, sexy or
merely happy? Perhaps, miserable? I must ask an ornithologist.

Monday, 10th December

We went to Angus's funeral at Golders Green. A. and I arrived early.
A uniformed and urbane attendant asked which funeral we were
attending. A. said Mr Menzies's at 1.15. 'No, no, my dear,' this
horrid man said, 'always at twenty minutes past the hour, twenty to
the hour, and the hour itself.' We were ushered into the most bad-
taste waiting room I have ever entered. Brown brocaded wall paper
such as you do not get in the Bewlay Pipe Shop, frosted glass
windows, blue serge chair covers. Another official rushed in to say,

'Are you attending the Oppenheimer funeral? If not, please pass along.' The coffins as though on a conveyor belt. Derek Hill[*] joined us. The actual service took ten minutes. There was a very poignant incident. When the coffin started to slide, Piero, Angus's Italian servant, ran forward and placed some small token, which I could not see, on the coffin lid, retired to his seat and broke into heart-rending sobs. We were quickly ushered out, past the clergy-man who shook hands, round a corner, through an arched passage-way into the garden of rest, or whatever it is called. Looked at the wreaths. Those of the previous funerals already stacked within the cloister. A. said she must lunch with the family, Angus's brother Michael and his children. So Derek and I left together. We wanted to go out by the way we came in. The door under the arched passageway had been shut. We tried to open it, and saw through the cracks of the boards, a coffin being wheeled on a bier down the passageway. Retreated immediately and passed through the garden into the street. Derek and I lunched in Hampstead. Alone Derek is always charming and sympathetic. With people and above all at parties he is sometimes too vigilant. I went to his house and he showed the small head of K. Clark which he is now painting for Murray's. Since he asked for my opinion I said the nose was too hooked and the chin too defined. He has made K.'s chin if not exactly double, then blurred. Also a portrait of Walter Buccleuch[†] in robes of the Thistle, or Archers, with a plumed hat. Derek's likenesses sometimes fail with the mouth of his subjects. This is commonly the feature which portrait painters get wrong I notice.

Tuesday, 11th December

Rosamond [Lehmann] dined with me at an Italian restaurant, Alpino, opposite Buckingham Palace mews. It was the cheapest meal I have had for years; the bill was £3.25 including VAT and service. True we both ate little, but we had a whole carafe of wine, which we left unfinished. I said to Ros, 'Don't complain to mutual friends of Jim's meanness, because I know I *am* mean; but I have pressed you to eat more, darling.' She said, 'Many women would do

---

[*] Derek Hill, b. 1916; landscape and portrait painter.
[†] Walter Montagu-Douglas-Scott, 8th Duke of Buccleuch, 1894–1973.

just this,' which surprised me, because I made my remark in jest, and it never occurred to me that any women would really be so bitchy. As we were sipping our coffee by the window – and I had to move from facing the window because the passing traffic made me giddy – side by side, someone tapped on the glass. I turned and saw Osbert [Lancaster]'s large, dear old face pressed against the pane. We beckoned him in and he joined us. We agreed how difficult it would be to dine in London clandestinely. He had walked from the Beefsteak where he sat next to Cyril Connolly. And A. who was dining this evening with John Betj and Elizabeth told me later that Cyril wanted to dine with them but Elizabeth sent him away because she only had three cutlets.

Wednesday, 12th December

I did not intend to go to Angus's memorial service in St Peter's, Eaton Square. But at my Properties Committee the items which concerned me came first on the agenda, so at 11.30 I slipped out. Sat right at the back of the church which was crammed with friends. Sachie [Sitwell] read a short address from the pulpit. I could not hear one word, but A., who was sitting with the Menzies in the front pew, said it was good. Sachie lunched with me alone at Brooks's afterwards. He insisted on taking off his black tie in the cloak room, putting on another which was so sombre that I noticed little difference to the mourning tie. The operation necessitated much awkward fiddling with old-fashioned collar studs. Sachie full of gloomy forebodings. Influential city friends warned him that 'we' had only three months to clear out of England. Another told him to hoard his cartridges, for there would be shooting within that time. He told me he is constantly asked by the BBC to say a few words over the air about his deceased friends. He is also being bothered by someone who is writing a book about the Sitwells. He complained that he was asked most indiscreet questions about his differences with his brother, and Osbert [Sitwell]'s relations with David Horner,[*] not to mention his mother's trouble half a century ago.[†]

---

[*] Companion of Sir Osbert Sitwell.
[†] In 1915 Lady Ida Sitwell was sent to prison for fraudulent practices arising out of gambling debts.

Sachie said almost piteously, 'I have to write. What else can I do?
I don't know how to shoot, or fish.'

A National Trust dinner at the St James' club organized by
Robin [Fedden] (who loves these dinners), in honour of Ralph
Dutton's retirement on reaching 75. Michael Rosse[*] paid a charming little tribute to Ralph, who murmured that he was too moved to
make a speech in reply. I sat next to Myles Hildyard[†] who when I
arrived went and changed the cards in the dining room so that we
should be sitting together. But I was so wedged in, so hot, uncomfortable, and unable to drink because of the heat that I found little to
say to Myles. I don't like these all-male dinners. There is something
subfusc, cheerless and drab about them. Yet on the whole prefer the
society of individual men to that of individual women. But men *en
masse* I don't care for.

Friday, 14th December

Tony Mitchell motored me to Charlecote where we met the Lucys
and two young men from the V. & A. who are rearranging the state
rooms as they had been in 1870. It was so strange to be one of a
party in re-Victorianizing rooms which I had been instrumental
thirty years ago in de-Victorianizing. I think the young men are
right in Charlecote's case, although I maintain that this date was the
nadir of British taste, a taste which improved slightly later. One of
the two was covered with beard and whiskers, bushy and fearful, and
he had a paunch. Looked like Lord Tennyson, but with an extremely common voice. His companion told me that the bearded
one simply loathed the eighteenth century, and only liked the nineteenth. Now why loathe any century? He is an example of the
prevailing pedantry of specialism.

Sunday, 16th December

I read that Henry Yorke has died. For years he has been a recluse,
depressive and alcoholic. Hardly a soul has seen him. Patrick Kinross
lunched with the Yorkes a year ago, and Henry hardly spoke, and

---

[*] Michael Parsons, 6th Earl of Rosse, 1906–79; m. 1935 Anne Armstrong-Jones (née
Messel).
[†] Myles Hildyard, MC, b. 1914; squire of Flintham Hall, Nottinghamshire and local
historian.

when he vouchsafed a word to Patrick it was one of abuse. Yet when I saw Dig Yorke at Nancy's funeral she said, 'Henry's very well. Do come and see us one day.' I knew better than to accept this invitation. I used to see a lot of the Yorkes in the early Thirties when they lived in Rutland Gate. He was slim, handsome, bright, sophisticated, but I did not then realize a novelist. He had dark hair, olive complexion and a brisk manner. I never liked Henry's novels, and tried but failed to re-read one some months ago. To me they had an astringent, raucous, unmelodious flavour, without a theme one could catch hold of, or analyse.

Yesterday we lunched with Diana Westmorland. She was blazing with fury against the Trades Unions and Mr Gormley in particular, for saying over the air that he did not care a damn about the inconvenience he was causing the public, and he was going to have a jolly good Christmas. She wanted to write him a letter. What should she write? I said, 'The Dowager Countess of Westmorland presents her compliments to Mr Gormley and begs to inform him that he is a shit.' A. was rather shocked that I should use such a word to Diana. Her retort was, 'No. I will write, "Fuck off to Russia!"' A. was appalled, and said, 'What would your father think of such words?' Diana rocked. Lord Ribblesdale, that epitome of Edwardian nobility, would probably have said the same.

Diana told us that Mrs Gulwell bruised herself the other day. Until she saw the bruise she took no notice of the bump she gave her arm. When she did, Mrs Gulwell sobbed, and said, 'My lady, I can't carry on any longer. I must retire.' Diana's retort was, 'You must. There's no alternative.'

Wednesday, 19th December

Now I see in *The Times* that Hamish has died after a short illness of which I knew nothing. I suppose it was cirrhosis of the liver. The last time I saw him was in the Droghedas' box at Covent Garden into which he and sister Mary gatecrashed during an interval, somewhat to Joan's displeasure. He was then purple in the face. For years I had not wanted to see him, and when he last stayed here he was very boring with interminable stories of the Thirties and his archaic, juvenile jokes of our undergraduate days, for he never grew up and his values remained those of his Edwardian father, the spendthrift Lord Rosslyn. Yet if ever there was someone who began with every silver spoon, except money – this he always got hold of through his looks, charm and desirability – and frittered away his life it was Hamish Erskine.* At Oxford he had the most enchanting looks although not strictly handsome, mischievous eyes, slanting eyebrows. He was slight of build, well dressed, gay as gay, always snobbish however, and terribly conscious of his nobility, which came solely from his father's side, not his attractive mother's. The toast of the university, he was tossed from one rich limousine to another. Somehow I don't think tossed from bed to bed, for he was not very sexy. He loved being admired and given expensive presents, which he casually left lying around and lost. I still have one of these no doubt ill-gotten presents, the gold wrist watch with initials engraved on the back which I wear now; I hasten to add it was in part payment of money lent him and never returned to me. At Oxford he was everything I, then a simpleton, would have liked to be and now despise, namely a shallowly sophisticated, lithe of mind, smart society figure – everything I was not. For long I distantly loved him and was attracted by him. Then I grew out of him. He had natural intelligence which he never cultivated, although he had a smattering of erudition and would talk about books, music and art in an amusing superficial way. He had an affected mincing, screwy little manner, dancing on the tips of his toes, smoking endless Balkan Sobranies and always boozing. Latterly he was completely superannuated and to the young must have seemed a primordial little Edwardian monkey, something left over from a past age, not to be taken seriously. Oh dear, the sadness! He who was envied and admired by hundreds of his young contemporaries will be utterly forgotten in ten years' time, as though he had never lived at all.

The present crisis is most upsetting. Having listened to Barber's excellent broadcast I then heard Healey the Shadow Chancellor's broadcast. This man deliberately misrepresented what Barber said. Healey had the mendacity to maintain that Barber's budget was aimed against the working man, whereas it was nothing of the sort. It merely taxed the rich man, which is not altogether a bad thing. The evil of misrepresentation, the calculated lies of politicians! Then the simultaneous news of the Arabs shooting and killing over thirty innocent travellers (we always assume travellers to be innocent) in

---

* The Hon. Hamish St Clair-Erskine, MC, 1909–73.

Rome airport, the three bombs in London planted by the IRA, the squabbles of the European Community meeting, everything is so atrocious and evil that it is a wonder we do not all go raving mad, or commit suicide.

Little Hamish had his glorious hour, or year. He was incredibly brave during the war, escaped from prison camp, walked across Italy to rejoin the Allied troops, and won the Military Cross. Like Mummy's Jock Hume-Campbell* he was the decadent aristocrat *par excellence*, easily adapting in a crisis to standards of living hitherto beyond his ken and, one would have supposed, wrongly, beyond his endurance. And he descended to taking the jobs of '*dame de compagnie*' to Daisy Fellowes† and Enid Kenmare.‡ Even these jobs he could not hold down, because he was incapable of rising before midday. Daisy told me once that Hamish's first duty was to blow out the spirit lamp of her tea kettle through a little silver trumpet at 5.30 p.m. He could not be depended upon even to fulfil this degrading function.

While still at Oxford Hamish was engaged to Nancy [Mitford]. She was very much in love with him – she was five years older – and he presumably not in love with her. I remember them now, dining with me in the George restaurant when we were undergraduates, Hamish drunk and indifferent, Nancy gazing upon him with adoring eyes. This engagement petered out, and Nancy soon recovered, but not to the extent of not being contemptuous of Hamish ever afterwards.

Thursday, 20th December

This morning I took my poor old dog, Fop, to the vet to have more teeth out and his anal troubles investigated while under the anaesthetic. I begged the vet, if he found he was beyond recovery from yet another operation, to let him go. I was quite calm. I never said goodbye, nor patted him. I merely took off his lead. The vet, Riley, a nice man, took him in his arms. I just cast one quick glance at

---

* Sir John Home-Purves-Hume-Campbell, 8th Bt, 1879–1960; J.L.-M.'s godfather.
† Marguerite, 1890–1962, dau. of 4th Duc Decazes; widow of Prince Jean de Broglie, m. 2nd The Hon. Reginald Fellowes.
‡ Enid Lindeman, of Sydney, Australia, m. (4th) Valentine, 6th Earl of Kenmare (he d. 1943).

Fop's old grey head which was not looking towards me. The vet said, 'I quite understand,' and I left hurriedly. He said he would telephone. During the afternoon A. and I drove to Badminton to collect dead bracken. I thought that because the vet had not telephoned perhaps Fop had come through the operation. Late in the afternoon while I was out he rang. A. said to me, 'The vet had to let him go.' I followed her into the house and said, 'What I must do immediately is to remove all the dog baskets to the attics,' and started to do this before taking off my heavy coat. While carrying his special basket from the library I burst into tears. A. was angelic, comforting and sensible. I recovered quickly, and now merely have the ache of sadness at losing the companion of twelve years, day and night. This house is cheerless without the two dogs, and their departure marks the end of an era, the heyday of Alderley with which they have been so intimately, so essentially associated. *Eheu!* you darling old friends.

Christmas Day, Tuesday 25th December

Parkside having been given a miss last Christmas, here we are back with the beloved Droghedas. Derry [Moore] and Rhoda Birley[*] staying and Alan Pryce-Jones[†] not. He chucked at the last moment, as one might have expected.

Garrett said this morning in a school-mastery voice, 'Who is coming to church with us in St George's?' Previously neither he nor Joan would contemplate church on Xmas morning. Now that he has the Garter a sudden devotion has overtaken him. We were given seats in the choir, Garrett and Joan ensconced in the stalls. During the moving service I felt inspired to write, just to write. I realized that it was my first purpose in life. Had I anything to write about? That didn't matter. I must write. It was nice to be praying for the Queen who was beside us. The new Dean gave a fine sermon about the unimportance of the material things of this world. A far better delivery than the late Dean's, that horrid Robin of Worcester. This is a saintly-looking priest. When the service was over I lingered with Derry in the cloisters, and found myself directed through a

---

[*] Rhoda Pike, widow of Sir Oswald Birley, portrait painter.
[†] Alan Pryce-Jones, b. 1908; man of letters and reviewer; Editor of *Times Literary Supplement*, 1948–59.

doorway. I whispered enquiringly to Derry, who said we had entered the Dean's house for a drink. Upstairs Joan lent forward to catch me and introduce me to, I supposed, my hostess. As I was about to shake hands I recognized Princess Margaret, and just had time to bow. She was looking sorry and slight. But she was friendly, smiled and said, 'Happy Christmas'. Then Tony Snowdon caught my hand. He looks grey, his hand shakes, and he chain-smokes, one cigarette after another. I asked him how he was. He said laughing that he felt worse since his operation. I don't know what his trouble is beyond general unhappiness. This stands out a mile.

The same old business ensued. Princess Margaret wanted to go. It was time, and she approached Tony, who said, 'No, I want to go on with my drink.' So I said to him, 'No, you must toss it down, and hurry along.' 'I won't be hurried,' he said. Princess M. then said, rather crossly, 'Then I shall have to walk home by myself,' and began to leave the room.

Listening to Joan playing Debussy I thought, how irritating music can be. I want it to go in one direction. Instead it slopes off into another, which I don't like as much as the direction I would like it to go into. I once believed I might have become a composer had I been educated, for I used to invent the most lovely tunes which I was incapable of scoring, or even humming.

1974

Tuesday, 1st January

So ends one of the saddest years of my life, as far as the death of friends is concerned. Apart from numerous acquaintances, like Maisie Cox* this week, Henry Yorke, Hamish Erskine, Angus Menzies, Nancy Mitford, Joanie Harford, Ralph Jarvis, William Plomer, Bob Gathorne-Hardy and Don Nicholas have gone. And, by no means least, beloved Chuff and Fop. Also I think the year has been more infamous than the war years, because barbarities of a kind far less excusable than war-time barbarities have happened in endless succession, the assassination of perfectly innocent people at the hands of the Irish and Palestinians. The morale of the British Mr Average has never been lower, his values more debased, his covetousness, greed and lack of self-respect more conspicuous.

Last night before going to bed I had a blazing row with A. who insisted that I was going to London next Monday instead of the Tuesday, as I had previously told her, because I wanted to enjoy myself, whereas she knew perfectly well that my only need for going was a dentist's appointment for ten o'clock on the Tuesday morning. I lost my temper, stamped, threw my slipper on the floor because I could not throw it at her, and cursed and swore, 'Anyway why the hell shouldn't I want to enjoy myself?' Slammed the door and went to bed without saying good-night. How infinitely foolish old people can still be. This morning I went into her room, apologized profusely and we embraced tenderly.

Sunday, 6th January

Why are feet cold immediately on getting into bed? During the evening mine are warm, and while I undress and walk barefoot or in slippers in my bedroom and bathroom they are still warm. The moment I am lying flat they become as cold as icebergs, and have to be warmed by my electric blanket. Then for the rest of the night

---

* Lady Cox, wife of Sir Trenchard Cox, Director and Secretary, Victoria and Albert Museum, 1956–66.

they remain warm, even if I am obliged to get out of bed and get back again.

Yesterday we lunched with Eliza Wansbrough. Gavin Faringdon[*] was there. I have not seen him for a long while. He must have had a stroke because he shuffles slowly into the room, then stands immobile, as though unable to continue, or to sit. And his legs start shaking. He is rather pitiable. His mind is as sharp as ever, although he does not volunteer subjects of conversation. Those cat-like eyes are now benign. He almost purrs, and is gentle. Such a contrast with the old Gavin, his lithe, panther movements, his dangerous eyes, wit, and his forked cruelty. He was a most dangerous man, evil I think, and malevolent.

Eliza said after luncheon that she was incurably pessimistic about affairs. Indeed never have affairs been worse in my lifetime. In an unboastful way I want to record how often I have been right in foreseeing events. I foresaw the present confrontation between Government and anarchy, and wanted it to happen three years ago when the Conservatives got in. It would have been better then. Feebleness has been this country's undoing. No national service, the exaltation of godlessness, cynicism, the terrorism which cannot be checked except by another form of lawful terrorism. I think it very possible that there may be fighting within four months. If Heath gives way to the Unions this time, the moderates who make up 80 per cent of the population will be in despair. The extremists will press their demands and have to be resisted with force by a super-leader.

Higham has written that he has read the whole of my 1942 diary and thinks it splendid; 1943 which I am now typing out is certainly better. So what next?

Monday, 7th January

How is it that when one has collywobbles and longs to relieve oneself, one can usually hold out, sometimes five minutes, until one reaches a lavatory? Then while one is unbuttoning, the agony and need for release are so great that one can barely, sometimes *cannot* wait? I mean why is it that the actual arrival at the place of release, seems to break down all the pent-up control one has gallantly been exerting?

---

[*] Gavin Henderson, 2nd Baron Faringdon, 1902–77; Labour statesman.

A. is shocked that Olive Lloyd-Baker,* that highly respectable, respected county lady, lately High Sheriff of Glos., and dressed soberly and becomingly, has suddenly transformed herself. She now has short, closely cropped grey hair like a man (rather, a man of the pre-long-haired age, of my father's generation), and wears a man's jacket and trousers, and tie, in fact Radclyffe Hall[†] rig. I say that her inhibitions of a lifetime have been released after 71 years because she has overlapped the age of permissiveness. She was always a secret Lesbian and now has thrown her cap over the windmill.

Thursday, 10th January

Soame Jenyns[‡] in Brooks's tells me he is hoping to go to Pekin on some mission if he can get a visa, but this is proving difficult. He was once there in the Thirties, and recalls the Temple of Heaven as one of the two most beautiful buildings in the world, the other being Chartres Cathedral. It is small but the courtyard and the scale are perfection. Soame says that of a friend of his called Prescott, a great eccentric, one of many memorable remarks was: 'I dislike luxury, but I do like grandeur.' Soame is constantly badgered by people writing biographies or theses about Ivy Compton-Burnett.[§] He says that women particularly are very proprietary, and several female writers make out that they were her intimate friends. Whereas, says Soame, she had no intimate friend but Margaret [Jourdain], and would not even speak about her books to him, who knew her better than any of these female claimants.

   Yesterday I went to Hamish's Requiem Mass at St Mary's, Cadogan Street. The large church was not full. It was an execrable service, in English, not one word of Latin, no incense, no music, the priest facing the congregation, breaking wafer and swigging wine, wiping the chalice, directing the congregation when to stand (for prayers!), when to sit (for Gospel?) and everything reversed just

---

* Miss Olive Lloyd-Baker, of Hardwicke Court, Gloucestershire; landowner and neighbour.
† Miss Marguerite ('John') Radclyffe Hall, 1883–1943; novelist (*The Well of Loneliness*), famous explicit Lesbian and partner of Una, Lady Trowbridge.
‡ Soame Jenyns of Bottisham Hall, Cambridgeshire, b. 1904; ceramic expert; descendant of Dr Johnson's friend Soame Jenyns.
§ Dame Ivy Compton-Burnett, 1884–1969; novelist.

for the sake of change. It was undignified, unspiritual, and common-place. Patrick [Kinross] who sat beside me said, 'No wonder these ritualistic changes killed Evelyn. No wonder you have lapsed.' 'Yes, I jolly well have,' I said.

After attending the Duff Cooper award-giving, at which John Julius[*] spoke fulsomely about Lane Fox's[†] book on Alexander the Great, A. and I dined with the Hutchinsons.[‡] We had a happy dinner in the kitchen. Jeremy was saying how awful it was that his nephew, young Rothschild, was second on the Palestinian guerrilla hit list after poor Mr Sieff, shot last week. A minute or two later the telephone rang. It was Freda Berkeley asking Jeremy to come quickly to Warwick Avenue where the Rothschild house was on fire. We dashed there and it *was* on fire, but not fired by Arabs. Apparently an electric radiator in a linen cupboard had started it.

Saturday, 12th January

Paul Methuen's[§] funeral at Corsham today. While A. went to pick up John Pope-Hennessy at Chippenham station I attended a trustees' meeting at Ivy House, where the heir Captain Methuen – very old and decrepit – lives, and the nephew John. The nephew has a wild look in the eye and may be 'retarded' if not mad. My trusteeship unfortunately ends with Paul's death although I still have to help clear up things. Christopher Medley[¶] and George Howard[**] remain as trustees and both are executors. We were talking about the very rare plants in the hothouses, suggesting that Kew might be consulted, or even presented with those they wanted. John Methuen remarked, 'You can leave that to me. I will consult the Bath

---

[*] John Julius Cooper, 2nd Viscount Norwich, b. 1929; s. of Duff and Lady Diana Cooper; writer and broadcaster; m. 1st, 1952, Anne Clifford; 2nd, 1989, Mary (Mollie), dau. of 1st Baron Sherfield.

[†] Robin Lane Fox, b. 1946; author and, since 1970, weekly gardening correspondent of the *Financial Times*.

[‡] Jeremy Hutchinson, QC, b. 1915; cr. Life Peer, Baron Hutchinson of Lullington in 1978; m. 1st, (Dame) Peggy Ashcroft; 2nd, June Osborn (née Capel), a dau. of Diana, Lady Westmorland.

[§] Paul Methuen, RA; 4th Baron Methuen, 1886–1974; painter, zoologist and land-owner.

[¶]. Yorkshire squire and trustee of Methuen estate.

[**] George Howard, 1920–84, of Castle Howard, Yorkshire; a Governor of the BBC from 1972; Chairman, 1980–3; cr. Baron Howard of Henderskelfe, 1983 (Life Peer).

Corporation Parks Supervisor for advice.' Those municipal philistines! And when we were making a date for the next meeting George Howard, whose wife Cecilia is dying of cancer, said, 'I will certainly come if I possibly can. But owing to Cecilia's illness you will understand if I am unable to.' At this John Methuen, his cousin, remarked in a jolly tone, 'I daresay our next family reunion will be at Castle Howard.'

A. and I were put in the third pew at the head of the nave. The church was crowded. Paul's coffin was beside me. I was puzzled by the extreme narrowness of the head end, almost a point. And he had a broad head. I remember Mama telling me that he was the best-looking young man she had ever seen. The service was conventional and dull, no music which he would surely have wanted. The poignant moment was when the hearse piled high with flowers slowly moved down the long avenue in front of the house, the avenue which is no longer used by motors, towards the great gate piers at the end. The coffin was interred at Beanacre where Norah lies. Diana Kendall's[*] sublimity and courage throughout were very impressive. This girl devoted her young life to looking after Paul. For over twenty years she never left him, and I am certain that he would never have lived so long nor so contentedly without her ministrations.

Wednesday, 16th January

I suspected from the first that Filipinas were liars. It turns out that our Susanna who came over here on the pretence that she was widowed in 1972 and was childless, has a husband alive and eight children. She disclosed this to friends who at once repeated it to us. Furthermore, she has put an assumed name on her passport. Not only she but the London agents have deceived us. They assured us that, as we earnestly requested, the Filipina we selected wanted to work in the *country*, so long as she might be with her nephew of whom she was very fond. It transpires that the agents never asked her whether she wanted to work in the country. She did not know whether she was going to London, Birmingham or Glasgow. As for the 'nephew', she met him for the first time in her life at the agent's Manila office just before her aeroplane took off. Now she wants of

---

[*] Mrs Wray-Bliss, secretary to Lord Methuen.

course to go to London and earn God knows what a week. I told her that on the contrary I would have her deported to Manila. I believe we may have some control over her, now we know how she and the agents have behaved.

Saturday, 19th January

Yesterday I had a temperature and kept in bed, reading a few pages at a time, then snoozing. Not unpleasant, and A. adorable, waiting on me. Today much better already, thanks to the kindly drug which the doctor has prescribed. Lying in bed, with the windows shut, I can positively sense a first inkling of spring; that premonition of a disturbance of the emotions which I dreaded in my youth, and which even today upsets me. Absurd of course, nevertheless disturbing, 'that damnable spring'. A tortoiseshell butterfly suddenly appears fluttering desperately against the window. Where has it been all these months? Not on the curtains, which were mended a fortnight ago; perhaps behind the tapestry against the wall. The wintry evening sun obliquely falling upon my large tapestry panel picks up the gold threads and the enchanted garden which, seen from my bed, is receding into infinity; the figures, ugly when you look at them closely, for the women have huge Yiddish noses, become romantic from a distance; and for several minutes I watch, spellbound and yearning, the Arcadian scene framed within the leafy blue-green boscage, and think if this be heaven, let me get there quickly.

How extraordinary Charlotte Bonham-Carter is. When after Paul Methuen's funeral we had tea with Diana Kendall in the library at Corsham, there was Charlotte sitting in one of Paul's large Chippendale armchairs, holding a plate on to which Alvilde was piling cakes and sandwiches. She had missed the funeral and had come for the tea. Unlike most of the guests who pecked at a cake and sipped half a cup, Charlotte was tucking into a huge meal, saying she had not eaten since dinner the previous evening. I think she was quite unaware why she had come. She was about to motor herself in the dark and through the fog back to Hampshire.

Thursday, 24th January

Had a long talk, as usual, with a cab driver on my way to Covent Garden. He told me that they have to buy cabs from one firm which has the monopoly. They cost £2,500 each. Since they must conform to certain regulations, cabbies cannot buy any ordinary car and fix a taximeter to it. To make money they have to cover a certain number of miles per day, 100 I think he said. In wet weather such as last night the queues in London are so bad that they cannot make their 100 miles. So they dread wet weather. As do we who can never get a cab.

Don Pasquale at Covent Garden. We were invited by the Drog-hedas to the Royal Box. The David Cecils, Norwiches, Ian and Mrs Parsons were guests. Ian Parsons is head of Chatto's it seems; said he much wanted to meet me, and to A., who arrived first, 'He is my favourite author.' All very fine but where does it get me with Chatto's, for they are now hedging whether to take my Stuart book even if I do what Norah suggested before Xmas, namely cut out 3/5ths owing to paper rationing? I am depressed by this. I sat next to Rachel Cecil who is a sweet little thing. Is she too sweet to be true?

Joan said when I arrived, 'Darling, I do want to talk to you. How I wish I could have you to sit beside me at dinner, but I can't, alas, alas, etc.!' The reason being that she had to have David Cecil (quite rightly, for he is older and far more distinguished than me) on one side and John Julius on the other. John Julius is young enough to be my son, and is not all that distinguished. (1996: He jolly well is now!) When I told Eardley, he said how horrifying this snobbish protocol was; that he would not know people who were slaves to these idiotic and contemptible conventions; and so forth. And I was a fool because I condoned such behaviour by knowing people who indulged in it. (Broadly speaking I do favour social conventions. Because they keep the wheels of good manners oiled.)

Friday, 25th January

Alvilde came into the library at six while I was typing, to tell me that the wireless announced the death of Jamesey Pope-Hennessy – murdered, most foully, by three young men, while sitting in his flat, at eleven o'clock this morning. His young servant was out shopping, re-entered, was attacked in his turn and, badly wounded, rushed into the street, his hand cut to ribbons. The police station is opposite James's flat, a thing I have often wryly wondered about, I mean whether they were aware of the strange comings and goings thereto and therefrom. But this is a hideous tragedy. My first fears are about what may be disclosed. One man has been arrested, bleeding in a bus at Marble Arch. I think it must be a case of drug addicts, or something extremely sinister. Although I have not seen James for seven years, when he last stayed here in January 1967 so disastrously, yet I always loved him, albeit I did not wish to see him again. I sent him a postcard from Italy in October to remind him of my existence and of my affection. Lately he has been much in my thoughts because in 1942 and '43 I saw him or spoke to him practically every day. We were inseparable. He was one of the most brilliant creatures I have known, but, alas, he was a bad friend.

Saturday, 26th January

Several people, deeply shocked, have telephoned about Jamesey – John K.-B. who went to see John Pope-Hennessy at his request this morning, Diana Westmorland, Elspeth Huxley. I took courage and telephoned John this evening merely to say how deeply distressed we were and to offer any help acceptable. John practically in tears said that having to identify James yesterday was a nightmare, he was so lacerated. There is to be a Requiem Mass for him on Thursday at St Mary's, Cadogan Place at eleven, the same dreary church and time as Hamish's service a fortnight ago.

Wednesday, 30th January

Yesterday I went to Charlecote with Tony Mitchell to decide upon the hanging of pictures. To my surprise Alice [Lucy] was there, with her son Edmund. Brian died less than a week ago of heart failure. It was not unexpected and when I was at Charlecote before Christmas he went duck shooting in the park and came in for tea to collapse in a chair, speechless. Edmund is a nice boy with a girl in tow. She looked to me pregnant. They held hands, called each other darling and spoke of 'we', but as far as I could gather, not plighted.

Thursday, 31st January

I went up specially for Jamesey's Requiem Mass. It was strange to be attending this memorial to Jamesey who I remember saying to me that we could never die. When it was over I stayed behind to avoid the usual crowd of gossiping friends at the church door. I lit a candle for James, then left. His brother John was still on the pavement. He shook hands and thanked us for our letters. Poor John, his face was swollen as though he had wept for a fortnight. Walking away I ran into Patrick Kinross in Sloane Square. We had a drink at the Royal Court Hotel. Patrick complained that all the funerals and memorial services he had to attend were a great interruption to his writing.

Friday, 1st February

Dining with the Somersets tonight Caroline and I agreed that whereas one must be critical in discussing one's friends, one ought not to be bitchy. Does this not go without saying? She added in her frank way, 'I think I have heard you be bitchy.' 'Oh, how dreadful!' I said. She then corrected herself, 'Well, I daresay I am wrong. Perhaps you have not.' But her first, unpremeditated remark has worried me a little.

Tuesday, 5th February

We dined with John Cornforth, and met Q. Terry[*] and wife. He is the youngish partner of the late Raymond Erith, and works in the same traditional manner. He spoke feelingly of Erith who was clearly looked upon by the East Anglians as a man of distinction, if not genius. Terry said that on his return from attending Royal Fine Arts Commission meetings he [Erith] would often be physically ill for three days over the horrors he had witnessed submitted to the Commission and, worse still, over the Commission's acceptance of them.

Wednesday, 6th February

Dined with Seymour Camrose[†] and Joan Aly Khan[‡] at a house in Hobart Place which I was not certain to be his or hers, perhaps both's. The Michael Trees[§] present. Anne Tree told me she was the

---

[*] Quinlan Terry, FRIBA, b. 1937; architect; in partnership with Raymond Erith from 1967.
[†] John Seymour Berry, 2nd Viscount Camrose, 1909–95; Director, The Daily Telegraph plc.
[‡] Princess Joan Aly Khan (née Yarde-Buller) m. 2nd, 1986, 2nd Viscount Camrose.
[§] Michael Lambert Tree, painter, m. 1949 Lady Anne Cavendish, dau. of 10th Duke of Devonshire.

happiest person in the world, and this made her feel guilty. Born rich, upper-class and married to the only man she ever wanted and a man who had a host of women at his feet. The man, Michael Tree, is a very nice, v. brainy bumble-bee who sucks a pipe and is the best friend of David Somerset. No doubt he harbours hidden depths. Anne Tree said she regretted that as children she and Elizabeth [Cavendish] were never allowed to learn about the Devonshire treasures for fear of their becoming what she termed 'swanky' with other children. The consequence was she lacked education in the arts, which she is now deeply interested in. Says that the two girls were never given proper allowances for the same reason, in spite of the limitless money in the background. Her mother is a saint, and her father laboured under a lifelong regret that he had no regular profession. I told her I remembered his saying he wished he could have been a dentist. She confirmed that this was true.

Then to the Nureyev ballet film, *Don Quixote*. Nureyev has such star quality that one cannot take one's eyes from him for a second so long as he is on the screen. When he is off it is another matter. One of the women said he was the most beautiful man of the age.

These immediate days are perhaps politically the most critical of my lifetime. Much talk about the devastating situation, and Seymour thinks anything might happen overnight, like a Communist take-over.

Thursday, 7th February

I lunched with Norah Smallwood and young partner, John Charlton,[*] the historian amongst them, to discuss the Stuart book. At first they much wanted me to make the Cardinal of York the central figure, and the Countess of Albany a satellite round him. But I made them understand that of the two she was the more positive, interesting figure, and I must take them separately. So they have agreed to my making two sections, thus jettisoning 3/5ths of my former book. This is a disappointment to me. Norah discovered they had engaged a Communist in their packing department at Chatto's. The man made huge mischief, and turned the other

---

[*] John Fraser Charlton, b. 1940; publisher; director, Chatto and Windus, 1967–93.

packers who had been with Chatto's for years and were
previously contented workers, into malcontents. So to get rid of
the Communist they were obliged to dispense with the packing
department altogether and so sack the lot. She said there was
no other way, without causing great difficulties with the Union
concerned.

I went to the V. & A. workshop to look at the Corsham putto.
Hempel, the man who is restoring it at a cost of £1,000, told me
that having worked on Michelangelo's *Dionysus* in Florence for so
many weeks he was positively certain this nasty little putto is
Michelangelo's work. He said he didn't care a rap for John Pope-
Hennessy's disagreement. Hempel said, 'He may be a scholar, which
I am not; but I am a craftsman and I have now got the feel of
Michelangelo's work at the tips of my fingers.'

Then to the Society of Antiquaries where I was admitted
formally. The ceremony involved being called before the President,
a distinguished man with a beard, bowing to him, having my hand
shaken and being told I was admitted, bowing and retiring to my
seat amidst applause. Five of us were admitted, and I believe the
applause for me was a little louder than for the others but I will not
swear to it. Perhaps I boast. While drinking tea before the ceremony
I felt completely out of sympathy with the Fellows I found myself
among. A lot of old fogies of the dreariest description. Why did I
join this dank association?

Went to the Lucian Freud exhibition. Only a few of his pictures
are beautiful. Among these a small head of Jamesey, his hand to his
chin. I remember this in his flat. I wish it were mine. The over-life-
size heads are revolting, namely Debo's and Duchess Mary Devonshire's.

Saturday, 9th February

Friends who know the writer James, now Jan, Morris say his much-
vaunted change of sex is purely exhibitionist, and has upset his
children, who now have no father, two mothers, and a difficult
situation to contend with at school. After the change one of the
friends was motoring to London with him. Inadvertently he said to
Morris, 'You are a kind man to give me a lift.' 'Not a man, please,'
was the response.

Sunday, 10th February

William Rees-Mogg[*] telephoned this morning. We had a long conversation about the situation. I said I applauded the attitude of *The Times*. He asked what were the views of the people round here. I said the shopkeepers in Wotton were strongly against the Unions. I asked why instead of holding an election had Heath not tried for a coalition government? He said Heath and Wilson would never work together. Then why not Whitelaw and Jenkins? He thinks Heath may just get back. I asked how he would be any better off in that case? William said if he increased his majority he would have renewed authority; if he scraped through he would reach a compromised, face-saving solution of the miners' dispute. If Wilson scraped through he would be bound to press for a coalition, because no foreign power would advance him the money we have got to get. This is encouraging. I said I thought this crisis as serious as that of 1939 because the enemy we were fighting was a hidden enemy.

Lunching with the Sam Lloyds was a nice couple. He a dear old buffer with a round, red face, Sir David Stephens.[†] He is Clerk of the Parliaments in the House of Lords. He knows all there is to be known about every single member of the Parliament, in the Commons as well as Lords. To my praising Heath and upbraiding Wilson, his comments were negative. Yes, no, with a seeming sympathy for the praising nevertheless. Then he admitted that neither he nor his wife was allowed to have any political opinions whatever. On my return I looked him up; he is two years younger than I am.

Sunday, 17th February

A letter from Rosamond [Lehmann] yesterday which I opened with trepidation. She much likes my 1942–3 diaries, and is flattering. This is a relief. When I telephoned her this morning to arrange how to fetch them in London tomorrow, she said, 'They are your masterpiece.' Well, if something I wrote over thirty years ago before I published my first book is my masterpiece, has my writing not deteriorated sadly since?

---

[*] William Rees-Mogg, b. 1928; Editor, *The Times*, 1967–81; Life Peer 1988.
[†] Sir David Stephens, KCB, 1910–90; Clerk of the Parliaments, House of Lords, 1963–74, and keen gardener, living near Cirencester, Gloucestershire.

The Rector told me that our Hillesley neighbours, the Waddingtons, said to him on Saturday, 'We must now leave you in order to
receive our weekend guests.' 'Who are they?' asked the Rector.
They are a wife and two children living in London. The husband and
father is a prison inmate of Leyhill near here. The Government pays
these three individuals' railway fares each weekend to Bath, and their
board and lodging with the Waddingtons, and their meals at the
prison during Saturday and Sunday.

Last night we dined at Westwood Manor with the Denys Suttons.
The Tony Powells and Roger Manners the other guests. Lord
Roger is a stockbroker. He says the City has come to a standstill.
It expects a complete economic collapse any day, when we shall be
in the same condition as Germany was in 1923. We must expect
chaos, the £ to be worth 1 penny, if we are lucky, and the oil sheiks
buying up our industries. A jolly prospect. All agreed that no single
politician dared tell the people the truth about the ghastly situation.
The English will not face up to a situation such as they have never
experienced since 1066. After church this morning Mrs Hesse-
Phillipson explained why her husband has been absent for the past
three weeks; he has been working day and night trying to save his
business. My nephew Simon, who before Christmas was telling us
how affluent his firm was, now says it may go bust and he be thrown
on the streets.

Monday, 18th February

Lying in bed reading at nights I hear with my right ear a distinct
buzzing, as of distant bees, coming from the space between bed and
fireplace. It is nothing to do with water pipes for it takes place hours
after any of us have used water, or turned on taps. It is not mice; it is
not flies.

Already primroses and violets are out in this village. And under
the wall between coach house yard and back drive a daffodil or two
is unfolding a yellow head. Such mild winters as we have had lately
cause A. much anxiety. The wicked east winds of March are yet to
come.

I thought it was going to be colder during the night — and so it
proved, but moderately — when I heard the owl at four o'clock. His
note was not the customary slow hoot, but an hysterical rise and fall,
either of distress or jubilation; certainly not of complacency.

A. and I to *Rigoletto* with John Pope-Hennessy in the [Royal] Box. A fine performance with a young Australian girl as Gilda, Peter Glossop as Rigoletto. Lovely scenery by Zeffirelli, which I had seen in a previous performance at the Garden. John was much moved by the music. I thought the stabbing scene at the end an unfortunate reminder of poor Jamesey's death last month. John seemed sad and rather lost. I have never before thought of him as a pathetic person. Collected this afternoon my typescript of the diaries from Ros. Funny how she genuinely seems to have enjoyed them.

Friday, 22nd February

Diana Westmorland brought to luncheon yesterday dear old Sister Whittick who is staying with her for the rest of the winter. W. looked after D.'s sister, Lady Lovat, for years when she was ill. She has been with many grand people, and was full of stories. Was with the Dowager Lady Lytton,[*] who towards the end lost her memory and yet still wrote to her twin sister, Lady Loch,[†] as she had always done every day of her life. One afternoon Sister asked her whom she was writing to. She said to her sister. Sister W. said, 'But you wrote a letter to her already this morning.' Lady Lytton told her to post it nevertheless. Sister saw that the envelope was addressed to Lady Betty Bunker. Lady Betty Balfour was her daughter. Bunker was the name of her maid. Lady Lytton would take hours dressing to go for a walk. She would leave by one French window into the garden, and walk straight through the next Fr. window back into the house. On sitting down on the nearest chair she would say, 'How nice it is to be home again.'

Walking by Goose Green this afternoon the low sun was shining slantwise across a field of plough. From a low level I looked eastwards across the field, with the belt of Newark Park trees in the middle ground and the blue Wiltshire downs just visible in the far background. To my left the plough was pale golden brown, to my right it was all shadow. Ahead it was a sea of sun *and* shadow. I fancied the sun and shadow plough to be a vast range of moon mountains. And I knew that henceforth on this despoiled earth of ours we must concentrate upon what of smaller compass and scale it

[*] Edith Villiers, m. 1864 1st Earl of Lytton, and d. 1936.
[†] Elizabeth Villiers, m. 1862 1st Baron Loch, and d. 1938.

has to offer and be grateful. After all there is an infinity to be found in minuteness now that the earth's greatness is so hideously contracted – a strange paradox when science tells us how the universe has expanded.

Monday, 25th February

Michael Astor[*] has just seen Christopher Sykes,[†] living in his rectory in Dorset. Christopher has recovered from a stroke in that his mind is clear, but he cannot walk upstairs more than once a day. Camilla on the other hand suffers from such a weak heart that she is expected to drop dead at any moment. She is quite incapable of looking after him and he her. In his forthcoming book on Evelyn Waugh he has encountered a difficulty. Although Christopher, like others of that enclosed circle, was devoted to Evelyn, he has after prolonged study discovered his character to have been a truly dreadful one, with little to recommend it and much to condemn. It must be awful when a biographer becomes disillusioned with his subject after spending ages and energy in pursuit of it.[‡]

The Astors are once again installed in Bruern Abbey after two years' demolition of back regions and re-adaptation. The house seems as large as ever but must now be more convenient. All the rear untidinesses swept away, and the back regions made part of the charming courtyard. Yet the interior lacks the genuine air. The new work is slick-shoddy. No decorative features to any of the rooms, albeit filled with lovely things and pictures. The resonance of the new vaulted dining-room so bad that none of us could hear a word spoken. Michael very distressed about this trouble. Matters made worse by the shrieks and hoots of Mrs Francis Haskell,[§] a Russian with a raucous voice: he a saturnine man, A. thinks a caricature of Isaiah Berlin in looks and speech. Very clever and sharp. Another couple the Darbys of Kemerton Court. She is a

---

[*] The Hon. Michael Astor, 1916–80; s. of 2nd Viscount and of Nancy, Viscountess Astor, MP; patron of artists, writer, and Chairman of the Committee of the London Library.

[†] Christopher Sykes, 1907–86; m. 1936 Camilla, dau. of Sir Thomas Russell Pasha, CMG; traveller, journalist, writer.

[‡] Nevertheless, *Evelyn Waugh* was published in 1975

[§] Francis Haskell, FBA, b. 1928; Professor of Art History, Oxford University and Fellow of Trinity College, Oxford from 1967; m. 1965 Larissa Salmina.

6

34 ANCIENT AS THE HILLS

daughter of Alec Douglas-Home,* like him marmosetish, but pretty, with lovely eyes and hands. Clever too, and attractive. Darby a nice, intelligent young man, an economist.

Wednesday, 27th February

Looking at a photograph of some anonymous mid-Victorian gent with long hair, bushy mutton-chops and fuzz around his inscrutable, patriarchal chin I can for the first time in my life envisage him as a human being, instead of a stuffed, insalubrious dummy, as heretofore. Because so many people today look like this, all hair in the wrong places, facial I mean. In the same way two years ago one could see a Donatello youth, a Bronzino youth in the tube train every day. Unfortunately that style of haircut is already obsolete. Such a pity. The tendency today is to readopt the grizzly aspect and do away with the Florentine Renaissance long hair devoid of beard and side whiskers.

Thursday, 28th February

I sat in the Hillesley polling booth tonight as a teller beside a bearded, unscrubbed man, so nice. Looked 60 and told me he was rising 40. Works in Rolls Royce at Filton, and is in charge of men. Is a Tory yet is critical of Heath's government, of property speculators and also of Trades Unions. Told me that among his co-workers there is no prejudice against the coloured people, so long as they obey the rules.

David Higham with whom I left my diary typescripts yesterday in London telephoned this afternoon with enthusiasm. Has already read half of 1943, thinks it first-rate and a winner. Begged me to let him send the book to Weidenfeld and not to Chatto's. Also wants to have it photostated because he is sure it will sell in America and get serialized. I said if serialized I must be allowed to approve the selection. I could not have salacious bits picked out, juicy bits about friends and foes. Higham said that would be difficult. I foresee trouble. On reflection I decided that I did not want to go to Weidenfeld, and would prefer to stick to Chatto. Wrote to Higham to this effect.

---

* Sir Alec Douglas-Home, KT, 1903–95; 14th Earl of Home, but disclaimed earldom on becoming Prime Minister in 1963; cr. Baron Home of the Hirsel (Life Peer) 1974.

Friday, 1st March

We are finished. We may as well pack up. We have left it too late. We were warned we had three weeks to clear out of England. This was three weeks ago. Labour has got in. The consequence is a victory for the Unions who are the dictators of the Labour Party. I see nothing but total disaster ahead.

We went to look at a house in Bath which an Admiral's widow is selling. The Admiral has just died. Her only son died shortly before. Her old gardener has died. Her old maid of 40 years' service is retiring. She who never knew a day's illness in her life is suddenly stricken with middle ear trouble, and falls down from lack of balance. She has no relations. She can move to anywhere or to nowhere. But she must live in a few small rooms where she can manage on her own. She must sell three-quarters of her belongings. Yet this woman, not poor, accustomed to good living and servants, is in her old age in this condition. She did not complain. She imparted these facts dispassionately.

Bloggs Baldwin who lunched today (bringing Elspeth [his wife]) told me that at Eton he was bullied. At the end he won his Field colours and they wished to elect him to Pop.* He refused because he hated the arrogance and exclusiveness of Pop. He has never got over the bullying. He said the effect upon him was to make him a coward. John Strachey[†] who was at Eton with him was likewise unpopular for no apparent reason. One day the whole of Pop, arms linked, marched upon him, intending to insult and then de-bag him. A monstrous regiment of proud, herd-mentality superior boys. He stood his ground. Would not budge. The herd began with the usual taunt, 'What is your name?' Strachey answered, 'It is a better name than any of yours,' and looked defiantly at them. They did nothing, and like the bullies they were, melted away. The effect upon Strachey was to drive him into the Labour Party.

We have made a bid for a maisonette in Lansdown Crescent in Bath. It consists of ground floor and basement floor, and is hardly big enough. The ground floor however has one huge library which was made for Beckford, and one room behind which A. will have as a

---

* A prestigious Eton boys' society of long standing.
† Rt Hon. John Strachey, 1901–63; Labour MP and Secretary of State for War, 1950–1.

bedroom. Below will be my bedroom, looking into a north court, cellar-like. When we move we shall have to get rid of seven-eighths of our beloved possessions.

Monday, 4th March

Walked with Midi through the fields and Foxholes Wood. She said laughingly that all her life she had been an outsider. In the Twenties she did not belong to the Twenties set; she was not accepted by her husband's sporting friends nor by intellectuals as one of them; she was not accepted by county people as one of them, owing to her being a Socialist, and not a Tory. They regarded her as a bit of a traitor to her class. I said in other respects I had always considered myself an outsider too.

Wednesday, 6th March

Yesterday and today I spent at Snowshill with Robin Fedden. We attempted to improve the arrangement of some of the rooms here. We met trouble. I was at pains to stress that the only point of the interior of this house was its being an eccentric magpie's nest, and notably *not* arranged. Whereas Robin and I with our tidy ideas of how we would like a house of our own to look tend to scrap everything that we find trash, and to thin out and arrange too prettily. Robin is entirely without scruple. He is ruthless in rejecting things, regardless of what were the donor's intentions and wishes. I have touched lightly on this aspect of Robin in the appreciation of him which I have written for the Trust's News Letter. In a sense it can be accounted as his strength. This I see.

I called on the Haineses at Wickhamford this afternoon, having visited the church and ruminated upon my parents' memory, and admired Reynolds [Stone]'s slate plaque to them. Both Haineses talk at once, regardless of what I am saying to them. Moreover Mrs H. is stone deaf and Haines is a little senile. They were rather shocked by their old neighbour of 89 marrying. When I asked if it were not a good thing, they said nothing and pursed their lips. Haines then said, 'What 'as an old fellow to do with marrying of a young woman at his time of life?' I said he was probably lonely. Then Haines said, 'He has been carrying on for years. She was his secretary in the South African War.' I said, 'Can that be possible?

And if it is, she can hardly be a young woman still.' Poor old Haines was a trifle confused.

Sunday, 17th March

Audrey on the telephone, discussing the news, said, 'I think there will soon be class hatred in this country.' I, bearing in mind the vitriol of some Labour ministers and Trade Unionists against the so-called rich, replied, 'But I think there is already.' Audrey meant that the upper would soon be hating the lower classes if they didn't take care. But I said, 'That won't help them'. Audrey has the old-fashioned notion that the upper can still make life disagreeable for the lower.

Monday, 18th March

I motored to Sufton Court near Mordiford in Herefordshire, arriving at 2.45. This house has been offered to the Trust and those who have seen it were undecided whether we ought to take it, and asked for my opinion. For me the conundrum resembled several I encountered in the old days. I fear the house is not important enough, although the exterior is fairly decent and the surroundings overlooking the confluence of Lugg and Wye and the meadows towards Hereford, of which only a cluster of houses and spires and the cathedral tower are delightfully visible, have great merit. The most interesting thing about Sufton is Repton's original Red Book with the water-colour slides of what existed and what he intended doing. Today Repton's improvements can still be detected, although a good deal smudged. The owner Major Hereford a nice old bumble-bee, although younger than me. His deference to his wife, formerly headmistress of the school which occupied the house during the war, loquacious and didactical, saddened me. 'My wife who has such knowledge, such taste, such wisdom, etc.' There is a son by a former marriage, and a grandson. The Herefords have owned Sufton since the thirteenth century in unbroken descent, with a single kink through the female line. A wonderful territorial name and connection. Sad too that on the father's death while this one was serving overseas the trustees sold all the furniture. The remains are what the French would call *quelconque*, upholstered armchairs in jazzy plush and beaten Benares ware in evidence.

Talking to these people made me realize that, whereas among my intellectual superiors I am a rather stupid person, among ordinary minds I am fairly (only fairly) bright. The impercipience of the Herefords going on and on, without sensing the irrelevance of their chatter, was amazing. I was in a considerable hurry to get to tea with the old Poës at Leominster. With great kindness Major Hereford insisted on putting me on the route. He drove ahead in his car at a snail's pace, stopping every five minutes to get out and show me some famous landmark. When we finally reached the Leominster road he descended from his car once again, clinging to my open window so that the knuckles of his fingers went white. Nevertheless I had an affection for the major.

I reached the Poës' house late, at five. They were sitting like Buddhas with the tea on a trolley in front of them, impatiently waiting. I had telephoned this morning asking if they would care to see me. Answer in the affirmative. I thought I would bring pleasure into their old lives (Frida is a little older than Mama would have been). I don't think I did a bit. First of all they gave me a message to telephone *The Times* urgently. This was the editor asking me to allow them to cut out of my letter a reference I had made to the Pope's attitude to birth control as 'moronic and downright wicked'. Moronic I agreed was a bit strong. They would not have either adjective. I then said I was miles from home, had not a copy of my letter on me and suggested they scrap it altogether. But no, the editor wanted to print it. So I capitulated. Returned to the Poës. Frida with quivering hands started pouring tea and slopping it over the silver tray. So I asked brightly if she would like me to pour for her. She threw me a look like a dagger-thrust. Jack said quite crossly, 'You know Frida has poured out tea since long before you were born.' I accepted the reproof. Then the telephone beside Frida rang. I thought I am damned if I am going to interfere again. Awkwardly the poor old thing tried to reach the receiver. Jack said, 'Aren't you going to help Frida?' So I picked it up and answered it for her. A voice said, 'This is Dorothea speaking. Who are you?' 'Oh, I'm just a cousin, J.L.-M.' I said and handed the thing to Frida. I heard Frida say, 'Dorothea, I'm afraid I can't speak to you now. We have an interruption. But when the six o'clock news is over, *if we are allowed to watch it*, I will ring you back.' For the next half-hour I talked brightly, senselessly, and left them. Not a great success I fear. Then I dashed at top speed in my tiny Morris to a meeting at Stroud of the newly formed Local Council under which Alderley parish will be governed. Was horrified by the lack of distinction of every single councillor. Not one educated man. This grotty lot now have planning authority which hitherto was exercised by the county council.

Thursday, 21st March

Poor David Lloyd's* only son Charlie has suicided himself in a wood behind Clouds Hill. This is sad for it means the end of the Lloyd dynasty. George Lloyd. would much have minded; also Blanche. I met the boy with David about a year ago in Brooks's. He was an uncouth, defiant sort of youth who was reading medicine. When I suggested that he might become a member of Brooks's he replied, 'No, no, this is not at all my sort of place.' He was 26.

Stopped this afternoon in the car and spoke to the old boy who lives in Wotton and is always on the road wet or fine. He was by Lower Lodge, Newark. He told me he would walk to Boxwell and back, a good five miles from Wotton. Is 75, rising 76. He encourages me. I ought to be able to do the same in ten years' time, with luck.

Sunday, 24th March

John [Kenworthy-Browne] telephoned to say he had read my letter in *The Times*. 'You do bare your soul,' he said. I have pondered over this gentle warning.

Thursday, 28th March

Yesterday I received a letter from Fr Michael Napier of The Oratory, strongly deprecating my *Times* letter, and pointing out at some length that overpopulation is no problem, and underpopulation in many countries is. His letter is so ill-judged, so blinkered and stupid that it has merely confirmed the views I expressed that the Catholic Church is lamentably at fault in its fatuous anti-contraception attitude. I shall have to answer him at length. He ends by saying that doubtless I intend to resign from The Oratory Arts Committee, and coldly thanks me for my past services! A. is so incensed that she

---

* David Lloyd, 2nd Baron Lloyd of Dolobran, 1912–85; s. of George, 1st Baron Lloyd, statesman and proconsul, J.L.-M.'s first employer, and his wife Blanche Lascelles.

is sending a copy of the letter to Julian Huxley, who started the correspondence, and whose letter prompted me to send mine.

When I told John Fleming* who stayed last weekend, that in typing these days I frequently produced words back to front, such as 'eht' for 'the', he was surprised. 'I never do that,' he said. 'I suppose it's senility,' I said humbly. 'I suppose it is,' he replied.

This morning came a letter from Norah Smallwood who has read and enjoyed my diaries. She is handing them to Ian Parsons, the chairman of Chatto's whom I met in the Droghedas' box the other evening at Covent Garden. She also says that some things I write may be libellous. I cannot think which passages these are. I admit some are in poor taste, which is a different matter altogether. Now today I am finishing the reduction of my Stuart book, which has taken a good deal of time and work. I don't know that, patched as it is, it holds very well together. Contrary to what I thought when I first wrote the book, I now find the chapters on the Countess of Albany the dullest.

Healey's budget has come and gone. It penalizes the rich. This ex-Communist announced his intention of penalizing them further. His motives are wholly political. They do nothing to save the economy, nothing to boost industry. Everything this new government has done and said is intended to placate the Trades Unions. My worst fears, held since the Tories were returned in 1970, are being realized. The Tories failed at the start of their government to stand up to the Unions, which they ought to have done when they could have afforded the time. Towards the end they tried, but owing to fear of causing hostility, the wets weakened and failed. They merely exacerbated ill-feeling. The Unions brought down the Tory government before the expiry of their term. Now they are cock-a-hoop. Naturally. An odd corollary is that whereas the Trades Unions are dominated by Communists there is not a single Communist MP today.

At the Trust's Regional Committee meeting in Tewkesbury I asked John Cadbury† if any of his family were still practising Quakers. He said several were, including his wife and himself. I longed to ask for further particulars as to their forms of worship, but did not

---

* John Fleming, b. 1919; architectural historian.
† John Cadbury, 1889–1982; NT supporter and prominent Quaker.

like to. He is of course the most upright of men, yet very Puritan and sober. No drink, no fun, plain of speech, dress, in fact deadly.

John Fleming, who had been discussing Nigel Nicolson's recent book about his parents, reminded me that many years ago Nigel remarked to me, 'If I thought Daddy was a cissy I would shoot myself.' I can hardly believe this, but if so, it must have been said when Nigel was still an Oxford undergraduate. It amuses me.

Monday, 1st April

A most lovely weekend, full sun, and yesterday even sitting and lying in the garden, a thing I never remember doing here in March. Now today suddenly as cold and grey as Christmas. Eardley, who is staying, and I walked along the wide Sharpness to Gloucester canal. A totally different landscape to our Cotswold one. The canal is raised on artificial banks at either side. Low-lying Isle of Athelney kind of country, of water-meadows with sheep grazing. We walked from Purton lock some four miles towards Gloucester. The lock-keepers' houses are like Decimus Burton lodges in Hyde Park, of simple Doric order. We passed through avenues of tall rushes, or pampas grasses, with peacock and tortoiseshell butterflies flitting, and Patchy, Clarissa's sheep-dog, trying to catch them. Where are these butterflies today? I have never known such a spring for the lesser celandine, which shine like golden stars on the road verges. Each spring some wild flower has its special profusion.

The *Magnolia denudata* in the garden close to the Georgian gazebo is at its peak. Yesterday the white candles against the blue sky all visibly opening. The day before they still wore their little grey velvet caps to protect the buds from frost.

Thursday, 4th April

Tuesday morning I went to A.'s new doctor, John Allison, because lately I have been suffering from dizzy fits. He examined me, cross-questioned me with great thoroughness. At first he thought they might be a recurrence of Jacksonian, but after blood tests, assured me No. Trouble simply that my arteries are slightly hardening, and my pressure is very low for someone of my age. He said to me, 'Your blood pressure is that of a young man of 17.' I visibly brightened. So he continued, 'But don't suppose that you look like a young man of

17.' 'Or should behave like one,' he might have added. I lunched with Harold Acton in the Ritz. We had half a bottle of Pouilly between us; avocado pear, grilled *poussin* with carrots, strawberries and cream, coffee. The bill, which I saw, was over £12 without tip. When I think how I used to complain during the war if a bill for two at the Ritz was over £1.

Dined with Philip Magnus at Pratt's. He says Jewell [Magnus] is on tenterhooks lest if he dines further away from Brooks's than Pratt's (which is opposite the morning-room window across Park Place) he should be mugged. He is an absurd man, and so square that he makes me feel positively circular. Pratt's is the core of the Establishment. Every member calls the other by Christian name. They are all Brooks's, White's, Boodle's, Tory. I don't suppose a Socialist would be admitted through the portals. Everyone talks to everyone. I felt an outsider. Uncomfortable with these extrovert, heavy drinking, raffish fellows, yet envious of their unbridled self-confidence.

Norah Smallwood has just telephoned that they want to publish my diaries. Apparently Ian Parsons is mad about them, and read out passages to the weekly board meeting. Showed them to Dadie Rylands* who was staying with him. However thinks they should be a little pruned. I agree that much trivia can come out, so long as someone else does the pruning and I am allowed to approve the pruned. Parsons may do it himself. But I don't want the spice taken out. The publishers are frightened of libel always.

Friday, 5th April

This morning Simon telephoned that Haines had had a further, serious stroke and was in the Evesham hospital. A. with her usual sense and rapid decision said we must go at once. So after luncheon we drove to Evesham. While I waited in the familiar cottage hospital lounge I recalled those dismal visits to Mama who was here before her death in 1962. The moment I saw Haines in the men's ward I knew there was no hope for him. Very clean and pink he was, half sitting up in bed, wearing coarse striped linen pyjamas. He kept picking with his hands under the sheets, always a bad sign. Eyes not

---

* George Rylands, b. 1902; Shakespeare scholar and Fellow of King's College, Cambridge.

glazed, but unseeing and bloodshot; tears welling and nose running. I think he knew who I was, but am not sure. Nothing I said registered. He rambled incomprehensibly. I could barely hear what he was saying, but it was chiefly in praise of the nurses, I think, then the usual dear old Haines boasting of something or other he had fixed, some pipes somewhere at the manor, and an occasional flicker of a smile of the old self-confidence. I was deeply saddened to watch beside the bed of this old man who has all my life been a pillar of our family well-being. It was always Haines who was sent for in emergency, always Haines who solved every crisis, burst pipes, electric light fuses, car not starting, Haines who knew where my mother had put her rings for safety, Haines to whom we children when in disgrace turned for comfort and advice. The first person on return for the school holidays we dashed to see was Haines.

I stayed five or ten minutes, but it was impossible to make any contact. We drove to Wickhamford, knocked on Mrs Haines's back door. She opened it and stood framed in the doorway a picture of woe. When we kissed her she wept copiously, but was more controlled than I imagined she could be. No hysteria. We drank tea, and even in her extremity she had to fetch the best cups from the sitting-room and the silver spoons from the leather canteen. We washed up for her and left.

A parish meeting in the Grange at eight. Awful affair, awful in that I am confronted with rows of wooden faces, not one of which responds to a joke. Nothing on the agenda worth discussing and the new Wotton representative, the bank manager of Lloyd's, attending for the first time. Very efficient, very proficient, '*au page*', and correcting me for introducing him as *the* Wotton representative on the Stroud Council, whereas apparently he is one of three. I ought to have known. And I don't care one damn.

Saturday, 6th April

Jimmie Smith[*] and Elizabeth Winn[†] to stay. A. has to cook, drinks have to be supplied; they talk and talk, Jimmie knocks everything

---

[*] The Hon. James Smith, b. 1906; Governor of the Sadler's Wells Theatre and member of the Royal Opera House Covent Garden Trust.

[†] Daughter of The Hon. Reginald Winn and his wife Alice Perkins, sister of Nancy (Tree) Lancaster; professional decorator.

over and when he sits on a chair, or sofa, breaks the springs or the arms. E. Winn told me that when her aunt, Nancy Lancaster,* went to stay at Firle after the war, she said to the maid sent to attend to her needs, 'I don't want anything more now, thank you very much. I am just going to clean my teeth.' The maid replied, 'But wouldn't you like me to clean them for you, madam?' She has her own. But what a refinement!

Sunday, 7th April

A ghastly night. Woke suddenly at 3.50, and heard my clock strike 4, then 5, 6, 7, and was up at 7.20 for church and bell-ringing. After breakfast Lois L.-M. telephoned to say that Haines had died during the night. I much wonder if the time I woke coincided with Haines's departure from this earth.

Tuesday, 9th April

David Somerset was told by Lord Rothschild,† who is still head of the Government's Think Tank, that undoubtedly this government is determined to finish off the capitalists. David met Lord Balogh‡ and asked him why on earth he had not stayed in Budapest where he was born, and why he did not work for the economy of his native country Hungary, which was Communist; why in fact he did not live there instead of England. Bold of him. Balogh replied that he was not a Communist and did not wish to live in a Communist state. But that is precisely what he is reducing England to.

Saturday, 13th April

Alex [Moulton] and I were to have started on our long-planned tour last Tuesday, but owing to Haines's funeral fixed for Wednesday 10.30 at Cheltenham Crematorium, I had to postpone it by one day. Alex called for me in his 1973 Rolls, an exquisite travelling carriage which glides whether cruising at 40 or darting at 90 m.p.h. Extre-

---

* Nancy Perkins, of Virginia, USA, m. 1st, Henry Field; 2nd, Ronald Tree, MP; 3rd, Colonel Claude Lancaster of Kelmarsh Hall, Northamptonshire; in 1945 became proprietor of the decorating firm Colefax and Fowler; horticulturist; d. 1995.
† Victor, 3rd Baron Rothschild, 1910–90; zoologist and public servant.
‡ Thomas Balogh, 1905–85; Baron Balogh of Hampstead (Life Peer); b. Budapest; Fellow of Balliol College, Oxford from 1945; political economist.

mely comfortable, with leg room unlike many Rollses I have
known. The Haines funeral over in twenty minutes. Audrey and
Prue attended. Poor Mrs H. in floods of tears throughout. Old
Haines's coffin draped with a Union Jack. I watched it disappear
through that dreadful curtain, the remains of someone I had known
and accepted as part of life for 65 ½ years. Then turned away, made
casual remarks about the weather, rejoined Alex and, after two
minutes' thought about the solemn obsequies, reverted to jests and
foolery.

We stayed two nights at Portmeirion. Hotel clean and comfortable, food not good, and out to luncheon; the bill amounted to £33
each. Portmeirion a delightful Italian baroque fantasy village until
you look into the buildings, which are shoddy and will not endure. I
was touched to be handed a note from Clough Williams-Ellis*
asking me to be sure and call on him. Alex and I went on Thursday
evening at six. The old man – he is 91 – met us at the door of
Brondanw, took us round the garden, which is laid out on Hidcote
lines, of compartments. This evidently the fashion of that generation, Sissinghurst another example. He knows nothing about plants
and shrubs. Says he is a frame-maker, which is true. Lady W.-E.
came forth to greet us. We sat and talked for an hour and a half. He
is a marvel. Dressed in the usual fancy dress, of breeches and yellow
stockings, and odd folded-over blue tie. In full possession of every
faculty, only slightly deaf with an aid. He stood showing me plans of
the various buildings of his which he complains are being demolished, houses he built before the first war. Says he is outliving his
own creations, which depresses him. Said Lutyens had great influence upon him. I asked if Lutyens taught him. No one taught him.
Said he was an amateur. This is too obvious for his architecture bears
it out. It is flimsy stuff. What a charmer, so friendly and forthcoming. 'You and I,' he says, 'share the same sympathies and
antipathies.' She is a beautiful old lady, quick, perceptive and very
clever. Also very left-wing. Her eyes are blank. They do not appear.
She misses nothing so they must be there but they seem to be blank
orbs, expressionless, steely.

I enjoyed our tour. Alex is a good travelling companion, cheerful,
amused, interested, with splendid manners. In Chirbury church we

---

* Sir Clough Williams-Ellis, 1883–1978; architect and creator of Portmeirion
village.

read a wall epitaph which described a Georgian squire as having 'an obliging carriage'. I told Alex that his carriage was obliging. 'Yes, isn't it?' he replied, thinking I referred to his Rolls. The tour marred by my worry over the rash and spots on my chin which itch dreadfully, and look most unsightly.

Friday, 19th April

On Wednesday I cancelled our visit to Glanusk to which I had enormously looked forward, and went again to London for the day to see old Dr Flaxman. He took a favourable view of my spots and rash, being convinced they were nettle rash or an allergy. However I persuaded him to take a blood and urine specimen. The latter looked in the glass as pure as Pouilly Fuissé, as I observed to him. He agreed. I shall know the result of the tests on Saturday morning. One day I am better, the next the trouble recurs. What can it be? He says I am incurably neurotic. He is a dear old boy, friendly and nanny-like, but I wish he would not embrace me when I leave his surgery.

Yesterday walking with Patchy up the Kilcot–Tresham valley I got to the old rutted lane between steep banks where the cows never trample. I thought I had never seen in England such a galaxy of wild flowers for years. All the spring flowers out – primroses still, wood anemones, violets, and early cowslips and bluebells. This is a dream realm; I have always loved it, and pray it may be spared. I wanted to live, whereas at Easter when feeling ill and depressed I understood how when mortally ill one would be reconciled to extinction, anything for peace of mind as well as body.

Today, walking with Patchy from just below the monument at Hawkesbury down Stony Lane I came into the most beautiful combe of all the many I have walked through in these parts. It lay between Splatts' Wood and Frith Wood, and on the map is called Long Coombe: the gentlest slopes like something fashioned by a sculptor, so smooth and even, and at the far end across the Kilcot valley my woods, Foxholes Woods. I thought if God really means every man to survive into old age, which presumably he does, for young deaths are premature deaths, contradictions of the natural order of things, then he clearly means the sexual appetite to become exhausted for a purpose. And that purpose can only be to enable man to contemplate *Him* and save *his* (with a small 'h') soul. Now this purpose is acknowledged by all Christians to be the greatest of all. From which conclusion I return to the premise, which always used to be inculcated in us by the devout, that the sexual appetite is not a good thing in any case. Disputable of course. So where are we? as Lady Vernon* used to ask, and answer in her trembling tones – 'Nowhere.'

This morning I posted to Dr Roy Strong† my chapter on 'The Country House in our Heritage'. It is a hotch-potch made from old articles I wrote, with a few herbs added. Nothing to be pleased with although A. who read it said it made her cry, cry in the right way. Now I have three *mss* submitted. Norah Smallwood who is coming to stay this evening will doubtless give me the verdict about the Stuart book which is the one I worry about most.

Tuesday, 23rd April

Norah has given the verdict. They don't want the emasculated, rewritten book. Damn 'they'! They say it is neither one thing nor the other, and there is still too much extraneous matter, in the introductory chapter. She asked if I was prepared to have another go at it. I said No, not on any account. She asked if it might not after all be better to go over the original book, which had embraced all the exiled Stuarts, and greatly prune that. I told her that it was impossible. I had destroyed it in cutting it up for the second version. She was very nice. We sat in the sun on the white seat at the front door while A. and John Pope-Hennessy went for a walk. Then she went on to say how much Chatto's were looking forward to publishing the diaries, what title should we give the book, and suggesting that certain passages be omitted, ones likely to cause offence to the Trevelyan family, now alive, of whom a brother is one of their partners. I said, 'Norah, I had planned that a serious book of mine should appear next; I have already published one autobiography, and one novel which has not been a success, and which people thought (wrongly) was also autobiographical. I will not now have my diaries published unless I can get the Stuart book or some other published in between.' She looked astonished and we sat in embarrassed

---

* Doris, widow of Sir George Vernon, 2nd Bt, of Hanbury Hall (he d. 1940).
† Roy Strong, b. 1935; Kt 1982; Director, Keeper and Secretary of the National Portrait Gallery, 1967–73; Director of the Victoria and Albert Museum, 1974–87; writer and historian; m. 1971 Julia Trevelyan Oman, designer.

silence. She said, 'Please think the matter over, and let me know in a few days.' I shall not (I hope) change my mind, and have posted a letter to David Higham to tell them that I will not have the diaries published after all. A. says I am cutting off my nose to spite my face. This may be true, but this is how I feel. I just cannot reconcile myself yet to the fact that I may no longer be able to 'write', and have to fall back upon old material – rubbish like the diaries – written thirty years ago. Very depressed as a result of this weekend. Yet rather enjoy spiting my face.

In other respects the weekend a success. John P.-H. was charming; charming because he has little natural charm and when he endeavours to exhibit this exiguous quality attains it more readily than ordinary people, from whom one generally expects a modicum. I took him on Saturday to see Joan Evans. While they were talking I spoke to Mrs Oldfield who had called. This good woman told me she calls once a day. She finds herself in the unsolicited position of minder to Joan, simply out of good nature and compassion. Says the new housekeeper, aged 70, will probably leave because she never bargained for the odious task of cleaning up after and washing Joan, who is incontinent and whose habits are filthy. She does 'bigs' down her legs into her shoes, leaves puddles and worse on the carpets and in the bed; she gets drunk and has to be carried into bed. Her eating habits are awful (we witnessed this when she lunched a year ago, spitting gobs not into her hand but into the plate). This explains the extraordinary complaint Joan Evans made to me when I telephoned to ask how the new housekeeper was faring. Joan complained that she had a mania for cleanliness; made the house stink of disinfectant, and 'had an unwholesome distaste for excreta'. I thought I had heard wrong at the time.

John P.-H. said that K. Clark was writing (not for publication) confidential footnotes under each of the photograph portraits taken by Janet Stone and recently exhibited by her. They were then to be bound together and deposited in the British Museum. The notes were brief descriptions of each sitter and his and her merits and demerits. I am among these sitters. John said, 'You may well suppose the comments will be tart.' He said the best thing Jamesey wrote was his description of meetings and visits with members of the royal family during the preparation of his Queen Mary book. It could not be published for twenty-five years at least. Much talk of Jamesey whom he misses greatly.

Laurie Lee and Cathie* to lunch on Sunday. Laurie now bulky, heavy from excessive beer-drinking. A middle-aged child. Is a bit too facetious. He complained to Norah that nowadays he did not receive the welcome he used to get in his golden, romantic youth. But who does after 50?

Saturday, 27th April

On our way to Kemble station last Sunday with John and Norah we drove up to Hodges, meaning to walk round Eny's garden. But in front of the house Keith the gardener stopped us, and Nicole Hornby came up to us from the door. We told her what we had intended to do, and she said, Yes do walk around. Then A. asked how Eny was. Nicole said, 'She went this morning.'

Since by Tuesday there was no obituary of Eny of any sort in *The Times* I wrote an appreciation, which A. thought good, and I too long. However I posted it. On Wednesday on our way to London we attended the burial of Eny's ashes in the tiny graveyard of the pretty Georgian toy church at Pusey. Only her family there and a handful of special friends, the D. of Beaufort, Sally Westminster, Diana Westmorland and a very few others. Stand-up luncheon in Pusey House after. A rush visit to London to dine with the Charlie Douglas-Homes[†] and hear Valda Aveling play the clavichord. I strained my ears to catch the mosquito-like sounds. At times was transported into a sort of midget spiritual world, interrupted at intervals by the trains outside the house in Mornington Crescent. V. Aveling stout, dumpy, difficult to talk to, but knows her own mind.

At nights I am woken by my face tingling as though needles were thrust into every pore, and between the fingers of both hands little spots arise and tingle. What can this be? Tonight I mean not to have a bath, or even cider to drink. Perhaps the tingling will subside, if the blood is not heated.

Jessica Douglas-Home is beautiful, with eyes like burning coals. She says what comes into her head, gently but firmly. I sat next to her and she began with, 'What beautiful nails you have. Like shells.' 'I hope they are clean,' I laughed. Then, 'I suppose the Catholic

---

* Laurie Lee, 1914–97; troubadour poet and author; m. 1950 Catherine Polge.
† Charles Douglas-Home, 1937–85; Editor of *The Times*, 1982–5; m. 1966 Jessica Gwynne.

Church has got rid of you?' and asked me how long I had dissented, and when I last went to Communion, and what I did now. A strange, inscrutable girl.

Very depressed all this week about my books. Nothing on the stocks any more. I wrote to Higham who is abroad, and his secretary made Norah return the Diaries as well as the Stuarts. The only good news, and that by comparison unimportant, was a postcard from Roy Strong approving of my contribution to his country house book. I hardly care what anyone thinks of it.

Bitterly cold north-east wind blowing. Yet in the stricken woods the far side of the Ozleworth Valley I heard the first cuckoo.

Friday, 3rd May

On Tuesday David Pryce-Jones[*] came to see me. He telephoned a few days before to ask. I said Yes, in spite of the fact that Debo had warned me that his reason might be to pump me about Bobo [Mitford] whose life he wants to write. Debo, Pam and Diana are dead against it. Decca[†] whose friend he is has urged him to do it. I expected to be irritated by an intrusive manner. Not at all. He could not have been more understanding, more charming. However I began straight away by saying I surmised he had come to talk about Bobo, that the three sisters were among my oldest friends, and therefore I could not discuss this subject. He looked crestfallen, but the ice having been broken we discussed biography generally. At the end he begged me to write to Debo and point out that when he saw Diana he thought she favoured the project, and that if he (David P.-J.) did not undertake it, somebody else would, somebody very hostile, which he certainly was not. He hinted that somebody was already on to the project.

He and I parted on good terms. How anyone could want to write about Bobo in the first place beats me. She had no influence on the Nazi inner circle. What makes her character interesting, as distinct from her life, is that she said before the outbreak that if England and Germany were to go to war she would kill herself. While David P.-J. and I were walking in the garden we found Alvilde with Brian

---

[*] Writer, son of Alan Pryce-Jones.
[†] The Hon. Jessica Mitford, fourth of the Mitford sisters, 1917–96; m. 1st Esmond Romilly (d. 1943); 2nd, Robert Treuhaft; author.

Gascoigne.* A sharp contrast between the two young men, David
spruce and well-dressed, the other ungroomed, wearing an old goat-
skin jacket moth-eaten and moulting. Patchy thought he was
another dog.

Went to a trustees' meeting at Corsham on Wednesday. Mercifully George Howard and Christopher Medley were present; they
are the two who matter. Both firmly vetoed John Methuen's desire
to get rid of much of Paul's papers and books and files. For the old
man cherished all records of family concern, including the Field
Marshal's papers. John Methuen is a sort of yahoo without the
slightest sympathy for his uncle's interests, which were legion. I
cannot make him out. I felt the spirit of Paul hovering around us,
quizzical and anxious.

At last the maisonette of 19 Lansdown Crescent is ours today.
We have signed cheques for £19,000 each and sent them
off. Neither of us wants to go to the place in the least. And
the irony is that this evening I saw in Bath a small house for sale
in Darlington Place which I know would suit A. down to the
ground. Only disadvantages that it has four levels and only one
bathroom. But the garden is just what she would like. It is spacious
and cheerful. I am overcome with guilt about Lansdown Crescent
for it is my selfishness which has pushed her into this project.
Beckford's library is what got me. We cannot move into the
maisonette, me keeping the only room with an outlet, and A.
confined all day to a basement. So what are we to do? Oh I wish
I were less waffly and less selfish. I think A. hates the beastly place
already.

Saturday, 4th May

I admit that the Duke of Beaufort (or must I call him Master?) is
very good at doing his majisterial stuff as Lord-Lieutenant. Today he
presented Irvine, the custodian of Chedworth Roman Villa, with
the BEM. We members of the regional committee were assembled,
and a few friends of the Irvines. Irvine rather cock-a-hoop and a bit
cheeky, refusing to recognize the solemnity of the occasion, and yet
flattered. Mrs Irvine laughing too much. The Duke quite informal
and un-pomposo, yet solemn when he had to read the Queen's

---

* Son of Derick and Midi Gascoigne; jazz music composer.

letter to Irvine, stressing the sentence, 'Her Majesty particularly asked me...', etc. I have known Irvine ever since I first worked for the Trust. He certainly deserves an honour for long, devoted service in this remote locality. Lord Vestey,[*] owner of surrounding land, was present. Nice looking young man with over-good manners, in that when introduced to us, made the same remark to each with a switched-on smile, 'I am very pleased to meet you.' Later I talked to him about his great-grandmother Melba, whom as a child Alvilde loved so dearly in Australia. Again the same neon-light smile. A young peer's shyness I suppose, a sort of defence mechanism against the inquisitive stranger, yet contrived to be demotic. Intentions of the very best, and rather endearing. When Henry Bathurst[†] behaves like this one wants to shake him.

Sunday, 5th May

Yesterday A. and I motored to Wickhamford to see Mrs Haines. She very lonely, very tearful, and very self-pitying. Could not hear one single word we uttered. The evening before Haines died she was in the hospital and asked him if he knew that I had visited him the previous evening. Although he had been wandering all day he replied, 'Yes, Jim came. Wasn't he a sport?' Mrs H. rather shocked that he omitted the Master. It goes to show one absolutely must visit the dying even when one suspects they are unconscious of one's presence. One may well be wrong. They may well long to utter, and be speech-bound.

The cuckoo has at last arrived, in the plural. I heard him endeavouring plaintively to sing from the devastated woods across the Ozleworth valley this morning in the intense cold. No swallows yet. The young thrushes' nest is empty this morning. Yesterday it seemed impossible for such huge fledgelings to remain in so small a nest. Four of them. A. built a roof of wire netting and leaves over the nest weeks ago to prevent the rooks taking them. She succeeded.

---

[*] 3rd Baron Vestey of Kingswood, b. 1941; great-grandson of the Australian singer Dame Nellie Melba (Helen Armstrong, née Mitchell); Gloucestershire landowner (Stowell Park).
[†] 8th Earl Bathurst, b. 1927; of Cirencester Park, Gloucestershire.

Thursday, 9th May

On Tuesday went to London for the day to see David Higham who lunched with me. The long and the short is, he persuaded me that I was foolish to withhold the Diaries from Chattos, and he felt sure some publisher would take the Stuarts. So he is going to tell Norah this. Norah is always so irritated each time she hears from Higham, that she may after all decline to accept the benefit proffered. I am to retype the Stuarts, dear God, because it cannot in its reduced, cut-up form be submitted to a new publisher.

My rash has returned, three days only after I left off the anti-allergy pills. I have started them again. They make me drowsy and unwell. Such a bore to be bright scarlet about the chin and upper lip, like John Fowler.

I had a letter from Colin McMordie at Oriel asking if he might come and see us. He motored over from Oxford for dinner. He is twenty-four, starry-eyed, very intelligent and bright and very affected. It is flattering when the young ask to come forty miles for the pleasure of our company. He talked about his thesis and his future when he leaves Oxford. Must already be a graduate I presume. Was immensely clean and tidy, wearing a blue pullover with silk scarf and bell-bottom trousers, absurdly like skirts, and not becoming. The tightness of said trousers round the knees causing creases. I at my most avuncular had to send him away when we started yawning.

Thursday, 16th May

I took to London my pen-and-ink sketch by Inigo Jones to sell at Sotheby's. I am sorry to part with this rarity. I also took eight Battersea patch-boxes which belonged to my father. I had fairly recently put eleven of them in the glass-topped table in the upstairs passage because when lying around in the library they only made extra work for the dusters. The result of this consideration is that three have been stolen, I suppose by one of the awful old English women we have had over recent years. John K.-B. is kindly disposing of these things for me. I badly need the cash for wages.

Last weekend I stayed a night with Eardley at the Slade. Able to go because A. had two grandchildren staying. Nevertheless she does not like me going away without her. I enjoyed it. Fanny Partridge[*] also staying, and Mattei Radev there. Fanny let me read Peter Luke's forthcoming play about Lytton Strachey[†] in which Ralph Partridge plays a prominent role. He is made out to be a low-brow, conventional soldier hero back from the front during the First World War who meeting Lytton Strachey is civilized by him. Whereas Fanny points out that he did not in fact meet Strachey until well after the war and had always been a highbrow, having got a First at Oxford. Fanny strongly objects to much of the play; and it is interesting that someone so tolerant and candid as she in the traditional Bloomsbury way, yet objects when those she knew and loved are portrayed by a writer who never knew them. The play seems to be without much point.

On Sunday morning while the others were in bed I went to H. Communion in the charming little church of Prior's Dean. Only a Lady J., her old mother and a couple of gents present. No one of the peasantry attending. As usual too much interest in the presence of a stranger. I tried to slip away but not without being caught by Lady J. who bade me good morning, thanked me for coming, and asked where I had come from. The first guest doubtless ever to have come from the Slade.

Yesterday I attended a long pre-arranged luncheon at the Bristol Merchant Venturers Hall. About twenty Venturers present. All businessmen. I sat on the Master's right at a long polished table covered with rare plate and cups. They have some fine treasures, in silver chargers, salvers, Queen Elizabeth's saddle and harness used at her visit to Bristol in 1574. I approve of this sort of Society. Bristolians are immensely proud of the Merchant Venturers' traditions; the Society was founded in Edward VI's reign. Good wine, but the food absolute filth, I could hardly get it down. Nan Bernays arranged for me to be invited by the Master, and I should feel, and am, greatly honoured, in spite of the inedibility.

---

[*] Frances Marshall, b. 1900; diarist and literary reviewer; m. 1933 Major Ralph Partridge (who d. 1960).
[†] Lytton Strachey, 1880–1932; biographer and member of the Bloomsbury group.

Monday, 20th May

Liz von Hofmannsthal and Henry McIlhenny[*] to stay the weekend. Saturday afternoon I went for a long walk with Liz from the main Stroud–Bath road through Boxwell down to Alderley. She walks rapidly like a man. Since I last stayed with her in Austria for Easter of 1973 both Raimund and Angus who were present have died. Liz dyes her hair jet black, and I noticed that her scalp is likewise black which is not attractive. She is still extremely beautiful, but her character is cold. Henry flew from Ireland to Bristol, hired a huge Daimler with chauffeur who stayed in Wotton and hung around all Sunday till they departed after tea. H. tipped the Filipina £5 for one night's visit. He is a friendly and generous soul, but absurd.

Tuesday, 21st May

Dining with the Buxtons[†] at Cole Park tonight my host said, 'Read the inscription on the silver-mounted coconut.' It read: 'Given by Lady Puleston to Dr Philips for medical services, 1819.' I said, 'It ought to be mine, not yours.' Walked after dinner with Jan Badeni[‡] round the outside. It is a lovely secret house with Georgian front and Elizabethan rear, the whole surrounded by a moat. The garden and the trees make a fine setting, but the Buxtons' taste is negative.

Wednesday, 22nd May

Hastened this morning to Burderop Park near Swindon where was a big sale. Only told of it by Badenis[‡] last night. Too sad. A very old family house of the Calley family. Miss Calley recently died and left all to a distant relation who is selling just *everything*. A harlequin portrait of Prince Charlie, full length, in tartan jacket and trews, fetched £750. As a painting it was worthless. What I coveted was a profile drawing of the Prince said to be by Gyles Hussey, identical to

---

[*] Henry McIlhenny, d. 1986; collector and philanthropist; President of the Philadelphia Museum of Art, USA.

[†] John Buxton, of Cole Park, Wiltshire, author and don (New College, Oxford), and Margery (née Lockley) his wife.

[‡] Count Jan Badeni, 1921–95; Polish immigrant who served with the British Army in Second World War; m. June Wilson; of Norton Manor, Wiltshire.

one at Blair Castle and another in Don Nicholas's collection,
although in bad condition. I knew it would go for even more than
the harlequin. Dreadful to witness the end of a family home. I
dashed back to meet at Wotton an elderly lady called Sunter Harrison,* who is writing a history of the Puleston family. Boring and
unintelligent old thing, tho' nice and very 'how' as Vita would have
described. She told me that the first Puleston baronet jilted a
Miss Mostyn Owen and was challenged to a duel by her brother;
and that Elizabeth Lady P., whose portrait hangs in my library, was
the ambitious daughter of a Chester ironmonger. Today's old
woman tells me she is the ninth daughter of a brood of ten. Of
them eight have all died of cancer. Her husband was a GP studying
the hereditary symptoms of cancer, from which he too died, at the
age of forty.

Dined with Olda Willes;† she is 88. The dear Fulfords staying.
Sibell beginning to be senile, forgetful and frail to look upon. She
told me she was four years younger than Olda. Roger has finished
his fourth volume of Queen Victoria's letters. Is not editing any
more because the correspondence with the Q'.s eldest daughter
deteriorates after his finishing date, which is the year of the Treaty
of Berlin, I believe.

Joan Evans tells me that when Lady Salisbury called upon her
mother (then living in Hertfordshire) she drove in a carriage and
pair, with four outriders.

Thursday, 23rd May

A. and I went to Bath. No. 19 Lansdown Crescent maisonette is
now ours. We came away pleased, and think we can make it quite
cosy. Even though it was raining heavily today the semi-basement
room was light and cheerful.

Saturday, 25th May

Chatto's have taken back my diaries and will publish them. I am
now retyping the Stuart hash for the nth time.

We were invited to dine tonight by the Anthony Kershaws whom

---

* Mrs Sunter Harrison, local historian in Flintshire.
† Olda Willes, née de Brienen, widow of Thomas Willes and first cousin of Eny Strutt.

we don't know.[*] Very politely he had told me over the telephone
that Father Gerard Irvine was staying the weekend with them and
particularly asked to see me. The Kershaws live in a converted barn at
Didmarton. Barn has a good plan, but little panache. Indifferent
dinner; meat left eschewed on my plate. Because of rash I am not
allowed to touch one drop of wine for three weeks, which makes
social effort more onerous than normally. Yet it is surprising how
well and un-sleepy I feel after dinner. Mrs Kershaw a jolly, plump,
Elaine sort of figure. He, friendly, suave, square (diamond tie pin),
very affable, not untypical Tory MP. Father Gerard is an enthusiast,
not over kempt, decaying nails and teeth, but godly, gossipy and
widely informed. Said he was with the Harold Wilsons in Lord
North Street this week. Wilson on returning from Parliament said,
'My trousers came down in the House of Commons. All Prime
Ministers' waists shrink after a few weeks' office.' (I would have
thought the opposite was the case.) Father Gerard said, 'Why don't
you wear braces?' Wilson answered, 'I daren't, because *Private Eye*
might get to hear of it.' He says Wilson can be amusing company.
Mrs W. is highly sensitive, and gets terribly wounded by *Private Eye*.
That is because she is incorrigibly middle- class and decent. He is
lower-class, pure and simple, and so less sensitive and decent.

Sunday, 26th May

We lunched with Ann Fleming[†] at Sevenhampton. A pastichy sort
of house, nearly all new in correct Georgian or Regency taste.
What's strikingly beautiful is the contour of the park gently sweeping down to a lake, with two urns well placed against the trees.
Robert Kee[‡] was there, an intelligent, civilized man whom I met on
the only occasion I stayed at Ham Spray with the Partridges. This was
when he was married to Janetta. Also present the Stephen Spenders.[§]
He has completely lost the last vestige of good looks. When I think
of him at Oxford he was a radiantly beautiful seraph with a

---

[*] Anthony Kershaw, b. 1915; MP 1955–87; Kt 1981; m. 1939 Barbara Crookenden.

[†] Ann Charteris, widow of 3rd Baron O'Neill (Midi Gascoigne's other brother) and
(3rd husband) Ian Fleming.

[‡] Robert Kee, b. 1919; author and broadcaster; m. 1st, 1948, Janetta Woolley; 2nd,
1960, Cynthia Judah; 3rd, 1990, The Hon. Catherine Mary Trevelyan.

[§] Stephen Spender, 1909–95; Kt 1983; poet and man of letters; m., 2nd, 1941, Natasha
Litvin.

shock of gold hair. Now he is a collapsed pudding. He is bluff, untidy, badly dressed, spread, square in figure and deportment. Reminds me of Ralph Vaughan Williams in his old age. We talked about Mitfords and he referred to Decca as a Communist bitch. I should have said to him, 'But you were a Communist dog once.' We all agreed that it was rare for young people to know what they wanted to be when they left the university. Stephen said, 'I always knew from my earliest boyhood. I wanted to be a poet.'

Tuesday, 28th May

Charlotte Bonham-Carter asked us to dinner before we went to the Byron party given by Roy Strong at the V. & A. We arrived at eight. Already there were present six people. By nine there were twenty. We ate in two different rooms, balancing plates on our knees. Filthy food. I sat next to Cynthia Gladwyn and again we talked of Nancy. She told me how deeply distressed Nancy had been when she first discovered that Hamish to whom she was engaged, was 'what he was'. Charlotte, gallant old thing, organizing and drilling this huge party. Apparently she gives about one a week, usually on Mondays. How she can be bothered! The Mondi Howards[*] were there, and I shook hands. Then she came up to me, hugged me and said 'How could you be so formal?' But the truth is I had forgotten I once knew Cécile so well. She reminded me of incidents, walks in Hyde Park when 'you were the most handsome young man I had ever known. I was thrilled by you', and I had not the faintest idea at the time. O would that I had! Then the Byron party. A marvellously arranged exhibition. Alan Tagg[†] has brilliant powers of improvisation. One compartment is a supposed reproduction of Byron's room in the Palazzo Mocenigo, Venice. You look into it, and it is dark save for a few taper candles, and filled with cats, dogs, books on the floor, walking sticks, etc., just as the poet may have had it.

---

[*] The Hon. Edmund (Mondi) Howard, b. 1909; m. 1936 Cécile Geoffroy-Dechaume,

[†] Alan Tagg, b. 1928; worked as assistant to Cecil Beaton and Oliver Messel; decorative and theatrical designer.

We have definitely decided to sell this house. The last straw was to be told by the nice woman who puts her cows in our paddock that the Margerys told her, and the man who does the mowing, that they intend to leave in September. So we have written to the agent who has been badgering us for months, to say we will definitely sell. Feeling heartbroken.

Friday, 31st May

At last we went today to Glanusk to lunch and tea with Peggy De L'Isle. It was fun to be eating off silver with the Bailey crest, the same as my forks and spoons. Saw the portrait of Sir Joseph painted about 1830, still youngish, with firm little mouth, and his pretty second wife with eldest child, my great-aunt Spearman. Also bust of Sir Joseph in the private chapel where all the Baileys are buried. Bust taken of him later in life. He is ugly in the mouth and jowl; strong resemblance to photographs of my grandfather whose lower face is similarly simian. Not an engaging countenance. He must have been immensely rich and besides building Glanusk in 1828 owned about a dozen seats. He also collected pictures, one Velasquez at least, which Toby Glanusk, who was a soldier, sold during the war for nothing. I also noticed several Charles II or James II mugs, like the tankard I possess, also with heavy baroque chasing, which I have been told was put on by the Baileys in Victorian times. Peggy De L'Isle very friendly indeed, bluff and benevolent like Dreda Tryon[*] and Betty Hussey.[†] Her daughter Shân Legge-Bourke[‡] turned up for tea, a pretty girl with golden hair and fair skin. We had tea in the nursery. Shân's child of 9 was the centre of attention. To it we had to address our conversation. At its puny jokes we laughed. At its boastful remarks we marvelled. Adult conversation ceased entirely. I cannot believe this to be the right way to treat children. Had we been in France this child, if present at all, would be seen and not heard, and certainly not addressed. It would remain inconspicuously in the background, demure and unnoticed and if looked at, would curtsey.

---

[*] Etheldreda Burrell, m. 1939 The Hon. Charles Tryon, later 2nd Baron Tryon; he d. 1976.

[†] Elizabeth Kerr-Smiley, m. 1936 Christopher Hussey, architectural historian (*Country Life*); he d. 1970.

[‡] Shân Bailey, dau. of 3rd Baron Glanusk and Margaret (subsequently Viscountess De L'Isle), b. 1943; m. 1964 W.N.H. Legge-Bourke.

Wednesday, 5th June

Bobby Gore and Diana Cooper stayed the weekend, from Saturday morning till Monday morning. Bobby's wife has left him for good, and he is bewildered what to do next. I don't think he really minds. He is very sweet, appreciative and delightful company. His only minus is over-solicitude, which most decent people would reckon a plus. Diana is a marvel for 81, still of ineffable beauty. Complexion like that of a woman of 50. I saw her in bed, *en negligée*, and marvelled at what I saw – skin so smooth, taut and flower-like. She is interested in everything literary, social and world-eventful. She is only a very little deaf; otherwise quick as lightning and the cynosure of all eyes. She holds every stage because her mind is like a rapier. An extraordinary woman, and when one has her alone like this, she is very sympathetic, almost affectionate. One can talk to her about anything, just as I did with Vita. But she has not the quiet undemanding manner and the empathy of Vita. Nevertheless she is a joy, and a miracle.

Monday, 10th June

I had a horrid dream. My father was in his coffin with the lid off. I was in bed alongside, and could not move away. I was frightened because I thought how awful when the corpse begins to stink. Yet my feelings for him were very compassionate.

When we spent the day at Glanusk Peggy De L'Isle told me that the family still owned 80,000 acres, mostly mountain land, yet it strikes me as enormous. The Glanusk property marches with the Beaufort property. Their grandfather Glanusk, she said, helped Master's father or grandfather by lending him money. I can't believe Master would be pleased to be reminded of this. We lunched on Saturday with the Downers at Oare. I had a long talk with Alec Downer.[*] He is one of the most virtuous men I have met. He told me that while he was a prisoner of the Japanese, he learned that material values were totally vain, and only the spiritual ones mattered. He is a rich man, and to lose his possessions and money would cause him no distress whatever. He is an intimate friend of Heath in

---

[*] Sir Alexander Downer, 1910–81; High Commissioner for Australia in the UK 1964–72; m. 1947 Mary Gosse.

so far as anyone can be intimate with Heath. They are on Xtian-name terms, and Downer can see him whenever he wishes. Said Heath was 100 per cent good; he could fill the office of Archbishop of Canterbury without even a need to investigate his inmost thoughts. Alec said in his quiet voice and gentle manner, 'He is good in the sight of the Almighty.' Wilson, he said, was absolutely unreliable, a man of no convictions, shifty, yet a skilled parliamentarian.

Alec Downer is for the first time in his life pessimistic. He sees no ray of hope for this country which is rapidly on the Marxist slopes to perdition. When he told me that Lord Carrington was staying with him next week, I begged him to give a message from me. Tell him, I said, that the Conservative voters in the country are desperately frustrated; that we feel our leaders are muffling Conservative policy; that the party is timorous; that the time has come when Conservatives must no longer be pusillanimous; we must no longer be afraid of offending the susceptibilities of the Left. Alec for some inexplicable reason listens to my views, and is far too flattering of my writings. He has all my books, and made me autograph a number of them.

Yesterday we had the Rupert Loewensteins[*] and Denys Suttons to lunch. Denys and Rupert are right-wingers of a different sort to Downer. Whereas Downer is a Tory of old-fashioned integrity and honour, the other two are of the tough pragmatic sort. Both very clever men, they said the Conservative shadow government ought to bribe the Liberal MPs; that every man had his price, and they should be bought. Both men worried to death about the future. Rupert, a merchant banker, advises against having any stocks and shares. Don't invest in shares. Only have cash. All very fine; if everyone only had cash what would happen to the economy? Denys says – watch the art market. When the bottom falls out of that, you may be sure the end has come. But how does one recognize the bottom's impending dissolution?

Wednesday, 12th June

I lunch with John Cornforth. When I tell him that we are selling Alderley, he says that without a garden to tend A. ought to write

---

[*] Prince Rupert zu Loewenstein, b. 1933, financial adviser; his wife Josephine (Lowry-Corry).

more garden articles. He says she writes them far better than any other garden writer, i.e., Lanning [Roper] and Anne Scott-James. When I pass this dewdrop on to A. she merely pooh-poohs it.

Thursday, 13th June

I suppose I am rather shifty. Hugh Farmar[*] told me in Brooks's that he was worried about Wimpole's future. He had seen Mrs Bambridge[†] who has quite lost her memory and can't transact business. He asked me if she had left Wimpole in her will to the Trust? Then he said he had had this very conversation with Michael Rosse. I said I wd speak to Michael. He said, 'Don't', because Michael will think he (Hugh) has been talking to everyone on the Trust. 'All right,' I say, and promptly do tell Michael when I see him in the NT office. Then I meet Hugh Farmar in the street. I tell him that Michael is asking Hugh Grafton to talk to him (Hugh Farmar) about the matter. But I say, 'Don't tell Michael that I have said so when he informs you himself.' 'We are both behaving in the same mysterious way,' says Hugh Farmar. This is how affairs are conducted, perfectly honourably but deviously.

When the middle-aged and old buy porn, they should be pitied not spurned. It is sad that they who thirty years ago may have been sexually eligible can no longer get sex and must have resort to these subterfuges. Don't be revolted by them. Be understanding, be compassionate. All that is required of the old porn-seeker is that he should do it in secret and with circumspection. And never, never let on. Better still, never get on to the muck.

Norah Smallwood telephones to say that no one at Chatto's likes my latest choice of a title for the Diaries, which is 'On the Fringe', a good one I think. So does A. Norah says such a title is depreciating myself. Rot.

Friday 14th to Sunday 16th June

We stay at Firle. It is a cosy grand house with a French flavour. No stately rooms in it, and the only one of pomposity is the drawing-room with screens at either end in a Burlingtonian manner. The

---

[*] Hugh Farmar, 1908–87; Clerk to the Drapers' Company.
[†] Elsie, 1894–1976, dau. of Rudyard Kipling; m. 1924 George Bambridge.

sense of continuity is pronounced. Liz Hofmannsthal and Freddie Ashton[*] staying. I like him immensely. We had long talks about Desmond Parsons whom he dearly loved, was deeply in love with. Holds Desmond in veneration; thinks he was the rarest of the rare. Told me that his (Freddie's) love was not returned in the same measure as he gave it.

On Sunday morning A. and I and the Gages, plus George Gage's younger son Nicky, went to Holy Communion. We followed the service out of red morocco-bound prayer books, dated 1798, and in the prayers for the royal family the King's name 'George' scratched out and 'William' inserted above. After tea with June and Jeremy we walked back to Firle below the downs in intense heat, but by ambling did not get over-hot. Interesting information.

Duncan Grant[†] and Lydia Lopokova[‡] lunched on Sunday. Duncan very white in the face and shaky on his legs. Had to be helped from the dining-room. I sat next to Lopokova. A little old lady with mauve, mottled face full of character. She laughed and joked throughout the meal. She ate a lot of beans. I asked if they did not give her indigestion. In her funny Russian accent she replied, 'They stop my stomach.' Then we talked about constipation. George Gage said it was a melancholy subject. She said on the contrary it was gay. He asked her if anyone had ever drunk champagne out of her shoe. She said No. I said, Then we ought to drink out of the Russian boot she is wearing today. She said she was not wearing boots. I said she was. In a flash she lifted her foot over the table, like a ballerina of 20 instead of 90. She told me Nijinsky was the greatest artist though not the greatest dancer she had partnered. Her memory of recent events is shaky. She cannot take it in that Diana is now married to Gage.

Monday, 17th June

Stayed last night at Parkside for the Garter Ceremony this afternoon in St George's Chapel. We were given front seats in the nave and

---

[*] Sir Frederick Ashton, 1906–88; Kt 1962; choreographer; director of the Royal Ballet until 1970.
[†] Duncan Grant, 1885–1978; Bloomsbury group artist.
[‡] Lady Keynes, 1892–1981; ballerina; m. 1925 John Maynard Keynes, 1st and last Baron Keynes (he d. 1946).

were within touching distance of the procession. The beauty of it! The Queen looking radiant because her horse won a French race yesterday. Prince of Wales smashing. Garrett [Drogheda] of course the most elegant of the Garter knights. Opposite me Shân Legge-Bourke, wearing a turban and pretty dress. Everyone else a frump except A., very smart in white dress with little black spots and black sequin hat. The men all in morning coats, except me in a blue suit and white shirt. Derry in a mustard suit, all wrong. What a moving ceremony! The prayers appropriate, being exhortations to withstand evil and have courage. Much needed in view of events, the House of Commons being bombed this morning by those bloody IRA.

After the ceremony we returned to Parkside for a cup of tea on the lawn. Sir Gerald Templer[*] told Garrett while they were robing that the revolution would undoubtedly come before twelve months elapsed. Everyone is abysmally depressed. Jeremy Fry[†] told me he was in despair. Elspeth Huxley likewise.

Joan and Garrett perpetually bickering over nothing, or rather things manufactured by Joan, who behaves in a fractious, spoilt child fashion.

Tuesday, 18th June

An example of the lunacy of the age. This afternoon the front-door bell rang. I saw through the window a small van. Cautiously I opened the door. There were two boys, one with idiotic Maoish moustache, the other Pakistani, quite decent looking. They began spouting words which I could not understand. I asked them to stop. They began again. I said, 'Who are you? What do you want?' One said, 'We have to make twenty calls and have two minutes' interesting conversation with each person we call on.' Then mumbled something about sending children to the sea for holidays. Immediately they resumed spouting nonsensical verbiage. I said, 'If you choose to speak like lunatics I can't prevent you. But I am too busy to listen,' and shut the door in their faces.

---

[*] Field Marshal Sir Gerald Templer, KG, 1898–1979; Gold Stick to The Queen from 1963.
[†] Jeremy Fry, b. 1924; inventor and entrepreneur.

Wednesday, 19th June

Motored to Plowden in Shopshire. The farouche Mr Plowden turns
out to be gentle, and rather shy. A nice man not well versed in his
family and possessions; not abounding in visual sense. Has erected a
most unsightly television aerial against the shafts containing the
historic priests' hides, and a misplaced tennis court in full view of
the house. In the drawing-room I observed a pouffe of multi-
coloured leather stitched to resemble a tortoise. I lunched with him
and wife in the kitchen; all most simple and sympathetic. He showed
me round, fumbling through papers, searching in vain for particulars
of paintings and relics. Is very devout and had read my letter to *The
Times*. I was embarrassed and said I ought perhaps not to discuss the
subject with him. But he was generous enough to say he read it with
understanding. In the chapel he said he would show me the vest-
ments kept in a drawer which pulled out from the altar because the
Blessed Sacrament was away. A secluded old place, of slight interest
apart from the Catholic continuity since pre-Reformation times, and
the ancient territorial association. Nevertheless, the house a romantic
conglomeration of black-and-white gables and high brick chimneys.

On the way home I called on Noel Saunders[*] at his house in
Winchcombe, by pre-arrangement. I wanted to talk about my will.
He said he guessed why I had come because the other day
at Alderley he had told A. and me we ought to discuss with one
another each clause of our respective wills and wishes. I said we
each knew and approved the gist of the other's will but were shy
of combing through every detail which seemed to us presump-
tuous and intrusive owing to our having no children. Explained
my quandary and asked how best to resolve it. He merely said
he thought he could deal with the situation when it arose, i.e.,
on my death. This was not much help. In fact, no man
but oneself can help one in most quandaries concerning the conscience.

Thursday, 20th June

Caroline Somerset motors me to Pythouse where I introduce her.
We lunch with the House Secretary and wife. Caroline charms them

---

[*] Solicitor, New & Saunders, Evesham, Worcestershire.

all, is jolly with everyone, and absolutely natural. She is adorable and I could easily fall head over heels in love with her if I allowed myself. She told them the story of her being turned out of the lift in a Moscow hotel last month because she had a cigarette in her hand; and another of a policeman ordering her out of a bus and making her pick up an apple core she had thrown from the window. Humiliated she smiled winningly to the Russian policeman who did not respond by a flicker of amusement or interest in this beautiful woman. To my surprise Eric Craven* is an inmate of Pythouse. He is 81. He told me he was lonely, miserable, hated the other residents, and the food. He cannot drive a car, has no interests left. Life is a burden to him. Oh dear! The House Secretary told me Eric Craven drank.

Caroline took me to the Trees' Shute House at Donhead St Mary. Walked round the garden. The Trees have devised a stream which falls over steps so contrived that the water makes a different note at each fall. But by the time you have moved from the first fall to the second you have forgotten what was the note of the previous fall. We looked at a portfolio of Cecil Beaton caricatures. They are the cruellest things you ever saw, infused with vitriol and devilish hate. We wondered if similar drawings of us existed, and agreed we would, given the opportunity, wish to see them – even at the risk of being deeply wounded.

Friday, 21st June

This morning I endeavoured to get a Bath number for three-quarters of an hour. Three times I rang the exchange, three times the supervisor. Finally, I was driven so mad with rage that I shouted abuse down the mouthpiece and smashed the telephone to smithereens on the hearthstone. Pieces of it flew across the room to the windows. Instead of feeling ashamed I felt greatly relieved. And if it costs me £50 to repair it was worth it. I only wish the telephonist who was so obstructive and impertinent to me had been the hearthstone. Caroline reminded me yesterday that wrath was one of the seven deadly sins.

---

* Widower of Ruth Ashwin, whose family, now gone, were squires of Bretforton Manor, Worcestershire from the sixteenth to the twentieth century.

Saturday, 22nd June

Miss Sybil Connolly* flew over from Dublin to see the house with view to purchase. It is too big for her. A. says she is a very well-known dress designer. Not elegant and wearing a huge white straw hat which she had to cling to, and long white gloves. She talked non-stop. With her was her brother, so-called, who is 19 to her ?50 – by the same mother, she explained. A mystifying boy, fair, dandily dressed, 6ft 4ins tall, with large feet and hands. He is still at Downside which from his description is a civilized school. Told me he belongs to the school Vintage Club which encourages the boys to learn about wine. He is visiting the chief French vineyards these coming holidays. Said that most of the classes at Downside contained only eight boys each; that he was reading history; that Mary Tudor and Mary Queen of Scots were both 'out' with the boys today, which amused me. But his views on politics fairly sound. Although Irish himself, with a faint accent, he says he loathes the Irish. 'I would kill the bastards,' etc., at which his sister expostulated. When he said that Cardinal Conway was anti-Christ she expostulated again. I could see how proud she was of him however. Behind his exquisite manners – bowing before shaking hands with us, calling me Sir – I noticed his lips curl at his sister's foolish prattle. A terrifying youth.

The Griggs dine, bringing Joanie Altrincham whose ceaseless grousing and interruption of any interesting conversation is sometimes irksome. I could see how irritated John was with her, though he too has such exquisite manners that it was barely perceptible. He is both intellectual and entertaining – an enchanting man.

Sunday, 23rd June

Garden open today; weather overcast and grey, the first such day in an uninterrupted fortnight's sunshine. One woman whom we invited inside the house said to me, 'It is an honour to touch your books on your working room shelves.' An honour! Great praise from all for A.'s garden, which indeed is at its very best. Much lamentation that we are leaving. I feel numbed by the prospect.

---

* Dublin couturier.

Wednesday, 26th June

Desmond [Shawe-Taylor]* staying two nights for the Bath Festival. Last night in the Assembly Rooms the heat was such, though out of doors rather cool, that I could not return to my seat after the interval. Instead talked in his office to the Manager Mr Barter, whom I have known for years. He was slightly drunk and I knew was having difficulty in speech without lisping. I remarked that I was present when Princess Marina opened the Rooms in 1938. So he showed me his visitors' book with her and the Longleat party's signatures. Caroline Thynne must have been very young, for her signature in childish writing was spelt Caraline. Mr Barter made me add my signature, which I did but told him was cheating, because it was 36 years posthumous.

Went to Hanbury today with Tony Mitchell and Peter Hood† to discuss how to arrange the drawing-room and long room when the present tenant, Mander, leaves. He was there. All Trust officials hate him, but today he was very agreeable and brought us tea and chocolate cake on a tray.

Handel in the Abbey this evening. Very lovely. James Burrows, counter tenor, and John Shirley-Quirk, baritone. Both powerful voices; the first seems a contradiction of nature and is notwithstanding rather fascinating to listen to. Makes me uneasy all the same.

Desmond is such a fusspot that I don't wonder Jack [Rathbone] is driven mad at times.

Thursday, 27th June

Sally Westminster's Barge Party put off on account of rain and dreadful cold – electric fire on full blast in the library this morning. A. said I must go to S.'s birthday dinner at Wickwar. Keith Steadman‡ disagreed with me when I was protesting that we lived in a puritanical age. I said no ritual, no panoply, no magnificence was allowable. He affirmed that there was more licence now than ever in the past. I argued that the cult of stark nakedness on the stage and in the films was another example of puritanism, for it entailed

---

* Desmond Shawe-Taylor, 1907–95; literary and musical critic for *New Statesman* and the *Sunday Times*.
† Peter Hood worked with John Fowler at the decorating firm of Colefax and Fowler.
‡ Horticulturist and Gloucestershire neighbour; d. 1995.

stripping humans of all mystery, splendid clothes and dignity. Diana Petre[*] told John Leslie and me she was a Socialist, and claimed that it was downright wrong to put one's country's before one's own interests. We disagreed. She said, 'Well, you two never have.' We said that in fighting during the war we had done so, and might well be prepared to do so again. I admitted I would be more prepared to fight my own countrymen, if they were Marxists, than foreigners who weren't.

Friday, 28th June

In reading an excellent review by S. Spender on E. Muir's life, just out, I realise how little I think things out. How rarely I formulate an opinion.

How stupid I can be, too. When last night John Leslie came up to me and introduced himself, we talked of Rome where he lives. I said I had many old friends there once, but now they were all dead. I said, 'Did you know John Leslie?' He looked startled, and replied, 'I suppose you mean old John Leslie[†] who lived in the Palazzo Santa Maria Campitelli? He was a cousin of mine.' Only then I realized that he was John Leslie[‡] too. He is quite bald, precise, pedantic, courteous, square, but none the less intelligent. Wears a sapphire tie pin.

Sunday, 30th June

Staying this weekend with Loelia [Lindsay] at Send. She told me she had sold most of her Westminster jewellery and deposited the proceeds in a Swiss bank 'in case', as she put it. How many wise people have not taken similar precautions?

In the morning I slipped off to Holy C. in Send church without anyone seeing. When the service was over I tried to escape the church before the vicar got to the porch. But no. He was there in his surplice, asking me if I had come to live in the parish. Poor things, they long for new lambs to their flock.

The Lindsays took us to dine with the Waddingtons in a gruesome stockbroker's house in Sunningdale. Mrs W. looked very like

---

[*] (Mrs) Diana Petre; novelist; sister of Sally, Duchess of Westminster.
[†] Late of Little Westwood Manor, Wiltshire.
[‡] Sir John Leslie, 4th Bt, b. 1916; s. of (Sir John) Shane Leslie, author and biographer.

Clementine Beit, who was indeed staying. I nearly embraced her when we met, thinking she was Clementine. The real C. looked sad since their horrid experience [see page 174] and seemed distraught and nervous. Alfred [Beit] on the other hand looked incredibly young and unaffected.

Martin Lindsay is too stupid to be believed. He has a great desire to write and showed us a very boring article he has done on needle-work. Has in mind another, on what he calls equestrian 'statutes' in London, repeating the 'statutes' several times. He is frankly off the beam, and L. must be aware of this. Nevertheless she is a little on the defensive about him, and told us she never regretted marrying him, in spite of several friends' attempts at dissuasion. I love Loelia. In the car on the way back from the Sunningdale dinner she and I in the rear seat laughed so immoderately over a *bêtise* of Martin's that he became angry and asked if L. was drunk.

Monday, 1st July

On my way to Snowshill [Manor] this morning I stopped the car just before the village to watch the wind's effect upon a field of unripe barley. Waves drove across it in all directions but one, namely the west, whence the wind came. Then I turned and looked behind me. The colour of the barley was paler far, almost buff instead of grass green. In front the waves were like hares frisking at play, chasing one another, retreating, changing course and double tracking. I was fascinated and could have watched for hours.

A. had a brainwave in the bath yesterday. 'Diaries of Another Self, 1942–3' she suggested. We sent off a postcard for Norah to refute.

Tuesday, 2nd July

Got two tickets for the Bolshoi by some miracle. I thought the cast marvellous. Faultless discipline. Décor old-fashioned and shoddy; ditto costumes. Remarked how strangely sexless Russian ballet is compared with the English; that even Rudy, though Russian by birth, now anglicized, exudes sex. I thought this sexlessness to be the point of classical ballet. The animal in Nureyev detracts from the cold perfection of his technique.

Wednesday, 3rd July

June and Jeremy Hutchinson gave a musical party in their divine house in Abercorn Place, or to be precise a reception and supper there, but the concert was in Christopher's rooms close by. Christopher Osborn played Schubert, correctly without intense feeling; then Menuhin,* accompanied by his son Jeremy, played Beethoven. The son's playing full of feeling. This son Jeremy is attractive and gifted; Menuhin's other son is plain and has no apparent gifts. During the performance the latter had to leave the room ostensibly overcome by the heat (it was cold), and during supper spoke to no one. Poor boy, I felt sorry for him and understood the predicament, which no one else did.

I was placed next to Rhoda Birley and Diana Westmorland at the end of a long narrow table for thirty. Mr Heath sat exactly opposite me. I was unable to have one word with him, the noise was terrific, but I watched him like a lynx. When he meets you, greets you, he does it with cumbersome affability; that is the end of the matter. June introduced me. He shook my hand warmly (his is podgy), smiled and said, 'Of course, yes.' He has no social graces whatever. For this I like him. He is not faintly interested in women, and probably not in men either. He talked across June with Yehudi about musical scholarships. Has no small talk, and when at the end of supper June left and made Christopher's little Burmese friend sit next to Heath he did not address a single word to her, and went on talking with Yehudi. The poor child could not bear the honour beyond five minutes and discreetly left. Mr Heath seemed not to notice her departure. June then came up to me, gave me a great shove in the back and said, 'Now's your chance. Ask the leader all the questions you want to put to him.' And to Heath, 'Jim is a great supporter. He is madly right wing, and really supports Enoch', at which Heath gave a wry smile and turned away. Left his place in fact. No wonder, perhaps.

Diana Menuhin wore a thin bandeau round her forehead with one end dangling below her shoulder, rather becoming. She has reached a new age. She is no longer faded youth, but flowering old age, and

---

* Sir Yehudi Menuhin, OM, b. 1916; Life Peer 1993; violinist and conductor; m. 1st, 1938, Nola R. Nicholas of Australia; 2nd, 1947, Diana Gould, by whom two sons, Gerard and Jeremy.

again beautiful. On embracing me she said, 'Oh, you smell so good, I must kiss you on the other side.' 'It's not me, but Floris,' I said.

Monday, 8th July

A. was in London today. The evening was so still and beautiful that as I wandered round the garden, inhaling the smell of rose petals in the golden light, I wept at the prospect of parting with this place. I could not bring myself to look at the advert. in the *Sunday Times* yesterday. I felt positively sick with sadness. Then A. returned and was so full of orders, enquiries, bustle and fidgets that I longed to get away from her, and be alone with my melancholy.

With my bedroom window open at the bottom last night I was astonished to hear the distant noise coming from Kingswood way of what sounded like the whirring of factory machinery. Leant over the sill at one o'clock before turning out the light, listened to the distant hum and could not make out where it came from.

Tuesday, 9th July

At the MHA committee meeting this morning the report of the Finance Committee was considered. That committee means to increase the charges yet again by 20 per cent to meet rising costs. I warned that this will result in most of our residents, who are living on fixed incomes, leaving, and their places being taken, if we are lucky, by a different lot of richer folk.

Nigel Nicolson walked back to Brooks's with me and lunched. He has only received four really rude letters from strangers about his *Portrait of a Marriage*. The book has sold 100,000 copies in the USA already. He has received dozens of letters, mostly from American lonely hearts, asking for his guidance as though he were a marriage advisory bureau. He is now editing all Virginia Woolf's letters which will take six volumes. He is to spend two months in the year on each volume. He works with a fine discipline, and one American woman scholar to help him. V.W. never dated any letters; always headed them Thursday or Monday, without giving the month or year. He explained some of the difficulties he encounters. For example, V.W. wrote an exemplary letter declining the offer of marriage from a friend called Sydney Waterlow. It was phrased with impeccable tact, kindness, understanding and firmness. It was lent Nigel by Waterlow's son. The same day V.W. wrote to Lytton

Strachey: 'Sydney Waterlow has just left. I detest him. He entered the room bringing with him a smell of stale semen.' Now how can Nigel quote this one? She makes several unkind references to Raymond [Mortimer], saying he is a hopeless character, like a kitten playing eternally with a skein of wool.

I told Nigel about my diaries and he gave me some advice. Don't put in the day of the week and do put in square brackets the surname of a person whom you refer to a second time by his christian name. Don't print anything unkind about a living person, and beware of wounding relations, etc.

Nigel in talking about his *Portrait* said, 'Perhaps I made a mistake in allowing the *Sunday Times* to serialize it.' I said, 'Yes, I think you did.'

Before dinner went to Feeble [Elizabeth Cavendish]'s house where we were joined by John Betj. He autographed the book of his collected poetry which Gilbert Wheat the headmaster here [Rosehill School, Alderley] begged me to ask him to do for the school's prize-giving. I said to John, 'Just add under your name, *Poet Laureate*. This will give immense pleasure.' He did so. Then leant back and murmured, 'What a fraud I feel,' and a look of intense anguish passed across his eyes. He is much better than when I last saw him, has a good fresh colour. Feeble says he no longer drinks spirits, and only wine – no port – after six.

Dined with E. Winn in her charming flat on the top of number 14 Onslow Gardens. I think my bedroom in 1927 was a small part of her drawing-room. It was strange to lean out of the window and look at the unaltered view of the Square gardens across the road with the same trees in bloom after 48 years.

James [Pope-Hennessy]'s murder case is reported in today's *Times*. The disclosures are horrifying. He was choked to death by a hair-net thrust down his poor throat. James, who in his way was highly fastidious and extremely nervous; James, young and attractive and fascinating, referred to by thugs as 'the old bloke'. Nigel [Nicolson], who asked to see the account in *The Times*, turned away with tears in his eyes. 'Awful, just awful,' he said.

Thursday, 11th July

Debo D. who stayed last night said that the two saddest events in her life were the selling of Swinbrook by her father when she was fifteen, and the elopement of [her sister] Decca with her first Communist husband. Strange, when one reflects that she lost one or two babies shortly after birth, lost Nancy, her mother, brother Tom and others.

Jeremy Fry who dined said that leaving Widcombe was ghastly, but the relief of being free from the burden of the house was now immense. Thought in a year's time he might start minding again dreadfully. He said he could never let a house of his because it would be a defilement. He invests his houses with human attributes. I like this. He says his business is all but ruined by the 'situation', and all the money he got for Widcombe has gone to pay the bank for his business deficits. A year ago his business was flourishing.

Sunday, 14th July

Talk with Xan Fielding before dinner at the Somersets'. He is a very intelligent, forceful man. Somewhat retiring and does not speak until he has things to impart. Then speaks with authority and vigour. He is small, well-knit, heroic and handsome. His eyes evince Red Indian ancestry. He speaks four languages as well as his own. He is courageous and did brave things in the war. He told me that M.L. had been an old friend, but was no longer one. He did him, Xan, a grave injury, tricked him over some financial deal. Nothing amazed him more than M.L. turning out a good parent – he did not say husband. He said he was a delinquent, not a rebel, which I had suggested.

Alfred and Clementine Beit stayed this weekend. She told me about their recent ordeal. The two of them were listening to the gramophone after dinner at Russborough. Suddenly the door burst open and three men, without masks but with revolvers, entered. They immediately pinioned the Beits and tied their arms behind their backs, and their feet to their arms very tight so that it hurt. Then made them lie face downwards on the floor. One man stayed with them as a guard with his revolver pointed at their heads. The other two fetched the staff of six, brought them into the same room as the Beits and tied them, not so tightly, and laid them on the floor. It was then that Alfred turned up his head and was hit so that he bled profusely. Clem thought he was injured worse than he actually was. When Clem stretched out a hand to hold that of the cook to comfort her she was sternly ordered to take it away. Abuse was shouted at them. Clem was carried off by one man, held in front of him, half shoved, half carried – very painful. As she passed down a passage she saw the back of a woman in a blue and white, neat tailored suit, with a head of black hair. The man piloted Clementine down some worn stone steps to the basement, saying, 'This is where you belong, you capitalist pig.' Clem warned him that the steps were uneven, and he might fall with her. He cursed her and told her to shut up. He threw her, bound, face down on a stone floor and left her. She waited seemingly for ages, then heard movements upstairs and voices. Didn't know whether it was the gang or the household, so remained quiet. Finally James the footman discovered her, and on releasing her burst into tears and embraced her. The others thought she had been abducted. The little housemaid had managed to untie her bonds and release the others upstairs. Alfred in a great state, thinking Clem had been taken away, was at the telephone when Clem walked into the room. His reaction was to say to her, 'Where the hell have you been?'

After the stolen pictures had been recovered and Rose Dugdale caught the Russborough household were taken one by one to the farmhouse to identify things. Immediately Clementine recognized the blue and white suit and the black wig worn by the woman in the passage. She undoubtedly was Dugdale. Dugdale's mother was my harmless friend Carol (erstwhile Timmins).

Friday, 19th July

I hate the people who come to look over this house. I regard them as desecrators of the house and garden; it is an infringement of my inmost citadel. One lot complained that the house was no larger than their own in Solihull. I was inclined to retort, 'Then why not remain in Solihull?' Another that the drive was not long enough. Incredible. I felt like answering, 'But you can easily extend the existing drive by making it twist and twirl round the paddock for as long as you want it, and make it come out of the same gate on the road.'

I feel worried and sorry for Dick and Elaine[*] [L.-M.] in Cyprus with the fall of Makarios and the usurpation by Sampson, who is just a bandit without conscience or scruple. Dick in his last letter wrote

---

[*] Richard Crompton, 1910–84, and his wife Elaine (née Brigstocke); J.L.-M.'s brother and sister-in-law.

that they would be all right so long as Makarios remained. It would be awful for them if they were driven from the island and obliged to leave their possessions behind.

We went on Wednesday night to the Gala performance at Covent Garden to celebrate Garrett [Drogheda]'s retirement from the chairmanship after seventeen years. Cleverly (I thought) I parked my car in a side street quite close to the opera house. The performance went on till midnight. It consisted of snippets from opera and ballet, which are always tiresome. Yet I was very impressed by the dancers. Thought Anthony Dowell[*] a most beautiful creature. His dancing the perfection of discipline. His compact drawing-board figure like an ephebe's on a Greek amphora. Antoinette Sibley[†] the quintessence of delicacy and desirability. A perfect pair. Then Nureyev and Margot Fonteyn danced together. Nureyev is already beefy and has quite lost the gloss of youth. Yet I have seldom seen a head carried more proudly. Fonteyn is far past dancing, at 54. Yet what poise and confidence in her movements, and how winning her manner. At the end of the performance we went to a champagne party in the crush bar. Agony. I could not hear a word. Could not bear to go on to the buffet supper on the stage. Left A. with the Berkeleys and escaped to my car. Got it out of its parking place and started off, but was stuck in a jam with Garden lorries in front of and behind me. The hold-up was caused by the police stopping all traffic until the Queen was to leave the opera house. I had one and a half hours' wait. Could neither advance nor leave the car to return to the supper party. Served me right, I suppose. I talked to the porters and lorry drivers. They were furious with the poor Queen. 'It is always the same whenever *she* comes here. Why can't *she* stay away?' etc. So I said, 'I don't suppose she wanted to come any more than you would. She has come out of duty, because the performance has been organized for charity. And what's more she has been working all today.' I knew this, because Lennox in the interval told me he received his accolade this morning with all the other honour winners. 'Anyway' – I said – 'if you had a President, just the same thing would happen.' 'All right, squire,' they said. I was not sure how derogatory this term was meant to be. Before the queue could move, one of the men brought

---

[*] Anthony Dowell, b. 1943; Senior Principal Dancer at the Royal Ballet from 1967; director from 1986.

[†] Antoinette Sibley, b. 1939; Prima Ballerina at the Royal Ballet.

me a tin mug of disgusting tea with, 'Here you are, chum.' They really are nice; but so self-motivated.

Arriving before the opera I behaved unbecomingly. A man in a large car had the evident intention of backing into an empty space by the pavement. But I nipped in frontwards, ahead of him. He reversed into my car. I was furious. He was furious. A slanging match ensued. Fucks and buggers flew around. A man on the pavement watched and gaped with interest and enjoyment. I refused to give way, locked up my car and stalked off. Not before the man stood up to me, face to face, with a most menacing look as though he meant to strike me. I was so enraged that if he had I would have hit him back. Within four minutes I felt ashamed.

When the performance was over a large sheet descended upon the stage outlining and magnifying the familiar slender figure of Garrett. He was introduced by Jennie Lee[*] in gold spangles who made a long and tedious speech in what sounded like Esperanto, and was her Welsh accent [in fact, she was Scottish]. Then Garrett spoke. He was not the least sentimental. He was the perfect paradigm of patrician ease. He was willowy, smiling, devil-may-care, casual; yet all the time absolutely controlled in what he said and his manner of delivery. Every word was audible, and to the point. He was his usual mischievous self; quite cheeky to the Queen, telling her that now she had found the way he hoped she might make a habit of patronizing the opera, yet respectful at the same time. He even hiccuped into the loud speaker slung round his neck, apologizing for the surprisingly amplified sound. Now, no non-gent would ever ride supremely over that sort of incident.

Saturday, 20th July

Motored Geoffrey Gilmour, who stayed last night, to lunch with Woman at Caudle Green. English farmhouse luncheon specially prepared by Woman for her Parisian guest, of roast chicken and summer pudding. She has no help whatever, does housework and gardening, and looks after her heifers. Finds it too much and means to let the house to her godson and build herself a bungalow for

---

[*] Lady Lee of Asheridge: Life Peer, 1970; Jennie Lee (Janet Bevan), 1904–88; Labour MP 1929–31, 1945–70; m. 1934 Rt Hon. Aneurin Bevan, PC, MP (he d. 1960).

£30,000. Then I motored Geoffrey to Ronnie Greville's[*] new house, Cubberley, near Ross-on-Wye, by Claud Phillimore[†] in 1972. It must be the last country house to be built. Derivative but charming. Walls white-harled over. Inside a long passage from end to end, rather like a gallery. One huge saloon with high coved ceiling. Cork walls, the cork laid in thin strips like wallpaper, and dyed mauve and pink, very pretty. Dining-room walls of orange felt; sounds hideous, and is bold and arresting. Lovely furniture. Altogether a most comfortable and desirable house. At the far end of the gallery is a colonnade or orangery, not used as such but as a sun room. The stairwell has a domed ceiling from which is suspended a huge chandelier, made to Ronnie's design. He, who used to be extremely handsome, is now 62, suffering from heart failure. His face a wreck of its former self. Hair thin and dyed ginger. Eyes tiny and rather sinister. Only his old, wicked smile recalls the Ronnie I remember. And of course his camp manner and gestures.

Sunday, 21st July

In church this morning we were a congregation of five, counting the rector. Gilbert Wheat, the headmaster, came in with his spaniel, Bruin, as usual. Bruin sits beside him in his pew, but when Gilbert prays devoutly becomes restless and wanders up to me. I stroke him while I try to pray, hoping he will not bark or howl. The rector takes this attendance as a matter of course, and does not the least object. In fact I am surprised he does not count Bruin as another soul, for he is so keen on totting up the number of communicants and putting them down on the register.

Monday, 22nd July

Whizzed up the motorway to Little Moreton Hall where I met Merlin Waterson and Elizabeth Beazley.[‡] Memories of this house go back to the ancient days when Papa *en route* for Scotland in the autumn used to stop and show us children round the half-timbered

---

[*] Ronald, 4th Baron Greville, 1912–87.

[†] The Hon. Claud Phillimore, 1911–94; succeeded his nephew as 4th Baron Phillimore, 1990; architect of country houses.

[‡] Elizabeth Beazley, architect; member of NT Executive Committee and architectural panel.

macro-dolls' house which he dearly loved. We agreed today that the black-and-white, or rather the black tar, was probably wrong, for it is not shown on any prints or water-colours earlier than about 1850.

Tuesday, 23rd July

Anthony Phillips,[*] very nice young man from the silver department of Christie's, called at midday to look through my silver. Did not think much of any pieces. Lunched with me, A. having gone to London. Told me he picked up an extremely rare engraved medal which had been given to the chief of a Red Indian tribe by English colonizers in the seventeenth century, in the Portobello Road.

Thursday, 25th July

Eardley who came last night motored with me to Arlington Court for the day, and a lovely day too, to see Woodrow and Newman[†] for the last time. They are retiring this autumn after twenty-five years. They have worked wonders here. Thousands of visitors pour through the place, which has little worth seeing. The two friends are, like all the retiring, beginning to criticize their successors, who won't understand the point of the odd assortment of Miss Chichester's things, and will not establish the close links with the house which they have done. Indeed they are probably right. Newman is a dear man, so kind and almost affectionate towards us. What a wonderful valet he would make. Mrs Woodrow now dead, sadly – gangrenous leg – and lamented by both.

Friday, 26th July

Lunched with Tamara Talbot Rice[‡] at Coln Rogers. House full of character, on the swift Coln stream, part low, part high, tower-like, stuffed with good things, a jumble, dusty, over-crowded. The John Pilchers[§] staying. Lady Pilcher the most enormous woman I have ever seen, face like the sun, a radiant yet grey sun. He a joker. Both

---

[*] Head of Silver Department at Christie's.
[†] Curators at Arlington Court, Devon (NT).
[‡] Russian-born wife of David Talbot Rice, historian of Byzantine art; she d. 1995.
[§] Sir John Pilcher, GCMG, 1912–90; ambassador; m. 1942 Delia M. Taylor.

very intelligent. Mrs Talbot Rice now an old woman, with Parkinson's disease. Oxford-educated. She told me that her husband David
Talbot Rice's uncle lived at Shipton Court. He had a truculent and
aggressive butler. One day the butler got drunk and attacked
the uncle, who in defending himself pushed the butler over
the banisters and killed him. A footman witnessed the scene and
blackmailed the uncle for the rest of his life. The uncle was fleeced
of all his money and a curse fell on the house. Pevsner's guide says
that the house was entirely gutted and redecorated drastically in
1903.

On Sunday evening while looking at the television I caught a
flash of Dick [L.-M.] eating in the restaurant of the Dome Hotel in
Kyrenia. Watched again at ten. Again saw him for a fleeting second.
I worry because the Cyprus news is worse, the Turks landing more
and more invading troops.

Thursday, 1st August

My sense of smell, like my memory, is deteriorating. The Michael
Hornbys bring us a huge incense plant. Everyone remarks on the
strong scent the moment it enters the hall. I can barely smell it; and
it used to be the most evocative and nostalgic of scents, recalling my
grandmother's drawing-room at Ribbesford. As for memory, today
A. went to Bath, making me promise I would be in at 4.30 when the
Filipina was to telephone to announce what time she was to be met
in Tetbury. At three I went to look at churches in Slimbridge and
Fretherne, and totally forgot. Result, great inconvenience and two
abortive visits to Tetbury to meet buses.

Yesterday while showing a man round the house and garden, he
noticed what looked like a loose sack suspended from a branch of
the beech tree in the paddock. It was a swarm of bees which had
attached itself to the branch. The cows in the paddock could easily
have bumped into it. It swung in the wind. We told the new farmers
in the farmhouse who keep bees. They came with a cardboard box.
Were dressed with nets over hats and gloves over jacket sleeves.
They cut the branch with secateurs, and having dropped the
attached swarm into the box and covered it with a cloth, walked
off with it. The bees after an interval woke up to the outrage
committed upon them and buzzed furiously. The farmer's wife said
that when angry bees give out a smell, not exactly of honey, but a

sweet smell. All creatures give out a smell when aroused, it seems; certainly humans do.

Friday, 2nd August

Picked up Audrey at Windrush. We motored to see Mrs Haines. Found her in a great state about Dick and Elaine. Overjoyed to see us, she insisted on giving us tea which we didn't want. When we told her we had received a message this morning through the Foreign Office that they were all right, she said the news gave her more. pleasure than a thousand pounds would have done. Yet she insisted on telling us how the worry had kept *her* awake at nights, how *she* had cried for twenty-four hours non-stop, how we could have no idea what torment and worry *she* had undergone, how ill it had made *her*; not once did she express real concern for Dick and Elaine. Then became very upset when we told her that Simon and Lois had separated. Kept on saying how awful it was for the two children. Whereas in fact they are too young to understand or suffer.

Went back to Audrey's Mill House for supper. I thought how reflective of Audrey's personality this place was. Picturesque, isolated, overgrown garden, tumble-down house, the water rushing through the mill race, the huge ash tree, the moorhens, the swallows high in the sky. She is a child of nature, out of touch with the world, child-*like*. Told us that her two King Charles spaniels and two cats slept on her bed, and often the 17-year-old cat *in* her bed. If one admires something she has she wants to give it to one. Her bedroom was spartan, and rather pitiable.

Saturday, 3rd August

The Filipina on being paid her wages this morning revealed that in spite of her promise to us a month ago to stay until we moved in the autumn, she was leaving in ten days' time, when her holiday was due. We told her this was dishonest. All she did was to snigger. Then I paid Margery and got nothing but growls and complaints from him.

I now long to get away from them all. I loathe and detest them. All they want is less work and more money. They have no decent feelings, no regard for truth. They are spoilt and rotten. I hope unemployment leaps to astronomical proportions, and that they are humiliated and come begging cap in hand for work. I shall be prepared to undergo every personal deprivation for the satisfaction of seeing them reduced to starvation. And now I feel better.

Sunday, 4th August

At Pusey in pouring rain and bitter cold we were made to walk after luncheon slowly round the hideous garden. Michael Hornby, such a learned man, knows the Latin names of every plant and shrub, pat. Both Hornbys work like galley slaves. To what purpose? Pusey would be far prettier if left the landscaped park that it was meant to be. A large flower garden round this eighteenth-century house is not what is needed. Strange how ever since Eny's death Nicole Hornby has been the very essence of sweetness and affection. She used to terrify me. Now she embraces us both and loves us because Eny was fond of us. We love her back for this.

Tuesday, 6th August

I had to be in London for N.T. meetings, and A. sweetly laid on a play and dinner afterwards for me, and the two Berkeleys. At vast trouble she got tickets for *The Life Class*, which has received rave reviews. At the end of the first act we all so disliked and were so bored by this tedious, vulgar, pointless play, in which a lot of young students say to each other 'Piss off!' and 'Fuck you!' that we walked out. Dined expensively, and not well, at an Italian bistro nearby. Only bright light of the evening was our waiter, an engaging Spanish boy who spoke very little English. In extolling the trout we ordered, he exclaimed, 'Very fresh, like me.'

Wednesday, 7th August

The area agent for the Severn Region explained to the Properties Committee that the only tenants forthcoming for Brockhampton Park were The Greeting Cards Manufacturers, for use as a staff rest home.

Friday, 9th August

Sally W. took us to Tortworth to see the house which is now the officers' quarters of Ley Hill Prison. House an interesting monster by Teulon. Carved on the gatehouse under which visitors pass was the word 'Welcome'. This had to be erased. Staircase something terrific with high hall like Wollaton, no doubt the inspiration in this case as so often with the Victorians. The library has two fantastic fireplaces of prickly carved finials and pinnacles and much polished brasswork, and tiles. The gardener to whom I talked said that 95 per cent of the inmates of this prison 'go straight' after release. I was amazed. He said you must treat the prisoners like ordinary human beings, which is what is done here.

Saturday, 10th August

Last night we dined with Ian [McCallum]* at the American Museum. He had staying Michael York and wife.† A charming pair and apparently our greatest film stars. I saw him impersonating Christopher Isherwood in a recent film. A clear complexion, so youthful that there is no difference between skin of the face and of the neck. Golden hair not very long and thin-spun, with slight sideburns. Curious nose, slightly beak-like and intriguing, fine wide eyes and large, provocative month. Shop-window figure, and well-dressed. An exquisite. Quiet, extraordinarily modest and unspoilt. Takes an intelligent interest in things of the mind. Does not drink alcohol. Smiles sweetly and seems surprised when addressed. Wife, Pat, a little gushing, much older with son of 22 she said. Includes husband in conversation in a possessive manner. He defers to her sweetly, but may be irritated by her anxiety. Says he may be obliged to become an expatriate because although only in England three months of each year, nevertheless is taxed so high that he cannot make money. They were brought over to Alderley this afternoon, and we were enchanted with both.

Sunday, 11th August

This morning at ten to eight I climbed the church tower to wind the clock. I have to walk up the narrow and steep twisting stairs sideways like a crab. The key to the door of the belfry is kept on a torn piece of wire netting in the lowest slit window of the turret. Coming downstairs I dropped it and spent hours after Communion searching for it. A. said that her attention so wandered at service that

---

* Ian McCallum, 1919–87; Curator of the American Museum, Claverton, near Bath.
† Michael York-Johnson, b. 1942; actor; m. 1968 Patricia McCallum, actress.

she found herself reciting the Blessing out loud, suddenly realized what she was doing and stopped. Then before breakfast I motored to Wotton to buy the Sunday papers for the village, the paper shop having ceased to deliver. After breakfast I delivered them to the village and had to stop and gossip with everyone at his or her door. All very grateful and neighbourly.

Monday, 12th August

Christabel Aberconway has died. She often dined with me when I was a bachelor in Thurloe Square. She told me she wanted inscribed on her tombstone 'Mount, mount, my soul!' from *Richard III*, and nothing else. She was beautiful, with a roundish face, and a porce-lain-like complexion in spite of heavy drinking. She was a devoted friend of Osbert Sitwell, very well read, and relished bawdy stories. Indeed she relished anatomical detail, which was unattractive. I introduced Bridget Parsons to her, and asked Bridget afterward how she liked her. She replied that were Christabel one iota less affected she would have been insufferable. Her affectation and batting of the eyelids were more exaggerated than anything I have encountered in any English woman, which is saying a good deal. Millionairess that she was, she liked to travel in buses. She was overheard by a friend of mine late at night on a number 14 talking to the conductor. She was rather drunk. 'Dear Mr Conductor, do you really believe there will be no peeresses in heaven?' I never knew her intimately, and did not enjoy her huge cocktail parties given every July in that beautiful Palladian house in North Audley Street.

Wednesday, 14th August

Dick's birthday, and I wonder so much how he is faring in Cyprus. The situation is worse again; fighting resumed. And no news of him.

I am reading Jan Morris's *Conundrum*, decently told tale of her change of sex. I now remember as a child desperately wishing that I were a girl, and feeling desperately ashamed of my wish. But on reaching adolescence the wish totally vanished, and I have never ceased being glad I am a man. But during childhood I certainly was passive. Ever since 15 or 16, I should say, I have on the contrary been active. The girl-wish stage may have been caused by funk, for I feared the first war might last so long I would have to be in the army, and the trenches.

We went to London for the day, to lunch with Norah Smallwood and Ian Parsons of Chatto's, and talk about the diaries. Both approved my suggested title of *Ancestral Voices*. David Higham disapproves, preferring *Diaries of Another Self*, which was A.'s choice. The heat in the restaurant was overpowering. I took off my jacket and sat in a thin silk shirt, sweating. Luckily an electric fan was turned on to me and I ceased dripping so long as it was kept on. Could eat little and drink nothing but iced water. Sat with Ian Parsons in his office after, he showing me what he thought should be excised. A charming, civilized, persuasive man, but timorous.

Thursday, 15th August

The Acloques[*] have bought this house for £102,500. This is the figure agreed upon after gentlemanly bargaining through the intermediary of agents. I am no longer heart-broken, but relieved. A. so relieved that she is able to sleep again. I am sure we are right. Had we waited three months longer we might not have sold at all, and been landed with Lansdown Crescent in addition. As things are, we shall not be certain that the deal is clinched until contracts are exchanged, documents signed and money handed over. The financial situation is so dicey that events might occur within the next few weeks, a complete national collapse, and the purchasers not able to pay. Then where would we be? We begin to be excited about our new dwelling. If only A.'s room were not underground. Her bedroom will be charming, I think, although facing north. But what will she do in Bath with a pocket-hand-kerchief of a garden?

On Saturday, a lovely early autumn golden day, Geoffrey Houghton-Brown and his sister came to tea. We sat in the Georgian summer-house in the corner of the garden, with our tray on the antique capital, sheltered from the wind, with nothing unsightly in view, and the thick trees screening the grey rough old back of the house and the lawn lusciously green for the month. It was an idyllic scene. Geoffrey looking better after his gallstone operation, yet still grey and drawn. A dear fellow.

---

[*] Guy Acloque, m. 1971 Camilla, dau. of 9th Baron Howard de Walden.

Monday, 19th August

A. left this afternoon to stay with Clarissa [Luke] in France for ten days. I started off on an East Anglian tour.

Drove in my Morris to the Sitwells at Weston for one night. Georgia is much older, almost bent at the shoulders. And very chesty. Sachie also very chesty. Both rattle and cough, the result of chain-smoking, I suppose. A delicious visit alone with them, Georgia permitting – she could hardly prevent – general conversation, thank goodness. Weston is not a distinguished national monument; but it is a real, living English country house, bubbling with family history, still in the making; full of ancient dresses and treasures, many added by Sachie, and portraits of him – new one by Graham Sutherland excellent but for the straight line of the mouth. Georgia says, 'Oh, but he is severe like that in the home. You only see him laughing, screwing up his eyes and his Plantaganet little mouth turning up.' It may be true; I wish someone would paint him laughing. Sachie showed me the attics in which he is trying to file his enormous correspondence. He buys hat-boxes from Herbert Johnson's shop for the purpose.

Tuesday, 20th August

A long day motoring in sparkling sun and heat, stifling. Passed by Stoke Bruerne and thought I would have a look at the pavilions, since I was partly responsible for Robin Chancellor* buying and saving them years ago. They were not open but a housekeeper came out of the back door, to whom I made myself known. She told me to come into the garden and talk to Lady Chancellor, Christopher's mother. The old lady, 93, reclining on cushioned chairs, holding a sunshade, on the terrace. Very beautiful and fragile like Dresden porcelain, and sweet. Told me to walk round the garden, then talk to her again. Spoke of Christopher with amused admiration. Then to Kedington church, in south Suffolk, at Sachie's instigation, miles out of my way. Well worth the detour, for this is the church of the Barnardiston family, Sachie's ancestors through whom he inherited Weston. I particularly liked the wig pole and hour-glass beside the pulpit, and Sir Nathaniel Barnardiston and his lady, one hand over

---

* Robert Duff Chancellor, b. 1921, of Stoke Bruerne Park, Northamptonshire.

the other's, resting upon a skull. The cobbled porch; the piers painted in the seventeenth century as though fluted columns. A church full of timelessness. And before that Gayhurst church, almost the best Georgian church I have seen – the plaster frieze over giant pilasters displays a bishop's mitre and alternate open bibles, one dog-eared, another creased, each different, a charming craftsman's conceit.

At Euston [Hall, Suffolk] by seven. Fortune [Grafton] alone, with whom I dined. Hugh came back from grouse shooting on Chatsworth moors at 9.30, clad in the warmest plus-four suit, looking enormous and hot.

Wednesday, 21st August

All day at Euston. Hugh drove me to Elveden Hall nearby. I had always wished to see the fantastic inside. It's like the Taj Mahal outside-in. Pevsner calls it an oriental extravaganza unparalleled in England. It must be unique for expensive marbles, fussiness and good craftsmanship. The old caretaker in showing us round said he had been fifty years on the staff. Came as hall boy. When house-parties staying, there used to be a hundred indoor servants. Eight in the Steward's Room. 'They were dreadful. No one would put up with them today,' he said. But people are only too glad to put up with anyone today. We walked to the Euston racing stables which the Graftons are transforming into a possible retreat for themselves. They call it Healey Hall in deference to the Chancellor of the Exchequer. Motored round the estate to watch the harvesting. Bumper crops. The great combines like dinosaurs, devouring the corn as they lurch across the fields. Hugh now intensely interested in his farming. Entered the Kent Temple, which is disappointing after Worcester Lodge. What has been done to it in the past lacks discernment.

Priscilla Napier to dinner. No time absolutely to click. Loud laughter. Hugh made me read her *Sheet Anchor*, an eulogium of her deceased husband in Miltonic verse, a trifle archaic I fear, though very moving.

Thursday, 22nd August

Motored to lunch with Rosamond [Lehmann] at Yoxford. Her cottage in the village street incongruously tiny. It had been an antique shop. It reminded me of the shop in *Alice through the Looking-Glass*, and Ros of the old woman who turned into a sheep. She was dressed from neck to ankle in flowered chiffon and walked heavily leaning on my arm down the village street, a strange spectacle in such rural surroundings. When I said A. and I might be visiting Australia with a view to emigrating, she was shocked that I could contemplate leaving my friends. 'Do you really mean you could leave me, for instance, without a qualm?' rather rattily. Airily I said, 'I suppose so – now.'

Then tea with Baron Ash[*] at Wingfield Castle. Hadn't seen him for at least twenty-five years. Much the same, although just celebrated his 85th birthday with Miss Eden his retired housekeeper who came over for the occasion and cooked him luncheon. He has one daily woman three days a week; and she cannot cook. Baron lives on tinned food and scraps. At nights he pulls up the drawbridge and says intruders can only enter by swimming the moat, and they would not swim back with much loot. He is as pernickety and absurd and as pleased with life, or rather *his* rather vacuous life, as ever. We parted great friends.

Reached Holt Rectory in time for dinner. Stayed three nights with Billa. Roy Harrod[†] is now senile, laughs and gets cross at a whim. Forgets everything. Has to write things down. Billa can never leave him for more than a few hours at a time, for he would get lost, or set the house on fire. She wonders if he has a tumour on the brain. Billa does far too much, with her Norfolk churches, her preservation work, the cooking, her children, grandchildren, *and* Roy. Dom[‡] and his recent wife, who is Christopher Hobhouse's posthumous daughter, came for the weekend. She, whom I have never met before, is now older than Christopher was when he was killed. She exactly resembles him, the same arrogant carriage of the horsy head, handsome, good figure, clever girl. It was fun to see her. I much liked 'Our Economic Correspondent'. He is humorous, jolly and gentle with his father.

---

[*] Graham Baron Ash, 1889–1980; donor of Packwood House, Warwickshire to NT, 1941.

[†] Sir Roy Harrod, 1900–78, Kt 1959; economist; m. 1938 Wilhelmine Cresswell, b. 1911, Norfolk conservationist and founder of Norfolk Churches Trust.

[‡] Dominick Harrod, s. of Sir Roy and Lady Harrod, b. 1940; economist and broadcaster.

Friday, 23rd August

Went round Felbrigg for the first time since Wyndham's[*] death. He would be pleased with what the Trust is doing, namely keeping the house as it was, and improving the walled garden. Young Julian Gibbs[†] and John Sutcliffe[‡] accompanied us. Both nice boys, but both hippyish. The first still rather coltish, the second sensitive and withdrawn from the world – a natural nomad.

Sunday, 25th August

Yesterday to Salle church, surely *the* finest of the East Anglian churches, finer than Tattershall, which I also revisited and used to rave about, and to Blickling, one of my favourite country houses of the world.

   Went with Billa to Eucharist in Cley-by-the-Sea church. Lots of locals, or rather visiting residents, dons and wives who rent cottages on the coast. On my way to stay with Myles [Hildyard] I visited Well Vale in the Lincolnshire wolds. Charming Georgian house outside. I looked through the windows and saw nothing of interest within. House at present empty. Was much attracted by the Georgian church in the park. Walked up to it. The cracked bell began to peal. As I reached the door Evensong was beginning. I slipped inside and sat at the end of a back pew. Two rows of box pews face the vicar's three-decker pulpit. An old man played the harmonium, a more nostalgic instrument than the organ. A moving little village service seemingly far away in the wolds. We sang the Magnificat and the Nunc Dimittis and the sermon was about the light which we as well as God can bring to others. Not as far-fetched as the theme sounds.

   Myles has living with him a young man called David, with an engaging manner. He does all the cooking and housework, has decorated the dining-room ceiling and opened the library, lights fires in every downstairs room, waits on old Mrs Hildyard, is cheerful and liked by all. Yet Myles lamented that he did not share

---

[*] Wyndham Ketton-Cremer of Felbrigg, 1906–69, squire of Felbrigg Hall, nr Cromer; man of letters and Norfolk historian.
[†] Julian Gibbs, b. 1949; NT regional representative.
[‡] John Sutcliffe, artist and designer of book jackets.

his [Myles's] manly outdoor interests. Some people are never satis-
fied.

Monday, 26th August

John [Kenworthy-Browne] came down by an evening train and
stayed at Flintham for two nights. He and I motored off one day
to Ossington church in search of Nollekens statuary for his book,
and to Radbourne Hall near Derby, the Chandos-Poles' house,
which is reputedly by Smith of Warwick. A fine house, decorated
by John Fowler of whom C.-P. thinks the world. House too perfect
in a way, too tidy, unrumpled. The saloon with Wright of Derbys at
either end and two huge Mortimers facing the windows. Portrait of
Prince Charlie over one fireplace, good and taken from Lemoyne's
after the Forty-Five. The Poles were 'out' in the Forty-Five. The
Bottesford Church monuments make a splendid collection. Really
these English churches are richer in monuments than any in the
world.

Friday, 30th August

J. [K.-B.] and I spent two nights in York, visiting Roche Abbey,
romantic, tucked away in a fold of hills, with rushing stream, Went-
worth Woodhouse, Sledmere, Burton Agnes. The two last have
become deadish owing to the numbers of visitors during the season,
un-lived-in. Sledmere more elegant than I had supposed. The long
library a striking room. I am amazed it has not a greater reputation.
The guidebooks sold out, and we could elicit no information from
the guides. Could not make out how much of the house had been
burnt out and reconstructed in 1912.

Sunday, 8th September

A. and I went two days ago to look at Arlingham church on Saul
peninsula jutting into the Severn estuary which belonged to the
Darells.* We spent quite a time in the church, and only when I got
home and looked at my Glos. book on churches did I find that
twelve years ago I visited it and made copious notes. I had entirely

---

* Sir Lionel Darell, 6th Bt, 1876–1954, author of *A Baronet in Ratcatcher*, m. Eleanor
Heathcote, sister of J.L.-M.'s aunt Dorothy L.-M.

forgotten. This isolated, once forested section of Glos. is today a tragic wilderness of death. Every single tree is an elm; and every single elm is a skeleton. I could not live there for anything. I believe that other trees in addition to elms are dying of mysterious diseases, for throughout my recent tour I noticed youngish oaks dying in Suffolk, even on the Euston estate, and ash trees in Lincolnshire.

Received a letter yesterday from old Lord Harrowby[*] pointing out that there is a house on the Sandon estate, dating from the 1740s, which has 'curious' features, namely meticulously accurate measurements with regard to height of doors and windows. The floors are all level and the walls perpendicular. He and his archaeologist friends are bewildered by these phenomena. I am bewildered by his bewilderment.

Saturday, 14th September

I am going through old family letters and destroying those of palpably no interest, docketing those to keep and putting them in different envelopes according to persons and particulars. Came upon a bundle written to my mother at the time of her engagement in 1904. I am struck by the dearth of ideas in the majority of the letters, the commonplace observations, the lack of literary style and even sparkle – letters of my grandparents Bailey to each other when they were engaged in the 1870s, letters to Mama from Jock Hume-Campbell, Ronny Anderson, both of whom were in love with her, during the First War, from the front. Piteous letters, yet lacking glamour. Nevertheless I feel a vandal destroying so many of them. Yet I have kept the grandparents' and all the letters of the 1820s and earlier simply on account of their age.

This place is already going to seed, is becoming down-at-heel, since our selling it. Windows unclean, the garden a mess – Margery being away ill or feigning illness, we cannot be sure which. My emotions now are of one to whom a love affair has become sour. He wants to get clear of the old lover and the memories as quickly as possible.

---

[*] Dudley Ryder, 6th Earl of Harrowby, 1892–1987, of Staffordshire and Gloucestershire.

Monday, 16th September

Went by train to Derby; met by Christopher Wall and motored to
Sudbury [Hall]. We had a Sudbury committee meeting. After it
Debo asked me to stay the night at Chatsworth. I always take the
precaution of carrying a toothbrush, comb and razor. She said Decca
was coming to stay. So I did not resist. Andrew [Devonshire] was
also at home. He was extremely friendly and welcoming. I
was touched by his charming, open manner. Yet the rapidity of his
intensely clever, quickly changing mind does not always induce ease,
and I feel shy with him. He showed me a host of pictures he has just
bought, innumerable Lucian Freuds, of whom he is a notable
patron. The one of himself is after-life-like except for a livid red
swelling on the forehead, which does not exist now, and never can
have done. He has bought two by Anne Hill's* son-in-law,† one the
back view of a naked girl squatting in a bath, which I suppose is
erotic. I find it revolting.

Decca still resembles Nancy in face, although hers is rounder, and
less fine. She has a double chin, and wears ugly large round spectacles. Was dressed less chiclessly than I expected, but not well. Has a
deep ginny voice, which was explained by the amount she drank
and smoked. So un-Mitfordy, this. She is undoubtedly clever and,
like Nancy, sharp. Affectionate towards me without much feeling
behind the manner. Sophy Cavendish‡ almost grown-up, but still a
child, rather touching, with leanings to architecture, provided it is
Victorian or grotesque.

Before dinner I walked with Debo. She visited the cows, the
bulls, the stallions, the new additions to Rowsley Inn, the gardens,
the farm, talking to all and sundry and giving instructions. I said to
her, 'How are you able to cope with all this?' She said, 'It is my
passion. Stupid I know.' I said, 'It is far from stupid. It is marvellous,
and right.' Both Devonshires are like everyone else deeply depressed
by events. In saying good-night Andrew remarked, 'If I am driven
away from Chatsworth, which is likely, I shall never return, I shall
never set foot in Derbyshire again.' Asked what was going to happen

---

* Lady Anne Gathorne-Hardy, m. 1938 George Heywood Hill, bookseller (who d. 1986).

† Timothy Behrens, painter; m. Harriet Hill.

‡ Lady Sophia Cavendish, dau. of present Duke of Devonshire, m. The Hon. Alastair Morrison, s. of 2nd Baron Margadale.

with large establishments like his. I said the only hope of survival seemed to me the National Trust. 'Um!' was all he muttered. Yet here they still are surrounded by works of art of the greatest rarity, living in this enormous house, with old retainers, servants and butler and footman, and private telephonist on duty all day and night; and providing access to the public practically the whole year round. Long, long may it last.

Tuesday, 17th September

I was called by the telephonist at seven and simultaneously by Henry the nonpareil young butler with tea. Slipped out of the front door at 7.20 and was driven to Chesterfield station.

Debo showed Decca and me the Nancy Mitford room, which she opened to the public for this season and which is to be dismantled now. Decca and Debo address each other as 'Hen'. 'I say, Hen!' 'Never in your life, Hen!' They said it was Nancy's snobbishness which started the Hons' cupboard. It began as Hens'. Debo said Nancy was the secretest person she ever knew. She never revealed her inmost feelings to a soul. Never once discussed with her, or Diana, or anyone her sad love affair with Palewski. Nancy never really cared for her mother, holding it against her that she, Nancy, was unable to bear a child. She had the most preposterous notion that she caught syphilis from her Nanny, that Lady Redesdale knew this and refused to have her cured at the time. I said to Debo that such a means of contagion in Edwardian days was unheard-of, and surely impossible.

Friday, 20th September

Took to Audrey at Windrush several things from this place, dog baskets, family photograph albums, china, etc. Audrey said, apropos her son-in-law's family the Suttons, 'The trouble is that they inter-married with cousins so often that they have developed gonorrhoea.' An extraordinary and erroneous simplism almost as naïve as Nancy's about her Nanny giving her syphilis when a child What Audrey implied was that Suttons are sometimes soft in the head.

Jeremy Fry dined last night, and Midi [Gascoigne] stayed the night, she having left The Mount House this week. Jeremy still beguiling, handsome with dark hair curling down his neck, just the right length. Wears spectacles which somehow suit him. Elegant suit, long jacket, pale blue linen shirt with long, rounded points to collar. He has bought the topmost maisonette at number 19 Lansdown Crescent, above us, and over Miss Long's. Already is making alterations, and will be installed before we are. Has fanciful ideas about improving the entrance, and is extremely resourceful, unlike me. He drank a good deal and stayed till 12.30; got a bit boring as the evening progressed. He always holds the stage; must be in the limelight. Simply his charm and endearing manners, for is he not shallow and vain? I must ask him one day. He is lovable. Like David Herbert he carries off every unconventional impulse with aplomb.

Sunday, 22nd September

The Filers,* new purchasers of The Mount House, lunched. Arrived late which infuriated us, then stayed till six. But the reason of our submitting to this ordeal is that they are going to borrow much furniture from us, and so store and maintain it free. He is an extraordinary pushing young man, full of self-confidence, a bald-headed (although with all his own hair) thruster, like John Harris, only he is a business tycoon. He goes up to things and examines them with close scrutiny, remarking on their appeal, or otherwise, to him. Peers into the pewter mats, commenting on the motto and crest. Peers into the portraits, asking who they are of. Is anxious to buy anything and everything. Wants to have ancestors. Has the money. Pathetic. Handsome, looking like Keith Joseph.† Such people deserve to get on. He has already bought a farm near Hillesley with the object of winkling the owner out of the barn (Naboth's Vineyard) which faces The Mount House and the land round The Mount House, and installing the present owner as tenant of his new farm. There is no impertinence beyond his ambitions. I wish him well in his venture.

A. and I have been dismantling in earnest. Are sorting out books, and are disposing of hundreds and hundreds.

Two American tenants of Hidcote motored over to ask questions of Alvilde about Lawrence Johnston. The *he* is writing an article about L.J.'s creation of Hidcote. We have already reached the age

---

* James Filer, entrepreneur, and Britta, his wife.
† Rt Hon. Sir Keith Joseph, 2nd Bt, 1918–94; Secretary of State for Social Services 1970–4; 2nd Bt, cr. Life Peer 1987; Conservative politician.

when sleuth-hounds on the scent of personages we have known in the past approach us. L.J. was of my father's generation, and a close friend. I always thought him a dreary little man, like a major in a line regiment. Which he was, as well as a genius.

Thursday, 26th September

I motored to London on a mission of friendship and finance. Drove first to Heywood Hill's shop and literally threw several cases of books through the doorway, while my engine was kept running, hoping they would buy them. Then to Brooks's, unloading samples of china and the portrait of the Prince of Orange. Then to collect a parcel for A. from Clarissa's flat. Oenone* received me, very grown up and collected, and now handsome with her long face. Pity she says 'ja' – incapable of 'yes' which is English and just as short and expressive. Then to lunch with Isabel and Joe Napier.† Joe rising 80, Isabel much younger, still a Twentyish figure with her cigarette smoked from a long holder. Both touchingly pleased with the folding card-table with painted surface which I inherited from Nealie Thomson,‡ and which I remember Isabel once admired. She was overjoyed to have it, and when I carried it into her Pont Streetish drawing-room it did look nicer than at Alderley. I almost regretted having given it away.

Eardley and I went to *Cole*, the Cole Porter omnibus musical. Delicious music, and more astringent, less sentimental than Coward's.

Friday, 27th September

Went to Christie's. A ghastly young man with outrageously gushing good manners begged me, if not inconvenient, to step into a waiting room. No, sir, I am afraid, sir, it is occupied. If you don't mind, sir, stepping *this* way. 'It is like being shown a cubicle at Simpson's in which to change one's trousers,' I reflected. 'Oh, sir,' etc. Then I began unpacking. Diffidently I presented the first of my wares, an

---

* Oenone Luke, 2nd dau. of Clarissa and Michael Luke.
† Sir Joseph Napier, 4th Bt, 1895–1986; m. 1931 Isabel Surtees of Redworth Hall, Durham, J.L.-M.'s cousin.
‡ Neale Thomson, 1883–1963, Captain, Argyll and Sutherland Highlanders, of Hartlay House, Ayr; J.L.-M.'s cousin.

oriental vase of A.'s. With much tittuping and smirking the young man went off, came back to say that Mr So-and-So was, he regretted, too busy to see me. 'I am afraid, sir, very much afraid, it is Korean, mid-nineteenth-century.' He did not need to tell me it was no good, and I must take the lousy thing away. Inwardly I vowed that never again, never, would I so prostitute myself at Christie's, or Sotheby's, at least in person, and in future always through an agent. Then the English porcelain. A very polite, natural, middle-aged man called Hudson appeared, looked at them, advised which I had better sell in Bath and which bring up to him. Most helpful. Felt that much better. Off in pelting rain to Brooks's, to fetch the panel portrait. No taxi available, and the distance really too short. So I walked holding my overcoat over the picture, myself getting soaked. Michael Tree rescued me in the foyer and directed the supercilious, queenly young man to send Mr Somebody to me directly. I felt more important. Mr Somebody expressed considerable interest. 'Certainly is seventeenth-century,' he said. 'By Miervelt,' I suggested. 'Not improbable,' he said. 'There is an identical one at Blair Castle,' I said. 'Yes, this may be a contemporary copy.' 'Or the Duke of Atholl's may be a contemporary copy of mine,' I ventured. Picture taken away for more detailed examination by the experts. A. and I are pooling our proceeds in a joint trust to pay the exorbitant bills for decorating the Bath premises.

I commiserated with dear old May (Eardley's servant for 45 years) this morning about her back. The doctor told her nothing could be done for it. It is just worn out, he told her bluntly. She must continue taking pain-killers, and continue working until physically she comes to a standstill. She said she preferred to come to a standstill than to retire to her own lonely room. 'For what would I do there?' she asked pathetically in a tiny voice like a ghost's.

Stopped on the motorway for a snack. Did a dreadful thing. Could not open the small carton of cream to go with the slice of apple pie. Managed eventually to bite off a fragment of the corner. Applied torn corner to what I thought was the plate, and squeezed. A thin squirt of the cream shot across my table and landed in a pool on the lap of a respectable lady wearing wire-framed spectacles. I rushed to mop her up with a discarded paper napkin. A man shouted, 'Eh, that's my serviette.' 'Sorry,' I said, 'I saw it on the floor, and thought...' 'Yer didn't think,' he said. 'No, perhaps I didn't,' I said. Hadn't much time. I am becoming horribly clumsy. I run into people on pavements, impelled to collide with them, as though they are magnets to my steel.

Wednesday, 2nd October

In a book of country reminiscences published in 1907 the author, a great-uncle of A.'s, recounts how a Shropshire farm hand firmly believed that when the rays of the sun were visible through clouds, this meant that the sun was sucking up water from the earth with a view to dispersing it in rain. The author thought it very droll. But I was firmly of this opinion myself long after I was grown up.

Sunday, 6th October

I often think I am far-seeing and correct in my political judgements. Am certain I was right when in 1970 I said Heath ought, when the Tories were re-elected, at once to have had a confrontation with the Trades Unions and risked civil war. Even today I believe that a confrontation (which would undoubtedly entail civil war) would result in eventual victory for common sense, though it is no longer a foregone conclusion. As it is, this week's election may see a Labour victory and complete victory by the Unions, and so Marxism within two years. I was right about the danger of the intellectuals flirting with Communism in the Thirties, right about favouring Munich in 1938 because we were not ready to fight the Germans, right in knowing that Communism was a worse creed than Fascism, and right in deploring Churchill's insistence upon unconditional surrender and the consequent acceptance of the Russian occupation of Eastern Prussia, Poland and eastern Europe. Oh God, the pace things are rushing downhill now is sickening.

We cart packing-cases of china and objects and books to Newark Park. The packing seems endless. I counted the total number of meat dishes of my Crown Derby dinner service. It alone amounted to 45. We have dozens of others. Most of the old services have cracked and broken dishes and plates, very many are ruined by soda and detergents. I think the Edwardian days were the worst for damage by servants ignorant of good china.

Monday, 7th October

We motored to London two tea-chests filled with the Crown Derby
(I am keeping enough for our humbler needs) which in pouring rain
I delivered to Christie's. After luncheon went to Dr Allison in Basil
Street. He took scrapings from my arm rash, and boiled them in a
saucepan. Examined and pronounced them not to be a fungus, as I
had been informed by two London specialists, but eczema. Gave me
a special cream and said, if it was not gone at the end of a fortnight, I
was to return to him.

Dr Allison complained vociferously about the self-employed having to pay insurance according to the amount they earned. Said it
would probably drive him and his partners out of business, possibly
to America. He said he was so furious with his compatriots, who
were about to get their deserts in Marxism, that he had no pity for
them whatever. 'It is perhaps a dreadful thing to say, but I hope they
rot. They won't work and they won't allow anyone else to make
money when he works. They deserve to live in a Communist state.'

Tuesday, 8th October

Was taken to *Rheingold*, which bored me to tears. J.K.-B. was deeply
shocked that I had not studied and absorbed the libretto, which he
gave me to read. But after two scenes of nonsense from Wotan,
Albricht and those dreary bores, Fricker, Freia, etc., I could not
persevere. The performance lasted three hours without an interval.

Wednesday, 16th October

Met Peter Tew* the hearty old architect who worked for Paul
Methuen at Corsham; also for Moly Sargent† who lived with his
mother at 19 and 20 Lansdown Crescent. He said that he repaired
the library at number 19 after the bomb damage during the war.
There was very much damage, and he spent £4,000 on the library
alone out of War Damage Commission money. The ceiling was
down and most of it had to be restored, much of the scagliola
pilasters had to be repaired by Jacksons. He assured me that the

---

* Architect in Bath and environs.
† Sir Orme Sargent, GCMG, 1884–1962; Permanent Under-Secretary of State for
Foreign Affairs, 1946–9.

mirror doors over the bookshelves at the north end of the room were not there when he restored the room. They must be post-war innovations. I was much relieved and have decided that I can with a clear conscience have them removed. This assurance has come just in time, for the painters have finished in this room and we hope to move in on 11th November.

Tew said that when the bomb fell on the road outside number 19 (the bow front of 20 collapsed and had to be rebuilt) the tenant had a lot of Beckford's books which he had collected. The only shelves which were quite unharmed were those containing the Beckford books; and they were behind the glazed doors. Tew also told me that the bay to the right of the fireplace contained a secret recess. I said I guessed this when I saw his original plans of the two houses made for Sargent, for there is an unidentified space marked on them. He could not remember how one had access to the space, but his partner (who was another tenant of number 19, before the Strath-conas)* used to keep his silver in it. Tew is going to ask this man to meet me and show me.

Friday, 18th October

On the rare occasions when I am alone with Ernst he talks freely with me. Driving to and from Newark yesterday with loads of luggage to be stored there he told how at his home in Prussia a headless black dog used to jump on one's back while one was walking by a certain wood at night time. One did not see, one merely felt its weight and its breath down one's neck. The moment the clock struck 1 a.m. (Greenwich Mean Time midnight?) the dog vanished. He also said that in another place a castle would rise from a lake. Once two men were on the lake when this happened. Millions of serpents came from the castle and attacked the men, who resisted. The Queen of the castle, very beautiful, appeared and, with the sweetest smile, informed the men that resistance was useless. So it proved, for they were bitten to death. Ernst said there was logic behind every folk story. He said he believed in God but never went to 'shursh', as he pronounces it. I asked why he didn't and suggested that he might enjoy the boys' singing in our church. He said, with

---

* Donald Howard, 4th Baron Strathcona and Mount Royal, b. 1923; m. 1st, 1954, Lady Jane Mary Waldegrave; 2nd, 1978, Patricia Middleton.

finality, it was no good for he couldn't understand the psalms. Too much logic and not enough faith, I'm afraid.

The church clock here started gaining half an hour a day, so I asked Mr Preece if he would investigate. He put the clock right and said the trouble was caused by the hand falling when it was going downhill, as he put it. Then, I said, it surely ought to lose when it goes uphill. 'It doesn't follow,' he replied contemptuously.

I have had a letter from Brian Fothergill,[*] beginning 'Dear James L.-M.', to which I have replied in a friendly way, 'Dear Fothergill'. I dislike this half-hearted, unsure form of address. He tells me he is about to write a life of Beckford. I had nourished a faint thought of doing this very thing. Now I can't. Anyway I replied at length saying how interested I was, telling him about Beckford's library and offering any Bath help he might need.

Tuesday, 22nd October

We motored to Renishaw on Friday for the weekend. My first visit. For years I have longed to see it. I wish I had done so during Osbert's regime, for then it must have been more Gothic and gloom-filled than it is now. Reresby and Penelope [Sitwell][†] have brightened it up. For instance, the large drawing-room curtains, sky blue with no pelmets, and tweaked together along the tram-line in the French style, are innovations. An 1850 water-colour in this room shows curtains with bold pelmets. The room is dominated by the portrait, by Fosberg, of Osbert seated like a doge with a staff, his cane. Excellent likeness, and formidable. 'The eyes follow you round', in a menacing fashion. The famous Adam commode beneath the Sargent conversation piece is about the most beautiful piece of furniture in all England. The house still has much atmosphere, and is filled with family things and treasures, in the same higglety-pigglety way as at Weston. A. and I were given one room with double bed. Because of the immense size it was all right and we slept happily until A. started, as is her wont, thrashing around at 3 a.m.

---

[*] Brian Fothergill, 1921–90; historian and biographer.
[†] Reresby Sitwell, b. 1927; m. 1952 Penelope Forbes; succeeded his father, Sir Sacheverell Sitwell, as 7th Bt, 1988.

Ten people were staying. Delicious food, and an old family butler who obliges for house parties but will accept no recompense, no gratuity. Other guests were Elizabeth Longman[*] (pretty and whimsical), Felix Kelly[†] (sense of humour and right-mindedness), Sir Henry Lawson-Tancred[‡] (baronet and widower, intelligent, friendly); Lady Bowker (Levantine, a version of Anna-Maria Cicogna, glossy, gossipy, nice); Patrick Forbes, youngish (after dinner looking at Reresby's slides on the screen I caught him raising his head in order that a sagging chin should not be observed – but I did observe), a vintner; Rosie Forbes,[§] our hostess' sister, jolly, slightly boozy, smokey, glowing. Penelope is beautiful, stately and sharp. I can't understand why Sachie and Georgia hate her. Their hate is returned.

In the car Reresby told me that when Osbert began suffering from Parkinson's, David Horner (whom he calls Blossom) had an affair which upset Osbert, entirely dependent upon him for dressing and generally ministering. Later David Horner fell down the stairs at Montegufoni and was incapacitated worse than Osbert. So Osbert turned against David and treated him cruelly. David was intensely jealous of the Maltese who came to Osbert as handy-man, turned secretary and confidential adviser. Sachie refers to him as 'poor Osbert's catamite'. Reresby affirms that his father is very conventional and a strict observer of the proprieties. This is, I think, true. Reresby does not criticize his father and mother, and speaks sweetly of them in the face of much provocation.

Indeed Reresby is a very sweet fellow. The shape of his round face is Georgia's, but all the features are Sachie's. The voice is Sachie's. He has wide knowledge of many subjects, but is not creative. We can't all be, alas! He tells long stories, explains matters at inordinate length, expecting attention. Has a coarse streak. For example, in showing us into our bedroom he said to A., 'If Jim gets too randy you can always put the bolster in the middle,' and to Lady Bowker, 'This strange tap with double handles can be used by two Lesbians at once.' These sorts of remark make one squirm a little.

---

[*] Lady Elizabeth Lambart, dau. of Field Marshal the 10th Earl of Cavan; m. 1949 Mark Longman, publisher (he d. 1972).

[†] Painter; d. 1994.

[‡] Sir Henry Lawson-Tancred, 10th Bt; b. 1924 .

[§] Wife of the writer Anthony Rhodes.

After dinner the first night we were shown a film of safari, R. supplying commentary with a host's good-natured relish. One by one the company, headed by Penelope and followed by A., slunk off to bed, Penelope having given us a signal of permission, but unnoticed by R. I, being the politest in the party, was the last to slink. Before undressing I realized that I had left my reading spectacles downstairs. Descended and quietly re-entered the draw-ing-room to hear R. droning on, 'And in this slide you will notice in the far distance a giraffe with what appears to be two heads.' There was not a single soul in the audience. I snatched up my specs and while mounting the stairs heard R. still declaiming and chort-ling with satisfaction to himself. I find this aspect of Reresby lovable.

Next day R. pointed out how Osbert lacked taste. I had won-dered if O. painted the dining-room walls Pompeian red, which is very well, but the wall pilasters and the semi-dome surely ought not to be red. The Adamish doorcases he painted jet black.

Felix Kelly told me he had never met Sachie, and wouldn't for all the tea in China on account of his beastliness to Reresby who longed to be loved by his parents.

Saturday, 26th October

While I was motoring home this evening at five and approaching Alderley from Hillesley, a shaft of sunlight suddenly struck from the west across Foxholes Wood so that it reared in a sort of golden gallop above the valley against a sky of deepest storm purple. High up in the sky a flock of white seagulls circled against this purple backdrop. It was one of the most beautiful and moving visions I have ever experienced. I wanted to stop and watch until it vanished but a car was on my tail and I couldn't.

Yesterday Tony Mitchell motored me to Moccas to meet the present owner, Richard Chester-Master,[*] and his wife, a charming middle-aged couple. I rather dreaded the visit because of my indefinable, sacred feelings for Moccas. They were not affronted. The place is well kept up and the inside of the house less awful than when A. and I went as tourists last summer, although their eye is not

---

[*] Richard Chester-Master, of The Abbey, Cirencester, Gloucestershire and Moccas Court, Herefordshire, b. 1927; m. 1951 Priscilla Lutyens.

mine. Moccas still preserves the same magic for me, its profound melancholy, isolation and ineffable other-worldliness. The garden has been cleaned up in that the unsightly tangled shrubs have gone and the terraces of grass are mown. The two vistas up and down the Wye have been improved. Really it is the most sublime place imaginable. We drove in a landrover through the ancient deer park which the Chester-Masters are carefully replanting where necessary with sweet chestnuts and oaks. Hinds being led by proud antlered stags. We lunched at the Red Lion at Brentwardine, now somewhat tarted up and furnished with the C.-M.'s surplus antiques. Rural simplicity about to dissolve.

Last night in Bath Abbey at a Bach concert. During pauses between movements when the music momentarily stopped and the audience was not coughing there was a loud susurration, as of a flock of starlings, which perplexed me until I realized it was the gas lamps with hundreds of which the church is lit. We went back to Sally W.'s for a delicious supper of soup and cold partridge while watching Anthony Eden talking on the telly about his experiences with dictators. At 77 he is still a very handsome man. But behind that distinguished moustache there is a slightly rabbity mouth which denotes obduracy. He was interesting enough. Said Stalin was the gentlest dictator he had met, with the exception of Salazar, which confirmed my belief that the latter had been a good egg all along. In fact Salazar was the model of what an autocrat should be – devout, devoid of exhibitionism, traditional, intellectual, and yet firm.

Sunday, 27th October

Went to talk to Joan Evans, by way of a goodbye. She is a very generous woman. Was delighted when I told her that I was taking her carpet to my new library, and offered to give me two smaller rugs to cover the floor space at either end. I thanked her and said I would remember her offer if I found I had need of them. She also offered to lend some urns for the niches above the shelves. I shall not avail myself of these kind offers. I much enjoy talking to her, but I cannot be very fond of her. She is too pedantic, tart and withal pleased with her mental superiority. She said our relations were, 'if I may presume to say so', those of aunt and nephew. There are merely fifteen years between us.

Monday, 28th October

J.K.-B. met me at Brooks's before we left for a play. My old friend
Betty, the accountant, took us into the bombed ante-room round by
the back premises, for it and the coffee-room are boarded up. She
was emphatic that the bomb was not thrown through the window,
because as she explained no one could throw something as small as a
hand grenade through thick plate-glass windows and thick velvet
drawn curtains. Whereas this bomb exploded in the middle of the
room. I talked to the nice wine waiter, Michael, who was in tears.
He held himself responsible for the injuries to one of the two
apprentice waiters, whose parents are friends of his. He said he
persuaded these people to let their boy work at Brooks's, they being
country people reluctant to let their son go to London. I told him he
was not responsible for what happened in the least degree, though his
sentiments were understandable. I overheard Edward Mersey[*] say to
another member that if it was proved that Brooks's were responsible
(i.e., for allowing a stranger to enter the building), then the compensation payable by the club would be about £10,000, which he called a
pretty good sum of money for a boy of that age (17). It seemed to me
that £10,000 was little enough compensation for the loss of a leg
when one was 17. During the war I was in constant fear that Brooks's
would be injured by German bombs. It is true it had its windows
blown out and it escaped several nearby fire bombs. But it did escape.
Now it is severely damaged by an anarchist's bomb, thirty years later.

Sunday, 3rd November

Since my bed's removal I have been sleeping in Chloe's[†] room, the
far side of my bathroom. I hear the strangest sounds at nights, of
persons walking down the passage, step by step. I rush to the door,
open it swiftly, and there is no one.

All my books were taken on Friday. A thing I don't understand is
that the woodwork of the white bookcases has gone green
where the books stood, whereas the woodwork exposed to the sun
is still as white as when first painted. On the other hand where

---

[*] Edward Bigham, 3rd Viscount Mersey, 1906–79; m. 1933 Lady Katherine Petty-
Fitzmaurice, dau. of 6th Marquess of Lansdowne, who became Baroness Nairne in
her own right (12th in succession) in 1944.
[†] Chloe Luke, eldest dau. of Clarissa and Michael Luke.

pieces of furniture and rugs have been moved from the fitted floor cord the marks of non-fading are very much darker than they were originally.

I telephoned the Donaldsons to thank Frankie for sending me a copy of her *Edward VIII*. Jack answered and talked. We agreed that she has had rave reviews from all and sundry. She will make a fortune, deservedly, out of this book. She could not talk to me because she was hoovering the drawing-room. This is how the wives of Ministers of the Crown who themselves are intellectuals and successful writers are obliged to slave at housework, not from lack of funds but of servants.

Sunday, 1st December

A sort of perverse magnetism makes me run into people on pavements. I see an old woman approaching and say to myself, 'I must give her a wide berth.' Then a wilful impulse makes me bump her right arm so that I am obliged to stop and apologize. It is a contrary magnetism. I don't in the least want to bump, and it is not as though I lose my balance. It is as though a malicious sprite gets inside me and pushes me into people. And the more I am determined not to do it, the more inclined I am to do it.

Mrs Spurling* came to see me to talk about her second volume of Ivy C.-B.'s biography. We gave her luncheon. I expected a thin, tall, plain, jovial lady of 40. Instead I opened the door to a pretty, little girl of apparently 26. She is quiet, low spoken, so that one cannot easily hear what she says – she whispers like so many of the young – and dazzlingly bright. Is immersed in Ivy. Is sure she is as great a novelist as Jane Austen and that Ivy knew it. She told me that Ivy kept a notebook of phrases which, like Walter Pater, she picked out and popped into the mouths of a character; often she transposed a sentence from one character to another. No wonder her characters lack uniformity. Mrs S. is very interested in class distinctions, although she says that today these are so unpopular that it needs courage to mention them in a biography. I told her to have courage; she simply could not ignore them. She asked me if I considered Ivy middle-class? 'Yes, certainly,' I said. 'Give an instance,' she said. 'Well,' I said, she would say, 'I went to Hart-ford-sheer.' Mrs S.

---

* Hilary Spurling, writer and critic.

said nothing, but took this in. Half an hour later I heard her say in answer to my question what part of England she came from: 'Hartford-sheer.' Mrs S. remembers everything she has read. Quoted passages from Joan Evans's autobiography, and from mine. Told me she wrote to Joan who sent her a curt two lines, that she hated Ivy and would not see Mrs S. So I telephoned Joan in front of Mrs S. and fixed up for her to visit Joan tomorrow. Mrs S. absolutely delighted, for Joan knew Margaret's sister Eleanor, joint author of *An Adventure,*[*] very well, was in fact left Miss Jourdain's jewellery much to the chagrin of Margaret. Joan claims that Ivy ruined her friendship with Margaret. Mrs Spurling is almost as interested in Margaret as Ivy, for in the second volume M. appears throughout. She asked me many questions about her. Did I suppose that she found the entrée into country houses difficult in the Twenties? I said I believed not. She said M. had a great struggle to achieve her niche in the furniture expertise world, endured many snubs and slights, received less pay than an office boy, the prejudice before 1914 against women careerists being intense. Mrs S. has a husband and two babies, yet works all night, often going to bed at dawn. Hates the dawn chorus because it means she must stop work. We asked how she was going to manage when her children reached school age.

On 11th November we moved out of Alderley, and stayed the inside of a week with Sally Westminster at Wickwar. We came daily to Lansdown Crescent. Actually moved in on 15th to sleep. By now we are nearly settled. There are still things like curtains which we await. On Friday 22nd we said goodbye to Alderley for good, having removed the last remaining objects in the house. Left it quite empty, and vastly melancholy. In parting with the Margerys I had no regrets that I might never see them again, but a pang of intense sadness struck because this moment was the final break with the house, which I dearly loved and in which I had hoped to end my days.

Wednesday, 4th December

Cyril Connolly's death, sudden to me, is a shock. He was about the cleverest and most literary of my generation. His knowledge of the

[*] Moberly and Jourdain, published 1911 (anonymously); remarkable and often reprinted memoir of ghosts seen in the gardens of Versailles by Miss Jourdain and her friend Miss Moberly.

classics was prodigious. His wit, his style were highly entertaining. About the best critic of his time, more brilliant than Desmond MacCarthy,* and less sure, but more brilliant than Raymond [Mortiner]. I used to see a lot of him and his first wife, Jeanie, when they lived in the King's Road during the early Thirties. But Cyril always frightened me. He could be devastatingly rude, and snubbing. He had a very seductive voice, and when amiable could be enchanting. Like other brilliant men to whom literary ability comes too easily – Alan P.-J. [Pryce-Jones] is another – he was idle, and never fulfilled himself.

Friday 13th December

I dined with Patrick [Kinross] on Monday. He told me Cyril was very attractive as a young man, as I saw for myself from a snapshot P. has of him. P. has framed a host of photographs of his friends in a corner of his working room. He said Cyril was the first person he slept with, at Oxford. The next day Cyril left him a note in the porter's lodge, merely saying 'Alpha and Omega'. However he repeated the performance. He was a great bibliophile, and advised Christie's on books. But his knowledge of porcelain, on which he prided himself, was less sure. He had a very valuable collection of first editions, all kept wrapped in cellophane, and so never read or even touched.

All this week I have been rejoicing that in Bath Abbey there is Eucharist every Sunday at 12.15, according to the old rite. It comes after the Morning Service, and so the Creed is omitted. Last Sunday when I attended it was twenty minutes long, and was taken by an educated parson. And no Series 3 nonsense.

Anne Rosse lunched with me on Wednesday at the Ritz in that beautiful dining-room. I was rather dreading it because I had not been alone with her for years, probably twenty years. But I need not have dreaded it; she was enchanting, and affectionate, and mischievous as of old. Told me she was the great matriarch of England, with something like fifteen grandchildren, of whom some, Susan de Vesci's, are grown up. Spoke of Tony [Snowdon] mysteriously. Lamented that he was not a Messel. Takes after his father

* Sir Desmond MacCarthy, 1875–1952; literary reviewer and author.

then? I asked. Yes, I am afraid so, she said. And added, 'I am very fond of my daughter-in-law, however, and am going to see her this afternoon.' Said, 'I had better not discuss Tony now. It would take too long.' Seems pleased with the two Parsons boys. We talked of Jamesey [Pope-Hennessy] who stayed in a pub in some small town near Birr until nearly the end. Shortly before his death he telephoned Anne, saying he must see her urgently. She was about to leave home and could not ask him to luncheon. But he insisted on coming round to her. Disclosed that he had overheard youths say they were determined to 'get' her and Michael. Since he consorted with all the riff-raff of Ireland she was seriously alarmed. Says she will never allow Michael to walk into the garden alone; always with a gardener. What a bloody country!

Friday, 20th December

In the wonderful Turner exhibition a trivial thing struck me. When Turner painted the backview of women, which he was fond of doing, he made their necks into an isosceles triangle. Nape and back merge in a thick, wedge-like fashion which is not attractive. Why on earth did he do this?

The Badminton estate agent [Tim Mitchell] told us on Tuesday that he had just read the new Finance Bill from cover to cover. The measures to be taken against large estates are far worse than he had imagined. They are devastating, and estates cannot possibly survive them. Discretionary trusts are to be particularly penalized. Every ten years a transfer tax will be levied on them, and retrospectively. For example, 1975 will be the tenth year since Badminton was put in trust. Therefore it will be subject to this appalling penalization. He said the Duke hardly realized this, and he thought it better he should not. Caroline Somerset said to me that it meant the end of their hopes to live in Badminton; that David was terribly depressed. She said the class hatred being whipped up was having its effects. A friend of hers had asked Jonathan Miller to dinner, and told him she wanted to invite Caroline. The reply was, 'I *detest* all aristos.'

Monday, 23rd December

For several years we coveted Miss Taylor's little house, at the gates of Badminton, without ever having seen inside. It had been a sort of bad taste joke that each time we saw David Somerset we asked,

'How is Miss Taylor?' The old lady died suddenly about two months ago, after we had sold Alderley and bought and altered and decorated this place (Lansdown Crescent). To our surprise, about three weeks ago the Badminton agent telephoned to ask if we were still interested in the house, he having been told months, possibly years before by David, that we were. We have lately been to look round it. The agent added that others had applied to the Duke, and some very rich hunting people, who are his friends, had priority. This morning David has telephoned from London to say the hunting people are off and the house is ours, if we want it. We are in a great quandary.

Alvilde is madly keen on it. I am half-hearted. I have by now got to like being here. As for my library, I have never liked a room more. The Badminton house is small, there is no one large room. In other respects it is perfect, and the right size. We now have to make up our minds whether to rent it, treat it as a cottage for the summer, and live here in the winter months, I coming over here by day during the summer, and using this library as my office. My fear is that the two places will cost us more than Alderley did. Oh, what a huge worry!

Robert Henshaw* tells me that he has a friend who is governor of a lunatic asylum. One evening this governor said to an inmate who had been busily writing at a table in the public room, 'I am afraid you must go back to your own room now. It is time to go to bed. What have you been writing all day?' The lunatic replied, 'A letter to myself.' 'Oh, how interesting,' said the governor, 'and what is it all about?' 'What a silly question,' said the lunatic, 'how on earth can I tell until I receive it tomorrow morning?'

Friday, 27th December

On our way to Englefield Green for Christmas we lunched with Eliza Wansbrough who said she received thirty letters of condolence when her little pekinese was torn to pieces by an alsatian before her eyes – a dreadful experience. Then she said that when Martin Charteris's† mother Lady Violet Benson died, the Queen wrote him

---

* Resident of Bath; musician and conservationist.
† The Hon. Sir Martin Charteris, b. 1913; attached to the Household of HM The Queen since 1950; cr. Baron Charteris of Amisfield (Life Peer) 1978.

a nice letter of condolence, typewritten, of one page. But when he
lost his labrador she wrote him a letter in her own hand of three
pages. It so happened that on arrival at the Droghedas' Garrett said
we were to have a drink with the Charterises in Windsor Castle that
evening, which we did. There was no one else there but their nice
daughter Mary. Their house is the one which Wyatville inhabited
while he was altering the Castle. When the Charterises went to live
in it there was no central heating; it was perishing cold. I had a
lovely talk with her, Gay Margesson that was, and now is a tall,
distinguished, white-haired, pretty, middle-aged lady, of much
elegance. She reminded me that we first met with Jamesey. She had
not had J. in her house for years before his death. Saw him somewhere and was so appalled by his appearance and manner that she
funked it. Told me she was a lapsed Catholic, having been a convert
like me.

Christmas morning we all went to St George's Chapel. Rhoda
Birley, A. and I sat on the knife-board, as it were, below the salt, and
the Droghedas in their lofty stalls. It was like being in the Middle
Ages. Storeyed windows extremely richly dight (Early Victorian I
guess) in front of us; the stalls adorned with helms and plumes, the
Beaufort portcullis opposite. Choir sang divinely. Queen in very
pretty dress of white with fur collar and fur borders down the
middle. It surprised me that she was handed the collection bag by
a verger. Then to the Dean's house afterwards for a drink and Merry
Christmas everybody.

This Christmas much as usual. Long walks with Derry in the
Park, over-eating, sleeping and reading on the bed, dogless. Rushed
back here this morning to entertain David Herbert and Michael
Duff who is thin and clearly ill. When they left we embraced on the
pavement. Michael said, 'Do you mind being embraced in public?' I
said, 'Far from it – by you.'

Walking with Derry from the Copper Horse towards Windsor on
Boxing Day. The sun caught the Castle in sudden shafts of dazzling
light against a sombre sky. Nothing but the Castle was illuminated.
Then as suddenly the sun went off it as though someone with a
switch had turned the light out.

Tuesday, 31st December

I delivered the corrected galley proofs of my diaries to Chatto's, and went to Heywood Hill's shop. John Saumarez Smith* said, 'I hear you are publishing some diaries next year.' I asked him how he possibly knew. 'Ah,' he said, 'as a shopkeeper I keep my ear to the ground.' He said he hoped the price would not be too high. Agreed with me it would be a mistake to include illustrations of country houses. I told him I had said so to Chatto's in vain, and begged him to tell Norah Smallwood when next he saw her that he thought so too. I think the illustrations should be kept to a minimum, and should be of persons rather than buildings.

Oh God! am I making another dreadful mistake?

---

* Bibliophile and Managing Director of G. Heywood Hill, Ltd, booksellers.

INDEX

Index